WALKING WILD

Hiking the length of Kruger National Park

José A Neves

HPH Publishing

First edition, first impression 2025
Published by **HPH Publishing**
50A Sixth Street, Linden, Johannesburg,
2195, South Africa

www.hphpublishing.co.za
info@hphpublishing.co.za

Copyright © 2025 by **HPH Publishing**
First Edition
ISBN 978-0-903733-60-1
Publisher: Heinrich van den Berg
Proofread by Margy Beves-Gibson
Design, typesetting and reproduction by Heinrich van den Berg and Nicky Wenhold

Text by José A Neves
Photographs by the Panthera group members and guides
Cover photo by Clifford French
Copyright © José A Neves

All rights reserved. No part of this publication may be reproduced, stored in or introduced into a retrieval system, or transmitted, in any form or by any means without the prior written permission of the publisher.

Printed by *novus print*, a division of Novus Holdings

For my fellow Panthera

Contents

Foreword	6
Map	8
The Kruger Trail	9
A Lesson about Boots	17

Leg One: Crooks' Corner to Vlakteplaas Ranger's Post — 21
Winter, June 2019

Carnival	24
Poacher Tracks	31
Mopaneveld	37

Leg Two: Vlakteplaas Ranger's Post to Mopani Rest Camp — 48
Spring, September 2019

Run!	54
Red Rocks	65
Tropic of Capricorn	76

Leg Three: Mopani Rest Camp to Olifants Rest Camp — 87
Autumn, April 2021

Tripping Point	91
Fish Ladder	101
Stormy Weather	116
Images	127

Leg Four: Olifants Rest Camp to N'wanetsi Section Ranger's Post   143
Winter, July 2021

Kingdom of the Spiders   145
Hippo Haven   155
Into the Cold   163
Beads of Introspection   167

Leg Five: N'wanetsi Section Ranger's Post to Lower Sabie Rest Camp   179
Autumn, March 2022

Lions!   186
Rhinos and Medicinal Trees   201
Showers and Lightning   208

Leg Six: Lower Sabie Rest Camp to Malelane Rest Camp   217
Winter, June 2022

Selati   220
Biyamiti   233
Tlhalabye Hill   252

Reflections   260

Significant Sightings   266
Appendix 1: Booking, Water and Packing   267
Appendix 2: Safe Hiking in the African Wild   271
Acknowledgements   272
Bibliography   274
About the Author   278

Foreword

Wilderness cannot be conquered by individuals. When we walk in wild places, nature becomes part of us and enriches our souls. The wilderness is not something you can explain; it is something you experience, and once you have, you will be enriched beyond words. Sadly, true wild nature is becoming a scarce resource.

Kruger National Park is one of Africa's most protected and revered wildernesses, with significant endangered fauna and flora. Travelling on foot through this vast, diverse and rich landscape is the purest way to immerse yourself in this experience. The hike is challenging and, at times, it reminds you of how small and vulnerable you are.

Along the way, you cultivate a deep appreciation of our remarkable planet by sharing this space with every living, crawling, flying, sprouting thing. Living among its inhabitants teaches you to respect nature and the other species with which you share this planet, our home. The dream of The Kruger Trail started with a wish to protect this special place for our children, their children and all who follow.

The Kruger Trail is dedicated to generating public support and resources to ensure the Kruger National Park remains a part of our heritage for generations to come. All profits are ploughed back into conservation.

This is a journey not travelled alone. You learn we need the support of others and you build lasting friendships. You also gain an intimate insight into animals, insects, birds and their habits. You learn of trees that warn each other when danger approaches, and how everything every creature does has an impact on the biology of our ancient Earth. You may find evidence of Stone Age or Iron Age people who traversed the same paths you tread and gain a deeper understanding of how our carelessness places ecosystems in jeopardy. The Kruger Trail is made possible by the support of a dedicated team of guides, South African National Parks staff, and SANParks Honorary Rangers. To each travel companion, whether human or not, we tip our hat.

I read José's account of his journey through the Kruger National Park with great pleasure. In his meticulous and humorous way, José shares his experiences and those of his travel companions. His extensive research allows you to learn more about the flora and fauna of South Africa's precious national heritage. Together, he and those with whom he walked for over hundreds of kilometres, will lead you into this wilderness where you too can share in the wonder of nature.

Enjoy the journey!

Louis Lemmer

Chairperson of the Magalies Region of SANParks Honorary Rangers
Coordinator of The Kruger Trail

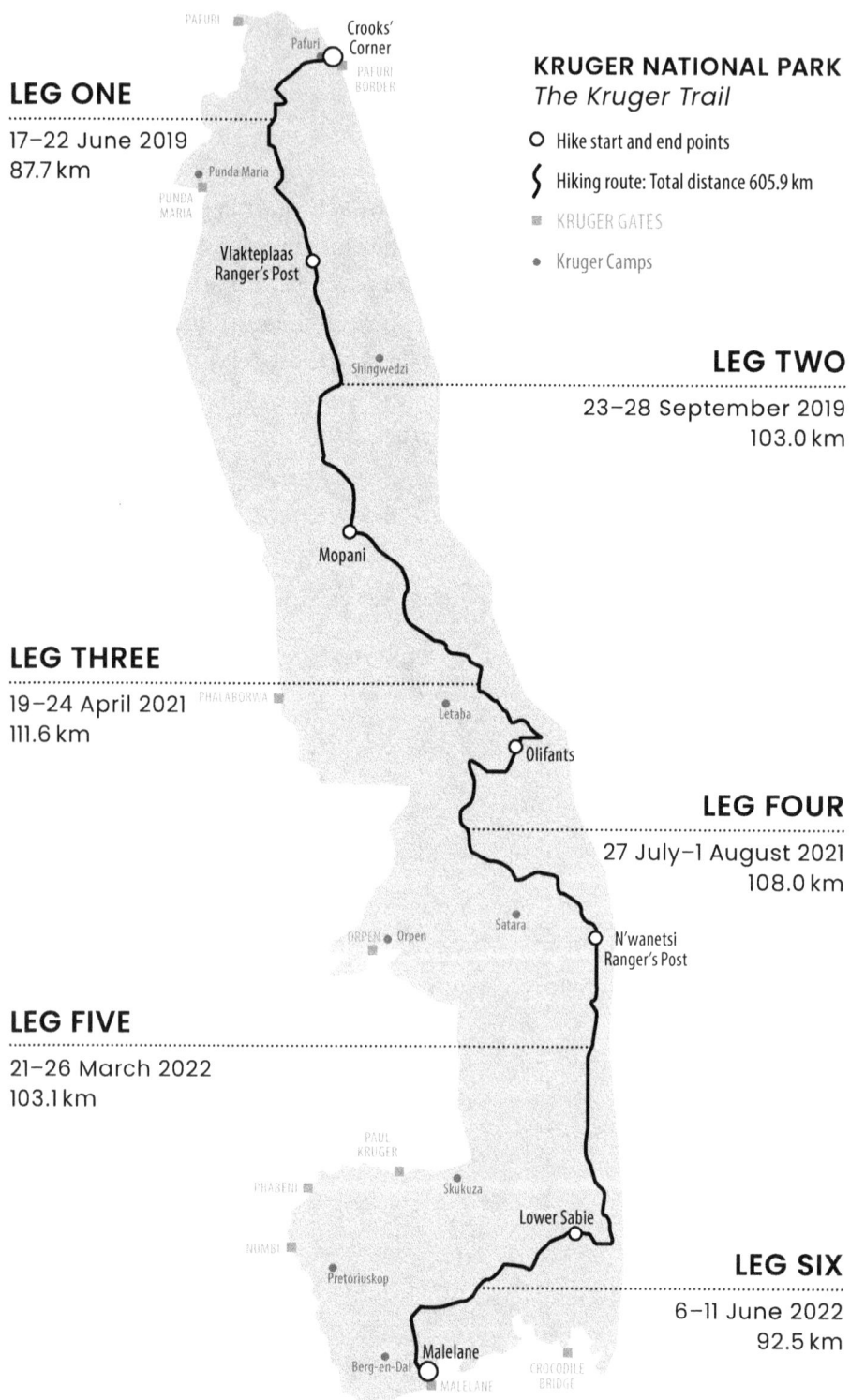

The Kruger Trail

We are closer to life when in the wild; the vulnerability of birth, defence of the young, the place of the aged, and where death coldly diffuses life back into the ecosystem. A part of the magic of the wilderness is the silence, coupled with the dusty dirt, the smells, and the feeling of being part of the circle of life. And, of course, we become hyper-alert to avoid becoming an inadvertent part of the food chain.

Many live surrounded by walls and hemmed in by roads. They may interact with domestic animals and landscaped lawns, but rarely meet nature on its terms. I get two responses when people learn I hiked more than 600 kilometres through the Kruger National Park; a place with large herds of elephant and buffalo, prides of lion, leaps of leopard and chuckling hyenas. They either admire what they regard as a courageous adventure, or they don't get why I wouldn't rather view wildlife from the comfort and safety of a motor vehicle. Both responses are valid, yet these words by Spanish author Javier Marias also resonate: "There's ... something that prompts us not to act and not to take that step, not to leave the house and not to move, not to speak to anyone and to avoid others speaking to us." But he assures, "Only the first step is difficult."

The first steps on the first day of The Kruger Trail – every time of the six occasions I walked it – were the most difficult as I worked to shake off city thinking. It was also the day newcomers were most likely to fall, distracted by the unusual task of remaining silent and walking with eyes on the ground to avoid roots, sticks and stones that could cause a mishap. It takes time to consider the profound lessons silence and mindfulness teach us.

The Kruger National Park is one of the world's oldest and most significant wildlife reserves and is located on the northeastern border of South Africa. Traversing its vast expanse creates an immersion in nature allowing for a deeper understanding of the distribution and life of mammals. The vigilant observer learns about predator-prey relationships and the multi-layered connections between animals, terrain and the seasons. You begin to appreciate the trade-offs in nature around economy and survival. The magnificent giraffe, for example, has an economically efficient and extravagantly long neck to access the tenderest leaves high in trees. Function and beauty in nature are never arbitrary.

My life, possibly like yours, has had challenges, mishaps, extraordinary encounters and considerable luck. I have travelled to 54 countries and met with six presidents. Yet the African bush still seduces this Portuguese-born immigrant to Africa. My eternal infatuation with nature means I am always open to enticement. My desire for adventure has sometimes threatened my survival and seen me stopped by fate. Before my 40th birthday, a cycling accident left me with life-threatening injuries. Five years later, determined to prove my recovery, I ran a 100 kilometre race in Japan, and after that I completed 10 Ironman events.

But fate continued to caution me. A speedboat ran over me in the sea and, not long after, my body erupted in searing blisters when I was stung by a swarm of bees on a training run. Both events required emergency medical treatment.

Later, there were events I revelled in. I went on patrol in the Bronx with the New York Police Department and fired weapons with the Federal Bureau of Investigation at a SWAT training facility in New York, as part of Young President's Organisation events. In the Philippines, I danced with Imelda Marcos, the wife of the disgraced Filipino despot, in her kitchen, at the invitation of Jean Saburit, a past-Miss Philippines beauty competition winner.

As a former, long-time Coca-Cola system executive, I am always busy and travel often. After hours, my passions are sport and wildlife, and this is how this tale begins.

I was returning to my car parked outside an isolated bird hide near the Letaba Rest Camp in the Kruger National Park in the winter of 2018. A poster pinned to the wooden slats at the exit caught my eye. A simple green map of Kruger Park, with a dotted path winding through six reserve sections, contained the words that stopped me:

Follow in the footsteps of giants.
Backpack the length of Kruger.

There wasn't a number to call, just an email address. I wrote and soon received a reply. I was told that The Kruger Trail is a backpacking hike through the Park, comprising six separate hiking journeys of approximately 105 kilometres each. Two Legs are undertaken each year, making it a three-year 620 kilometre journey.

The Kruger Trail is an initiative of the Magalies Region of the South African National Parks Honorary Rangers, and is the brainchild of Louis Lemmer, a dominee of the Dutch Reformed Church and chairperson of the Magalies Region of the Honorary Rangers. The concept of a hike the length of the Kruger National Park was initiated in 2016, after successful discussions with Park management led to the planning and investigation of potential routes. South African National Parks approved the project in 2017, and the first exploratory hike occurred that year.

The email noted the first two guest groups began in 2018. Groups are auctioned to raise funds for the Honorary Rangers who do voluntary conservation work in South Africa's 21 national parks, covering three million hectares or three percent of the nation's land mass. More than 2,000 Honorary Rangers help at entry gates; raising funds for anti-poaching activities. They run youth activities, and donate specialist advice on infrastructure and science. These amazing individuals have raised close to R 250 million for the country's reserves over the last decade. Their commitment to the environment caught my attention. The email noted five hiking groups were sold during a recent auction, and they would do Legs One and Two of the hike in 2019.

I asked whether any group had an opening and was put in touch with Lourens van Aardt, who successfully bid R 95,000 at the 2018 auction and secured the trip for an eight-person group. Chatting to Lourens was easy as we had a similar interest in sports. He has completed five Comrades ultra-marathons and is a golf and fishing enthusiast. I hiked the Indian Ocean Tsitsikamma Trail, while Lourens has on five occasions hiked that same coast on the punishing five-day, 41 kilometre Otter Trail. On one of the Otter Trail hikes, he took his daughters and some of their friends, and two years later, they did the Fish River Canyon hike together. He joked the hike 'cured' his daughter, Michelle, of hiking, but his other daughter, Jennifer, was hooked and joined Lourens for The Kruger Trail.

Lourens loves the Kruger and its surrounds. Years before, he worked at a mine bordering the Kruger Park and says, "...the bush got into my blood". When he learnt of the trail, he sent the news to Jennifer, asking if she was interested. "She emailed me back with, 'I am in.' I told a few friends, but did not find much interest. I was set on doing it. It ticked all the boxes – endurance, challenge and hiking through the bush.

"Although I had no members for the group besides Jennifer, I registered for the auction at the SANParks office in Pretoria. My wife and I attended the auction. Five slots were on the block. Seven or eight serious bidders were in the room, and others were bidding by phone. I bid on every slot, but stopped before the hammer. I had made up my mind I was buying the fifth slot. When the bid was awarded to me, I felt a rush of blood to my head. Excitement! Later that evening, I messaged Jennifer to tell her I had bought a group, and we were doing this. She later told me when she received my message, her words to her husband were, 'Oh shit.' She thought I would attend the auction, but not that I would buy a group," he laughed.

He dubbed the group Panthera, because his wife, Christine, was born under the star sign of Leo, and the lion is the king of the bush. "Also, the Lions have always been my favourite rugby team," he chuckled.

Panthera is a Sanskrit word meaning 'pale', but in Latin and Greek it means, 'predator of all animals'. Lorenz Oken first described the genus in 1816 and included all the spotted cats within the family *Felidae*. Reginald Innes Pocock revised the classification a hundred years later to define big cats with similar cranial features: lions, tigers, jaguars and leopards.

I wasted no time paying Lourens my share of the first Leg. I know risk is involved in hiking through a reserve filled with wild animals, but exceptional guides accompany each hiking group. Short walking trails were first established in Kruger Park in 1978, and all have good safety records.

The wild, which becomes our home for the duration of the week-long hike, is the terrain of large, dangerous game such as lion, elephant and buffalo, as well as an abundance of smaller, sometimes lethal creatures such as snakes and scorpions. Almost every life form in the Kruger has a place in something else's food chain. Although humans, for the most part, do not have to worry about ending up as dinner. We respect all that is natural when we venture into the wilderness.

The guides are qualified in Special Knowledge and Skills in Dangerous Game through the demanding Field Guides Association of Southern Africa certification process. They have advanced navigation and orientation skills, are proficient in rifle handling, enjoy camping under the stars, and have expert knowledge of flora, fauna and ecosystems.

The lead guide, I would learn, always walks in front, and behind him is a colleague. The eight hikers walk in a straight line behind the two guides – for optimal safety. Having one guide in front and one at the back, is a formation not used when walking in the wild. With animals, the danger is most often in front. So the guides walk to ensure optimal visibility and protection.

Guides are armed with SANParks-issued .458 rifles or their own weapons, provided they can fire a bullet at around 2,000 feet per second, to be effective against heavy, thick-skinned animals. While it is rare for the guides to fire their rifles, the protection of the group is paramount. Bullets must be flat-nosed, owing to the honeycomb nature of an elephant skull and to avoid deflection, which can happen with round or pointed tips. The rifles the guides carry, weigh around 4.5 kilograms. They are carried by hand; requiring an inordinate amount of strength given the distances involved. The chambers are left empty; with bullets in the magazine and 10 bullets carried in a leather pouch on a belt. While most hikers carry at least one walking pole, the guides are unable to because of their rifles. They also have a satellite phone in case of emergency.

Long distances must be covered with a heavy backpack, often over rugged terrain. Daily hikes range from 15 to 20 kilometres or more, and the weather can be harsh, with sweltering and often dusty days, even though walks are scheduled during the coolest weather.

Elephants in breeding or a lone buffalo are the biggest danger to hikers. Elephants have always been hunted for their ivory and because of this, especially in southern Africa, they have evolved to be aggressive to humans. Less than a century ago, five million elephants roamed Africa. Today, according to Animal Survival International, there are just 415,000. Anti-poaching efforts are succeeding in South Africa, with just 12 elephants lost to poachers in 2020; compared to 50 in 2017. On our hikes, we often witnessed the fear and rage of elephants up close, but we were taught simple, non-aggressive ways to deflect the magnificent beasts' anger.

Some say buffalo are the most dangerous animals in Africa. Buffalo attacked by lions are sometimes not brought down for hours or even a whole day; they will attack anything that comes close. Buffalo can never be taken for granted, and hunter lore is filled with tales of wounded buffalo circling back and attacking hunters from behind.

A bigger threat faces the Kruger National Park and other reserves. The footprints of man in pursuit of malevolent gains blot a landscape that should be protected and virgin, marked only by the tracks of animals, other than for controlled access to authorised groups. There has been no occurrence of hikers threatened by poachers, but there was evidence of their presence. Save the Rhino International, as an example, notes South Africa has most of the world's rhinos and is the country hardest hit by poachers, with more than 1,000 rhinos killed each year between 2013 and 2017.

The Covid-19 pandemic and determined efforts to combat the illicit trade in wildlife trophies, brought a glimmer of hope, and contributed to a declining trend in rhino poaching. Yet, in 2023, 499 rhinos were poached in South Africa against 448 in 2022. The Kruger National Park fared better and recorded a 37 percent decrease from 2022, with a total of 78 poached in 2023.

The serenity of this animal kingdom is also under threat from river pollution and climate change. Poverty fringes the park and when humans are in crisis, the natural environment is challenged.

The hike can be intense and is done in silence, with every member of the group alert. To walk wild in the Kruger is to hike with respect for every living thing. The Kruger has no signposted trails, so we hiked to landmarks or were guided by the GPS carried by the lead guide. Guides download satellite imagery to detect paths used by elephants and other animals. Game paths often lead to and from water, and most useful when headed in the direction we were going.

The Kruger Park is home to a diversity of animals and ecosystems. Each Leg of the hike offers a different experience, and no day is the same. On a hike, it is not just the large animals of tourist brochures, but also the small and near invisible ones, which are entrancing. Several researchers believe the biomass of insects in the park, equals that of mammals per square kilometre. This biodiversity is evident on a hike.

Tourists in vehicles tend to focus on the Big Five, a concept harking back to the 19th century, when hunters concentrated on the five most dangerous animals. Some visitors are more interested in the Rare Five. These are the aardvark, pangolin, black rhino, roan antelope and suni antelope. And then there is the Little Five. The leopard tortoise, elephant shrew, red-billed buffalo-weaver, rhino beetle and antlion. Ornithologists train their binoculars and cameras on the Big Six Birds of the Kruger: the martial eagle, lappet-faced vulture, ground hornbill, kori bustard, saddle-billed stork and Pel's fishing owl.

Many South Africans view the Kruger National Park with affection and even reverence. My first memory of the Park was on a family trip from Johannesburg in my dad's stately, green Valiant. I remember him getting out of the car to photograph a chameleon crossing the road. Perhaps the rules were not as clear in those days. Of course it may have been because, as recent immigrants from Portugal, neither my father nor mother could read English and were oblivious to the warning signs not to leave the vehicle.

When I was older, I visited the Kruger on a few occasions as a tourist. Although I never knew much about it or its history. Now, in addition to acquiring the technical equipment needed and preparing physically in terms of fitness for the hike with Lourens and the Panthera, I read articles, magazines and books about the Kruger. I learnt the park was named after Paul Kruger, the first president of the South African Republic. That territory was renamed the Transvaal six years after his death, when four colonies unified in 1910 under British imperial rule. The country became a Republic in 1961 and withdrew from the Commonwealth after increasing pressure due its apartheid policies. Democratic elections in 1994, saw the Transvaal in the north of the country divided into four. There is Limpopo in the far north flanking the large brown river of the same name; Mpumalanga, in the agricultural east; Gauteng, the industrial and commercial hub of the country; and the drier, North-West province.

The father of the Kruger Park, Paul Kruger, was a short man at 1.7 metres. He was a dour Calvinist with a vision. In 1884, the year after he became president, he set aside the area between the Sabie and Crocodile Rivers for restricted hunting. In 1898, he proclaimed the Sabie Game Reserve a 'no-hunting' zone to protect animals from unchecked hunting. In 1927, this reserve merged with the Shingwedzi Game Reserve to become the Kruger National Park.

The surface area of the Park, is 19,633 square kilometres, an area larger than Wales or Israel. The reserve hosts more than 760 species of birds, reptiles and animals and nearly 2,000 species of plants, including 336 species of trees. It lies between 200 and 400 metres above sea level, with 254 registered cultural heritage sites, and 130 Bushman rock art sites.

The Kruger is a renowned hub of advanced wildlife management. As an example, the fences between some of the adjacent private nature reserves on the southwestern side of the Kruger Park were removed to allow for wildlife migration in 1993. In 2005, barriers between the Kruger National Park and the neighbouring countries of Mozambique and Zimbabwe were removed to create the world's largest transfrontier park of some 35,000 square kilometres. This enhances migration and allows animals to enter the Limpopo National Park in Mozambique from the Kruger and the Gonarezhou National Park of Zimbabwe.

A Lesson about Boots

A fit 55-year-old with four full Ironman and six half-Ironman events, I knew I had to be in shape for the Kruger hike. In 2018, I crashed on the second day of the three-day, 265 kilometre KAP Sani2C mountain-bike stage race. This resulted in my right collarbone being torn from its ligaments. Surgeons inserted metal washers and a suture loop to hold it in place. I knew I needed to practise hiking to test my equipment and get my injured shoulder used to carrying a heavy backpack. My daily training included running, cycling, swimming and gym.

Three decades before, as a student, I hiked through the Outeniqua and Tsitsikamma forests of the Garden Route. My hiking boots from that time seemed in good shape.

I then decided to do three days of the Tsitsikamma trail in the nearby Wilderness area, a two-hour drive from Port Elizabeth/Gqeberha, where I lived. Tsitsikamma, a Khoi word meaning, 'place of abundant or sparkling water', has a spectacular trail that traverses indigenous Afromontane forests, with towering Outeniqua yellowwood trees, fynbos, cliffs, sparkling streams and Indian Ocean rock pools. Because of the short notice, I struggled to find someone to accompany me and finally, against my better judgment, went on my own. It was two months before the start of the Kruger hike, and I was eager to be prepared.

Friday midday, I parked my car at the Boskor sawmill near Tsitsikamma village. I set off on the gentle 6.4 kilometre ascent to Heuningbos Hut. I packed a few luxuries; meat for a braai and a mini bottle of wine for each night.

On Saturday, I faced the longest and most challenging day of the Tsitsikamma trail. It was a strenuous 14.2 kilometre hike, which included two big climbs, each with an ascent of 400 metres. I left just after sunrise hoping to walk in the cool of the day. The path was leafy and damp. I scrambled over wet roots and rocky outcrops. After six kilometres, on a stony descent to a river crossing, I felt stones under my left boot. My sock felt wet. Strange, I thought. I lifted my foot to look at the sole. It wasn't there. The outer leather was holding the inner sole in place. I kept the boot on, hoping it would hold. But a kilometre later, it disintegrated as the inner sole came away. I had packed flip-flops for the evenings and so, had plan B.

After discarding the leather boot, I pressed on, unbalanced, carrying a backpack weighing more than 20 kilograms, a flip-flop on one foot and a boot on the other. It was not long before the leather sole on my right boot also separated. I was again walking on the inner sole, and it disintegrated. After discarding the boot as responsibly as I could, I put on the other flip-flop. I now faced a tough seven kilometres, with a big climb to the second saddle and a three kilometre descent to Sleepkloof Hut.

The thong running through the sole between the big toe and second toe of the flip-flop, pulled out at the slightest pressure. I kept stopping to push it back in. Of course, flip-flops are not designed for hiking. The walking poles helped, but progress should have been faster. I now faced finishing in the dark. I thought about turning back but, by then, it was too late. It was a bit easier on the flip-flops going uphill, yet the heavy backpack took its toll and I often had to rest. I practised focusing techniques; choosing a tree or rock ahead as a goal, and resting only once I got there. When I arrived at the top of the saddle between the two peaks, there was Sleepkloof Hut far below.

I started the descent, knowing it was going to take hours. The slightest pressure on the strap of the flip-flop made me stop to feed the thong back through the hole. A snake slithered away on the downhill slope ahead of me. It was moving fast and I thought it was a Cape Cobra, but couldn't be sure. A few steps later, I almost stepped on a puff adder, disinterested in moving out the way. The poles took my weight and stopped the momentum, or I would have stepped on it. Relying on camouflage to protect itself, the puff adder is a thick-bodied and lethargic snake with venom that can cause severe tissue damage and even death. With my feet exposed, I gingerly walked around the snake, off the path in the longer grass. I was now as concerned about my safety as I was by the discomfort. I had a cell phone with me, but there was no signal. I was hours from any help. A snake bite would have been the end.

I arrived at the hut at dusk and spent another night alone. Well, not quite. Every time I went down the short wooden stairs from the hut to the cooking boma, a snake would hiss at me.

On Sunday, I did the short 3.2 kilometre hike to the Storms River Bridge in my flip-flops. The path was overgrown and muddy. I waved the walking pole ahead of me to clear the spider webs that tangled around my head. Before placing my exposed feet, I ran the pole through the vegetation to clear out any snakes, scorpions and spiders. What should have been a beautiful, relaxing walk through lush forest vegetation, was now challenging and dangerous.

Once I returned home, I sought decent hiking boots. I bought some Wolverine Black Cap boots, and walked round the house, happy with them. Although, I needed to test them in the field. I made plans to return to the Tsitsikamma forest and repeat the three-day hike with my sister Mia, and two of her art-class friends. They wanted to take four bottles of red wine and a bottle of sherry for the cold nights. I agreed to carry three bottles, as I needed the extra weight for training. We packed meat for a braai on the first night.

Mia handled the first 6.4 kilometres well, while clumsily carrying a bottle of wine. Her friend Sharnay, a beautiful and fit woman, thanks to regular morning walks through the verdant suburb where she lived, was up to the task. I was concerned about my sister's older friend, Bernie, who was determined to do the hike despite recent health issues. Bernie fell behind from the start, despite the easy pace.

We set off the next morning, an hour after first light. Progress uphill was slow and we frequently climbed over fallen trees or rocks. It was still cool and trees and mountains sheltered us from the early morning sun. I became concerned about the pace. After two hours, I checked my GPS; we had not even covered three kilometres. We would never make it to Sleepkloof Hut by nightfall at that pace since the most challenging climbs and the day's heat were ahead of us. We had a frank discussion and Bernie admitted she was struggling. Mia agreed to turn back with her. I needed the training and was determined to continue. Sharnay, who had easily kept up with my pace, offered to continue. Mia and Bernie said they would drive to Sleepkloof Hut in the afternoon and we would all stay there for the night. There was a lot of wine to get through.

Sharnay and I made good progress. By working hard with short breaks, we arrived at Sleepkloof Hut an hour before dark. We were surprised Mia and Bernie weren't there. I walked up the hill to pick up a phone signal. I called Mia, only to hear they would not make it to the hut as Bernie's leg was hurting, and she had opted to return home to Port Elizabeth.

Smoke rose from the shed where the fireplace was located and I got there to find a large kettle of water on the boil. "It's for the shower," Sharnay proudly informed me. "Go first. I'll heat another for myself."

I carried the steaming water to the shower with its primitive yet effective contraption. A bucket with a rope attached to the handle was rigged inside a cubicle. The bucket could be lowered for water, and then hoisted back up before the rope was tethered by a wire hook. On the underside of the bucket was a simple showerhead with a mechanism to regulate the flow. We had to add cold water to make the temperature bearable, but the bucket held more than enough for a leisurely hot shower.

Soon, we were both showered and refreshed. We made a creamy linguine pasta with ham and mushrooms. We chatted around the fire, huddling closer and closer as the cold night closed in, drinking fine red wine from aluminium coffee mugs. It was late by the time we let the last piece of wood burn to embers and made our way to the bunks in the cabin.

LEG ONE

Crooks' Corner to Vlakteplaas Ranger's Post
WINTER, JUNE 2019

Two weeks of training hikes in the Tsitsikamma forest prepared my body for hiking long distances with a heavy weight on my back. They also led to a new friendship as Sharnay and I often enjoyed meals with fine red wine, now drunk from crystal glasses.

It was time for the first Leg of The Kruger Trail. I met the first member of our group at OR Tambo Airport in Johannesburg. I flew in from Port Elizabeth, and Clifford French, a 44-year-old investment banker, flew in from Durban. We hired a car for the all-day drive to the Punda Maria Rest Camp.

It was good to get to know Clifford during the drive. By the time we arrived at the gate to the Kruger National Park, I felt like I was embarking on an adventure with a friend. As we entered, an elephant grazing along the roadside was a welcome sight. After a while, we paused behind a phalanx of cars viewing a male leopard sprawled in the shade of a tree. Two good sightings indicated a good start.

Punda Maria Rest Camp, the northernmost camp, has a subtropical climate and an intimacy and charm from when it was ranger quarters. Clifford and I set up camp next to the fence and close to a waterhole; it was a decision we almost regretted. Corrie Barnard and Arie Fourie soon arrived and set up tents opposite us. Corrie, at 67, was the group's oldest and most experienced member. He was fit, big and strong, and carried a well-worn bamboo pole taller than his six foot-plus. He accounted for every gram in his backpack from a list built up over years of hiking. Arie Fourie, 47, looking younger than his years, was an outdoor enthusiast, and an experienced hiker from Boksburg, who had already done two three-day hikes in the Kruger. In addition to being a paraglider, a fixed-wing and micro-light pilot, he also enjoyed skydiving and base jumping.

Pitching our tents close to the waterhole was not smart, as elephants bashing through undergrowth woke me up several times that night. A lion roared so close I felt it in my core. For now, I took comfort in being on the other side of the game-proof fence.

Henk and Antoinette Jonker travelled up from Centurion and arrived with Lourens van Aardt and his daughter, Jennifer van Aardt-Bester. Henk works for the same international commodities company as Lourens, who also lives in Centurion. Jennifer is an attorney. I was delighted to meet Lourens, who looked younger and fitter than his 61 years.

I met one of the guides, Bjinse Visser, and helped him fill water drums to be dropped off at the intended night stops. Except for the first night, where we would camp next to a natural spring. Sunday was Father's Day and I missed my daughters, who were worried about me being out in the open with wild animals. I wanted to call them, so I did not join Clifford and Corrie, who spent the afternoon with Bjinse, dropping off and concealing the filled water drums along the hiking route.

Later, I packed my tent and checked into a bungalow for a night of relative comfort before the hike. Our group gathered for a braai in front of my abode. I bought beer, sausages, steak and bread rolls at the camp shop, so we could dine without utensils. The second guide, Pilot Nxumalo, arrived as we finished our meal. He gave us SANParks indemnity forms to sign, and he and Bjinse delivered an informal briefing that included arrangements for an early morning departure.

Before I went to sleep, I posted a note in place of a profile picture on WhatsApp, saying I was not contactable from Monday, 17 June to Saturday, 22 June. The week-long technology detox is among the most worthwhile aspects of the hike.

Bjinse, a freelance walking guide with a background in mechanical engineering and injection moulding, would lead the first Leg. He had returned to South Africa after being in the motor industry in Canada and the United States. He worked with steel products and designs bullets and provides gunsmith services to lodges in the Hoedspruit area. Bjinse has logged over 7,000 hours on foot on wilderness trails and is a mentor and trainer to aspiring guides. He slept on the hard ground in his sleeping bag, with no foam base or mattress. Almost bald, lean and fit, he looked suited to life in the wild. He was lighter than my 80 kilograms, and later revealed he weighed more than 100 kilograms before he took up hiking. His tread was as silent as a cat in the leather hand-made sandals he hiked in.

Pilot Nxumalo, the second guide, is an employee of SANParks. Apparently he got his name because his father always had his American Pilot radio on. Naming is important in African cultures and is often used to convey the significance of times or occurrences. I have acquaintances with names ranging from Innocent to Surprise. Pilot told us he lives in Belfast with his wife and two children.

Bjinse and Pilot were armed with Czech-made CZ550 Magnum .458 rifles, issued by SANParks. The rifles shoot a flat-nosed 475-gram solid monometallic Dzombo bullet at more than 2,000 feet per second. We hoped they would never need to use them. The Dzombo bullet, named after one of the Magnificent Seven elephant tuskers, was designed by Bjinse and is preferred by most guides for its proven effectiveness against elephants.

Carnival

After a comparatively luxurious night's sleep in my rondavel, I was ready to start the journey. We left for the Pafuri Border Gate in convoy. Clifford and I squeezed in beside Bjinse for the hour-long drive in his single-cab van.

Much of the conversation was about Kruger Park challenges, such as poaching, rising elephant numbers and water distribution. We also discussed time and watches, and Bjinse spoke of a way of life different from my own, yet it resonated. Bjinse believes time does not have to dictate our lives. We should awaken at first light, eat when hungry, rest when tired, and sleep when dark. What we were about to embark on was a perfect opportunity to follow this natural rhythm. I looked at the digital sports watch on my wrist that I use for running, swimming and outdoor activities. Its lightness belies how heavily time weighs on my life. I decided to relieve myself of that burden while in the Kruger.

We parked the cars at the Pafuri Ranger Station near the Mozambican border. I left my watch in the car with my luggage. It was as if handcuffs came off; I looked forward to a week unfettered by time. After throwing the backpacks into a van, we clambered into a game-viewing vehicle that ferried us to Crooks' Corner. I was so eager to begin the hike, I hardly registered a jackal duo scurrying by and a black-chested snake eagle perched in a tree.

Crooks' Corner is a triangular piece of land at the northeast corner of the Kruger between the Luvuvhu and Limpopo Rivers. This is where the borders of South Africa, Zimbabwe and Mozambique meet. The Corner has long been a natural refuge for migrants, ivory poachers and gun runners who sneak across international borders.

After a group photograph, we put on our backpacks and gathered around Bjinse and Pilot for the first of our daily briefings. The rule is to walk in single file and in silence. Bjinse led with Pilot behind him. We were encouraged to change our position in the group now and then to give everyone a different perspective. We would stop only when there was an interesting or unusual sighting. If we needed to halt, a short whistle or click of the fingers would do. When walking and weaving through trees such as mopane with protruding twigs and small branches, we were told to push through and ignore the person behind following. Being polite and holding a branch for the person breaks momentum and slows the group.

Toilet protocols were discussed and we were instructed to do what was necessary on the path we had just trodden and not ahead because we would not know what might be there. Bjinse and Pilot carried small purpose-built aluminium spades for all to use. A hole is dug, and the toilet paper burnt after the deed, with the ash buried to minimise the intrusion into animal territory. Even in ideal conditions, toilet paper can take up to three years to decompose.

We were also encouraged to pick up a stone to carry to place it on a cairn at the top of Tlhalabye Hill, when in three years we completed the trail. I picked up a small, round pebble with excitement, even though at the time I did not fully appreciate its significance. Cairns represent calm or balance and can be a spiritual token. Cairns have been used since prehistoric times and are still common as hiking markers on trails where there are no other signs. When there are several possible paths, a cairn will point you in the right direction.

We set off at a brisk pace on a dirt road running through the tropical riverine forest that leads to the viewpoint at Crooks' Corner. I focused on the thrill of walking free in the Kruger and put out of my mind I was carrying the equivalent of a cupboard on my back. Bjinse wanted to avoid any Kruger visitors from noticing us because they were warned not to leave their vehicles, yet there we were, ambling along.

The first animals we came across were a small troop of baboons and then eland. The sandveld is one of the best places for eland, the largest and slowest African antelope. Despite their size, they are gentle and agile and can leap three metres from a standing position. We stopped for breakfast beneath a large shady tree and sat on fallen branches where the eerie, baby-like cry of a trumpeter hornbill amused me. Pilot pulled out a foldable stool that I came to envy. When it was time to leave, I was still fiddling with the timer on my camera, vainly attempting a selfie. The group was ready to go and my backpack was still on the ground. I was embarrassed and vowed not to hold up the group again.

A magnificent, semi-deciduous leadwood tree (*Combretum imberbe*) created an excellent opportunity to take a break and discuss its characteristics. They dot the landscape close to rivers and watercourses. Leaves were still on some branches even though it was winter. We stood in the shade of the trunk. Dead leadwood's remain erect for hundreds of years, owing to their resistance to termites and borer beetles. The wood burns slowly and the tree gets its name, in part, because its wood is so dense it sinks in water.

We stopped again at a dusty open space to analyse a congregation of animal tracks. The sand was cluttered with prints softened by the wind. Bjinse told us such tracks were like a newspaper of the day's events, telling stories about occurrences. Bjinse studies animal tracks and builds experimental three-dimensional models to imitate the lighting effects of the shifting sun, to accurately interpret tracks and the measurement of gait-length and patterns for a book.

Our lunch break was on a small hilltop shaded by two large trees. I sat on a fallen trunk and tucked into my ration of cheese wedges and savoury biscuits. I remained hungry and resolved to bear the burden of a few more grams to bolster my rations in the future. We soon fitted into the rhythm of nature and, like animals, we sought shade and rest during the day's heat. I lay under a shady tree and heard others snoring. I later gathered, I too contributed to the sonorous chorus.

The sun baked down on the afternoon walk over predominately sandy soils. A shallow layer of sand covers acidic basalt rock geologically comparable to the Kalahari and created by massive windstorms that swept the subcontinent millions of years ago. The basalt that dominates the eastern half of the Kruger is volcanic rock formed aeons ago by rapidly cooling lava. The dark, dense soils are rich in nutrient-rich organic material and are referred to as 'sweet' soils. Probably as a result of their vegetative suitability for animals. Small-leaved trees like acacia love this soil, as do the more palatable grasses. The western half of the Kruger tends to have coarse-grained sandy soils thanks to ancient granite rock and subterranean drainage systems. The high acidity of the soil makes it less fertile, with a lower clay content due to more rainfall and leaching. It is well wooded with abundant broad-leafed species. For the first time,

I appreciated how an understanding of topography and geology could make a visit to the Kruger more rewarding.

We headed west, with a gentle breeze caressing us. The wind carried our scent to the animals ahead. A large herd of buffalo moved out of our way, while the stragglers at the back gave us a grumpy stare before moving on. We saw giraffes, warthogs and playful vervet monkeys. Distinctive elephant prints were everywhere, but no pachyderms anywhere. Their acute sense of smell, fear of man and the wind in their favour, meant we had little chance of an encounter.

I looked forward to the night stop, not only for the release of the burden on my back, but also because we were camping at a natural spring that would serve as our water source. As we hiked a dry riverbed, occasionally clambering over large rocks, I imagined having a dip in the cool water or a swim. There was scant daylight left when we came to a steep and rocky place, shaded by large trees and a sandy promontory. While it looked ideal, I couldn't find a spring or pool of water I had hoped for.

We took off our backpacks and Bjinse pointed to where he and Pilot would set up tents, indicating the safe area between them where we should do the same. I asked Bjinse where the spring was, and he pointed to a mossy line of water trickling through a crack in the rocks. The almost imperceptible dribble puddled in a shallow dingy, green pool. The sliver of water continued in the velvety-green mossy cracks, ending in a bucket-sized pool of clear, still water. This was the spring from which we would wash and drink.

Before preparing the evening meal, we filled our water bottles and water bladders. The water scooped from the second pool was clear, provided care was taken not to touch the sides or disturb the bottom. I used water purification drops, while some chose to filter the water in addition to using the drops.

I cooked my first meal of the trail, making an acquaintance with instant noodles and packaged tuna. Bjinse, Clifford and I shared a fallen branch over which we prepared our meals by the light of a full moon. We spoke about honey, noting it is the only food known to man that does not spoil. Bjinse said he uses it to heal open wounds.

I was tired and lay in my tent for a short rest, only to awaken to a carnival of zebra hoofs on stone, noisy buffaloes, elephants trumpeting, and barking baboons. Everyone else seemed to be asleep. I slept again, until I was woken by the high-pitched scream of an elephant. All the activity not more than 50 metres from me was unnerving; thankfully, sleep overcame my fears.

We were up at first light and I calculated I must have slept for 11 hours. This was my first time packing up in the bush and the mood was festive. Arie watched me struggling to roll up my down sleeping bag and told me to rather stuff it into the bag. I noticed Bjinse and other experienced hikers did the same.

Lourens recounted later that he had told Bjinse on Sunday night at camp he loved animal sounds. "A faint smile crept across Bjinse's face, and in his understated way, he said, 'The overnight spot tomorrow might get busy.'

"After we had eaten on that first night, Jennifer and I chatted and soon fell asleep. I was woken by the loudest animal sounds I have ever heard! There was the trumpeting of nearby elephants, and a herd of zebra began barking. It sounded like the elephants and zebras were arguing over the small pool of water. This ruckus caused a herd of buffalo to stampede up the ravine past our camp and within metres of Clifford's tent. Hearing their hooves clattering on the rocks, I prepared for buffalo to run over our tent.

"All the sounds echoed off the high cliffs, making the experience far more dramatic. I expected to hear gunshots from Bjinse to save our lives. But after a while, things quieted down, and once my heart stopped pounding, I went back to sleep."

The first part of the day included numerous uphill sections, until we stopped for a short break under a large Lebombo ironwood (*Androstachys johnsonii*). This evergreen tree has attractive circular deep green leaves with white on the underside that provides good shade, even in winter. The wood does not burn easily and was used in the past for structural support in bridge building.

The morning sun was still low when we heard the harsh, rattling chatter of a greater honeyguide calling us to follow. It will fly in the direction of a hive of wild bees, stop and call again, hoping for a share of the spoils should the follower raid the hive. I had a chance to observe its distinctive tail with white spots illuminating khaki feathers.

Every animal was a thrill. Warthogs twice scurried past with their tails in the air. Despite not being the prettiest animal in the Kruger, thanks to their flat heads and wart-like protuberance on their faces, they are beautifully ugly in a way, much-loved by tourists. As we moved south, the soil changed from sandy white to red.

Suddenly there was a stampede of hooves coming at us on the path. Bjinse raised his hand and brought us to a halt. He whistled once, and then again to let the animals know we were there. The lead zebra stopped 10 metres from our group. It was a standoff. Someone behind me fidgeted and the zebra jumped backwards in fright and ran off; the rest following. I understood then why Bjinse had whistled. Zebra are twitchy and nervous and can frighten themselves into injury.

We stopped beside an expansive and leafless deciduous baobab tree (*Adansonia digitata*) for lunch. Baobab trees are hermaphrodites, meaning they have male and female reproductive cells, which is true for most plants. A baobab can produce from as few as five fruits to 200 in a year. The fruit is found inside a hard pod hanging from the branches and is tart. Folklore believes male trees have their branches pointing up, whereas female trees down.

I wanted a nap, and before dozing, I paged through the two pocketbooks I carried. One was *First Field Guide to Animal Tracks of Southern Africa*, published by Struik Nature. The other was *Pocket Guide to Birds of Southern Africa* by Sunbird Publishers. I looked for the track of the impala, the most common antelope in Kruger, and was surprised to find it was not included in the Struik book. Impala are affectionately known as the McDonald's of the bush owing to their prevalence and the similarity of markings on their hindquarters to the golden arches, but in black. They give a new spin to the term 'fast food'. I dozed off, thankful only sand flies, commonly called *miggies*, and not mosquitoes or mopane flies were bugging me, which would have been the case during summer. The fly, also known as mopane bee, is a tiny stingless bee species native to Africa. They annoy humans as much as animals because they look for salt and moisture around the eyes and mouth.

A pearl-spotted owlet swooped past during the short hike to the dry bed of the Mashikhiri River. After crossing a wide, dry riverbed there were impala for the first time. A sign we were close to water, as impala are never far from a water source. Six 25-litre water containers were concealed in thorn bushes beneath a baobab tree. The men each grabbed a container for the 100 metre journey to the riverbed, where we set up camp.

A lightweight plastic bag with an adjustable nozzle was hoisted into a tree and I had my first bush shower. I felt clean and refreshed after the lukewarm wash. Some complained about thorns underfoot, and future setups by our guides included elaborate flooring made of leaves or stones.

In the evening, we heard why we had hiked just 10.9 kilometres, or about half the usual distance covered in a day. Our guides were instructed to avoid an area where, four weeks before, the second group that started The Kruger Trail was forced to kill an elephant. Bjinse and Pilot were tight-lipped about the incident, saying only the hiking party surprised a breeding herd and a matriarch attacked them. No humans were injured. As I got to know Bjinse, his love of the bush, and the animals of the Kruger, I understood why the killing of the elephant was not something he wanted to talk about. Even though Bjinse is a master in the design of bullets and the manufacturing of his rifle cartridges, having his product slay a majestic creature is not something he enjoys. Bjinse has killed an animal just once, and that was when he defended a SANParks research group by shooting a limping and charging hippo, while crossing a river during the drought of 2015.

I went to bed over-confident because of the short distances on the first two days. Although, as a person who likes to ease into things, it suited me. On some of the future Legs, we would cover almost double the distance on the first two days, but I did not know that then. I slept well.

Poacher Tracks

On the third day, we started with a walk up the dry, rocky bed of the Mashikhiri River, a spectacular gorge feathered with ferns and brave trees clinging to rocky ledges. Plentiful, rotund dassies, or rock hyrax, with thick brown fur looked down on us from cliff tops. I was amazed at how fast they hurried up steep inclines. Their padded feet, moist from sweat glands, are manipulated for suction, allowing them to climb vertical rock faces. The two types of dassies in the area have long, tactile whiskers to enable navigation around rock crevices and tunnels. They spend their mornings basking on rock faces as, like reptiles, they have poor thermoregulation and need to warm in the sun before becoming active.

Bjinse pointed out a track in mud close to rock pools strewn with fresh buffalo droppings. The finely patterned track looked unnatural.

"Poacher tracks?" I offered uncertainly.

Bjinse said it was a crocodile track left as it moved upward to an almost dry pool of water some way ahead.

I felt stupid at my impulsive suggestion, but soon learnt I was not too far off the mark. Bjinse pointed to an arrangement of branches and tree logs positioned in an unnatural way. A previous hiking group noticed the unusual structure, and when the guides investigated, they discovered a poachers' camp.

Further along, we stopped for a welcome mid-morning break. Much of the hike had been uphill along the sandy riverbed. I took out a pen and notebook in the top compartment of my backpack to make notes. A zebra walked briskly past on the ridge above us. As we snacked, I asked the group, "On which side does a zebra have the most stripes?"

"Is it black with white stripes or white with black stripes?" Bjinse asked, as it seemed nobody had the answer.

"On the outside," I said to a mix of laughter and eye-rolling.

Encouraged, I asked another question, generally reserved for children on a game drive, "Why does a giraffe have such a long neck?"

The group was caught out again.

"Because its head is so far from its body," I said.

That was the cue for the group to rise and get ready to move on, saving everyone from more silly animal jokes.

The terrain began changing and the clusters of baobab trees looked darker because the soil was red with iron. Impala droppings were seen more often, which suggested water was near. Impala are adaptable in habitat and feeding. They switch between browsing and grazing according to where the nutrients are. I stepped on a clump of their oval dry pellets on hard ground, and I almost fell. It was as if I had stepped on ball bearings on a tiled floor.

We agreed to make a detour to visit a cave with Bushmen paintings; the location of which Bjinse had entered on his GPS. It was about a kilometre off route, so we dropped the backpacks beneath a tree without trying to conceal them. On the way to the cave, we stopped at a baobab tree with smashed pods lying on the ground. We suspected baboons had opened them. I tasted the nutrient-rich fruit inside the pod – tangy with a hint of citrus. A fan of the colourful feathers of a lilac-breasted roller lay beneath the tree. It must have met its demise there, but there were no clues as to which creature made a meal of it.

Bjinse's GPS guided us to a hill that stood out with its combination of rock, trees and thick bush. We went around it, looking for an opening to a cave that could have displayed ancient artwork, but without success. I was concerned about leaving our backpacks unprotected and was relieved when we returned to find them untouched.

The top of my backpack was unzipped and the pen was missing while the notebook was still there. I guessed I had failed to zip up properly after the breakfast break and it must have fallen out when I hauled on the backpack.

"Did anyone find a pen when we packed up after breakfast?" I asked.

Pilot looked at me with a mock frown.

"So, you littered," he said, a smile on his face.

Lourens offered me a pencil as a replacement.

We stopped for a brief lunch break beneath a baobab to make up time for the detour to find the Bushman paintings. I had my first toilet foray into the bush, aluminium spade and lighter in hand. Doing ablutions in the bush does not come naturally to me.

As we prepared to leave, I watched an eagle fly over a distant cliff. The Verreauxs' eagle is always close to the high rocky promontories they use for nesting and their preferred meal: dassies. We set off and were barely 100 metres away when Bjinse stopped and told us to put down our backpacks again. He pointed to two sets of shoe tracks. The vivid, damp imprints in the soil could only be from poachers. We suspected they had been on their way to the same baobab tree we stopped at for the lunch break. They must have noticed us as the tracks led away in a different direction to a nearby hill. Bjinse used the satellite phone to radio in the coordinates.

Hanging from a tall tree in the gorge near where the poachers' tracks were headed was what looked like a space blanket. A long cord hung from what must have been a burst weather balloon that had fallen back to earth. I felt deflated. We were supposed to be in pristine bush and there we were, surrounded by tracks from dangerous men and meteorological debris. Is there a single place where we can enjoy Mother Nature without signs of humanity?

Poachers are a real threat in the Kruger, with daily incidents and arrests. Increased hiking activity in Kruger raises the likelihood of them and civilians encountering each other, although none have been recorded. Guides prioritise the safety of the hiking group, especially as poachers can be armed with automatic weapons, typically an AK47, in addition to hunting rifles. They told us, should we come across poachers, there must be no reaction other than to retreat and take cover, with guides radioing in coordinates to the anti-poaching unit.

The afternoon hike took us over rugged terrain with plenty of climbing. It was overcast and windy, the coolness making the uphill walk easier. Animals tend to stay still and are more alert when it is windy, which makes them difficult to see. Dwarf mongooses ran on the rocky outcrops ahead of us. The sun-bleached white shell of a leopard tortoise surrounded by patterned individual panels, called scutes, lay at the foot of a rocky hill. As scutes grow with the seasons, the age of a leopard tortoise can be estimated by counting the ridges, similar to counting the rings of a tree trunk.

We cautiously descended a long rocky hill to a valley with a wavy strip of greenery tracing a dry riverbed. We wove through mopane trees and were told to stay close because we were likely to encounter and surprise animals.

As if to make the point, we soon skirted a gang of buffalo bulls grazing among the trees between us and the river. I knew I was tired when having to go around buffalo annoyed me. My backpack was getting heavier by the minute and I needed a break. I was familiar with this feeling from the closing stages of all the endurance events I have done.

Nevertheless, with the gathering dusk, I knew it was unlikely we would stop before arriving at the place where water drums had been left. I was relieved when Bjinse asked us to each pick up one piece of wood for the fire we would make that night. I knew then the day was done and I was excited about having a fire, too.

We made camp on the coarse sand of the dry riverbed. Six water drums were concealed high on the riverbank. A shower was rigged up behind the trees, with a lush mat of leaves to protect our weary feet. I made myself noodles and had a few sips of whisky from the last miniature bottle. I had packed six, one for each night, but I gave all away except for one. I wanted to dispense with the weight. I had also thought in addition to a technology detox during the hike, it would be good to take a break from alcohol. I did not pack whisky again.

A cold and dewy night below a clear sky found us sitting around the fire and chatting, but I soon went to lie in my tent for a short rest and fell asleep, missing most of the storytelling around the fire.

Before we left camp in the morning, Bjinse poured water over the ashes and scattered the damp residue among the trees. He swept sand over where we had made the fire. Bjinse is fastidious about leaving no trace of our passing other than the inevitable footprints.

Most of the day's hike was on a slight rise through mopane woodlands. The water pans and riverbeds were dry. A southwesterly headwind blew, and it did not help us to see wildlife other than a dassie and a few hares, plus a small herd of impala. They were the only animals we spotted all day.

We examined the large paw print of a spotted hyena, noting the compact step that, with its sloping back, gives the animal stamina and allows it to cover great distances. Being an expert on tracks, Bjinse pointed out the pressure points in the prints which revealed signs of its swagger.

My favourite walking spot was behind Pilot. I was careful not to hog the position, taking turns at the back, my second favourite place. On a few occasions, I stopped to let the group get some distance ahead. I savoured the solitude, before running to catch up, weaving through trees, before I was missed. Now, I look back on it as reckless and this feels like a confession. I was careful to avoid the cold stare from Bjinse I had witnessed whenever someone made a noise or stepped out of line.

Sometime during the morning hike, Arie lost a sole on one of his handmade boots. I sympathised, having been through that myself when training on the Tsitsikamma trail. Unlike my experience where the trail was wet, the ground was dry and Arie hiked unbalanced for three days on the inner sole of his right boot without it falling apart. There was no other option, given where we were.

Thorns are an issue despite sturdy footwear. I was behind Corrie at the back of the group when he cried out in pain. An acacia thorn, incapable of penetrating through elephant hide, had penetrated through the tread pattern of the rubber sole of his boots. A similar thing happened to Lourens on the first day when a thorn pierced through the sole of his well-worn boot and into his foot. He bought new boots after that, but those would cause him so much pain and distress on Leg Three he came close to abandoning the hike.

During one of the afternoon breaks, I leant my backpack and walking pole against a large acacia tree. It was a short break, so I chatted with the group. Once we prepared to leave, I found a spider web woven around my walking pole and backpack. I was amazed at how quickly it happened, and memories of the science fiction horror movie *Kingdom of the Spiders* I watched when I was young, had me ready to begin our trek sooner than usual.

It was mid-afternoon when we arrived at the crescent-shaped rock enclosure; our camp for the night and where water had been left. The shower was set up with the natural equivalent of a tiled floor but it had been an easy and cool hike, and there was no rush to use it. The sun was still up when I prepared dinner on the flat rock onto which my tent opened. Jennifer continued her welcome daily exercise of off-loading excess food to her fellow hikers. I had already spotted tuna, cheese wedges and biltong being dispensed, and I wondered what other treats awaited us.

We gathered around a waist-high table-like rock and while we watched a fiery sunset, we chatted about Kruger, the richness of its legacy and its challenges. The discussion highlighted our concern the Convention on International Trade in Endangered Species of Wild Fauna and Flora – or CITES as it is known – is not delivering on its promises to safeguard wild animals and plants. Talk drifted to social media and how it imposed political correctness.

A round of joke-telling lightened the mood. I pointed out to Henk and Antoinette my CDO was getting the better of me, and I could not understand why Henk walked with one red and one blue pole and Antoinette with just a blue pole.

"Henk, why don't you use both blue poles and let Antoinette use the red pole?" I asked.

Instead of a reply, I was asked, "What is CDO?"

"It's OCD[1], but in alphabetical order," I explained.

The evening breeze was warm and with a waning full moon there was enough light to move about without a torch or the headlamp most of us preferred. Everyone went to sleep early. I awoke in the middle of the night. I do not often dream, yet I dreamt every night in the Kruger.

I needed to relieve myself, but I had failed to do so before turning in for the night, as the safety protocol advised. I opened the tent flap and looked out. With the ample moonlight diffused by clouds, visibility was good, and I did not think to use my headlamp to scan for prowling eyes before exiting. In a most irresponsible action, I stepped outside in my underpants and walked away from the tents in the direction of the pointed horn of the rocky crescent. The moonlight making it easy to step over trivial crevasses and ridges. I stood there, out of earshot of the nearest tent, and did my thing. I savoured the stillness and the moonlit beauty before the recklessness of what I was doing hit me.

Suddenly, I felt vulnerable and a tightness took hold in my chest. I hurried to finish and scurried back to the safety of the tent. I was lucky, as a leopard, a lion, or even a clan of hyenas could have been loitering and I would have been easy prey for any silent killer.

---

1 Obsessive Compulsive Disorder

Mopaneveld

We awakened to a cool, overcast morning and were told to expect an easy hike with a moderate climb in the morning, and then flat terrain with gentle downhills for the rest of the day. The vegetation would continue to be mopane woodlands on mixed soils.

Before we left camp, we gathered for a scolding from Bjinse who was visibly annoyed. He told us he had to burn toilet paper that some in the group had not buried. There was some embarrassed fidgeting when he told us that he and Pilot were experienced trackers and were, by then, familiar with each of our boot prints.

The suitably chastened group set off, and it wasn't long before a Sharpe's grysbok darted away in alarm before us. Things were looking up after the uneventful previous day. We stopped for a break near a buffalo skull bleached white in stark contrast to its black horns. A martial eagle soared over a distant ridge. The largest eagle in Africa has dark brown underwings visible in flight; when perched, it is identified by a white chest covered in black spots.

Bjinse pointed out a distant mountain, unnervingly close to the horizon, where we would camp for the night. We crossed a gravel road leading to Punda Maria before we entered an expanse of mopane thickets adorned by a kaleidoscope of late autumn colours. As we were heading into the wind, animals would not pick up our scent, so Bjinse instructed us to keep in close file. He added that if we encountered a dangerous animal, and only on his signal, we should turn back and walk away briskly but never run.

I focused on the noticeable change in the mopane. Depending on the root's access to water, they look different, and yet are the same. When unsure if it is a mopane or not, I look for the unmistakable butterfly shape of the leaves. Mopaneveld is the dominant ecosystem in the Kruger, covering more than half of the surface area. The mopane tree (*Colophospermum mopane*) has three primary forms in the Kruger.

Mopane woodlands are found mainly in the northwest of the park on granite and gneiss.

Mopane shrubveld or scrub, including large stretches of stunted mopane, tend to be found on basalt, with little grass cover in the northeast and the central northern plains. The trees are smaller owing to the roots being unable to break through the clay to water beneath the surface. They are a source of protein for elephants that love to snack on their leaves and pods.

Mopane thickets are found in the sedimentary ecca shales around Punda Maria, and within another long strip of shale down the centre of the Kruger from south of Satara Rest Camp.

The surface was sandy, yet firm, even on winding animal paths softened by animal traffic. We skirted countless dry waterholes with deep footprints from elephant and buffalo. I imagined the squelchy, sucking noise as they lifted their legs out of what would have been thick mud in their search for water.

Antlion pits were plentiful in the softer sand. Antlions are insects known for the fierce predatory habits of their larvae that dig holes in the shape of an inverted cone to trap prey, primarily ants. When their pupae phase is over, they morph into antlion lacewings, often mistakenly referred to as dragonflies.

We wove around the endless, monotonous, stunted mopane. The white flanks and plain grey back of a chinspot batis perched on a branch, was a stark change from its drab surroundings. The bird never moved despite our proximity. An outcrop of rock and boulders supported a deciduous, rock-splitting, large-leaved rock fig (*Ficus abutilifolia*), with a good covering of leaves in spite of the early winter. The smooth, twisted, pale roots were visible in their age-old crawl across the rock face.

I felt deflated when we came across shoeprints again, seemingly headed to the gravel road we had crossed. We surmised they were Mozambicans illegally crossing the Kruger to go shopping in South Africa. Two sets of distant power lines also spoilt the picture and I realised our trajectory would take us beneath them. Bjinse cautioned we would probably become aware of more evidence of Mozambican shopping migrants there, too.

Later, we broke out of the mopane shrubveld into a service clearing beneath the power lines. To our left, some 200 metres away, we saw an elephant for the first time, a lone, mid-sized bull that turned to face us.

After watching the elephant, we carried on to the distant mountains on the vehicle inspection track for the power lines. The pylons are positioned about 400 metres apart to support high-voltage direct current over 1,420 kilometres, from the Cahora Bassa Dam on the Zambezi River in central Mozambique, to the Apollo inverter station near Johannesburg. Cahora Bassa is the largest hydroelectric scheme in southern Africa, with five turbines generating power, most of which is exported to South Africa.

The Kruger authorities are aware of migrant shoppers from Mozambique following the power lines and have tried to stop individuals from taking this life-threatening path, without much success. We came across two more sets of shoe prints on each lane of the vehicle track.

Conservationist Mitch Reardon wrote in his book *Shaping Kruger*, "Many refugees used the Cahora Bassa powerlines to navigate their way westwards across remote and otherwise largely featureless bush country. Some lions, specialising in human prey, began staking out the powerlines."

Anita Froneman, in a 2021 *Leisure Wheels* article, wrote, "This part of Kruger was the setting for one of the most gruesomely disturbing periods in Southern African history. If you travelled in a straight line, you need to cross 45 kilometres of wilderness to get from the Mozambican border and the first South African settlements. We will never know for sure, but it seems highly likely that the man-eating prides of northern Kruger were probably the deadliest maneaters Africa has ever seen."

This path of desperation and sorrow was leading us to clouds getting heavy and dark with the promise of rain. Our attention was diverted by the tracks of a honey badger. The reputation for fearlessness of these rare animals is well deserved, helped by thick skin resistant to arrows and spears and most natural predators and dangers. They have a symbiotic relationship with honeyguide birds and often team up with them for a prize of honeycomb and bee larvae. Soon after, we picked up the track of a leopard, the softened edges indicating it was a full-sized male that had passed two hours earlier and headed in the same direction as us.

The trees were becoming taller and fuller, and we soon connected with a smallish dry basin that explained the change in vegetation. We followed the catchment area at the beginning of the Shisha River. Rain drizzled, and I delighted in deep inhalations of unpolluted air mixed with the earthy scent of rain on dry soil. The smell of the first rains after a dry spell is pleasant and is referred to as petrichor, where the combination of plant oils and geosmin released from the soil is carried in downdrafts of ozone.

We stopped beneath an enormous mopane tree on the riverbank for lunch, and to take shelter from the persistent drizzle. If it had been up to me, I would have carried on in the drizzle instead of taking cover. I love rain and intemperate weather and will go out for a training run in showers. The contrast in this mopane tree with the shrub-like mopanes on the sandy stretches on which we had spent most of the day, was striking. It was hard to tell it was the same genus.

With the drizzle over, we packed up for the short afternoon hike. Because it was cool and we were close to the finish, there was no need for an afternoon nap. A lone warthog watched us from the safety of the opposite bank. After a pause to check for cars, we broke from the bush cover and crossed the tarred road connecting the H1 main road to Punda Maria. A parked vehicle was close to the roadside water pan, but we crossed behind it out of view.

A herd of impala ran off in alarm when we approached the waterhole on the other side of the road. This waterhole was different to the others; it had pools of deep water but overall, the water level was low and parts were dry. A serene African fish eagle was perched on a sun-bleached dead tree, its white chest glistening in the setting sun. As we approached the water's edge, the eagle hunched as if to take off, but our quick pace on a divergent path gave it comfort, so it sat, imperious upon its perch.

An abandoned water pit was our camp for the last night. It was built as part of the discontinued Water for Game initiative of the 1970s, when hundreds of boreholes and dams were created to give animals greater access to water, until it was discovered this well-meaning effort created an ecological disaster favouring some animals over others.

Later, I asked Bjinse about this. He said that by 1961, the Kruger was fenced on its western boundary, preventing animals like zebra and wildebeest from migrating to find water. In the 1970s, as part of the Water for Game initiative, artificial boreholes and dams were increased to allow animals access to water and help smooth out big surges and dips in animal numbers caused by droughts.

The thinking at the time was this measure would help rare antelope such as tsessebe, roan and sable. Still, it became apparent artificial water resources favoured some species over others. The populations of bulk grazers such as buffalo and zebra, as well as wildebeest, white rhino and elephant grew. As lions spread through the landscape to follow antelope, there was a marked decline in already rare tsessebe, roan and sable. The measures meant to help them were killing them. The greater numbers of bulk grazers shortened the grass those three antelope species used to hide their young, while they fed, leaving them exposed to predators.

Biodiversity was also affected, as the impact of herbivores on the grasses and trees was spread throughout Kruger. It turned out the strategy did not stabilise fluctuations in animal numbers, which continued to follow rainfall patterns. By the turn of the century, science and animal management strategies were adapted. The importance of fluctuations in natural populations was considered and the water policy was revised. This resulted in the closure of more than 150 boreholes in Kruger. Numerous earth-walled dams in the park were dismantled or fell into disrepair, as were the maintenance roads we hiked.

We soon found ourselves in an area filled with tracks of all sizes, including those of an immense pride of lions. The bloody bottom jawbone of a zebra lay amid the paw prints. Hyenas had cleared the bones after the big cat feast and left behind part of the jawbone. I was about to prod a lion dropping with my walking pole when Bjinse warned me about the smell; protein-rich lion scat has a vile scent that lingers.

Two saddle-billed storks landed on the opposite bank but soon took off again, probably because of the abnormal presence of humans. Their wings in flight are a striking contrast in black and white. As we turned to head into the setting sun, we found tell-tale signs of the zebra kill. Drag marks led through the dry section of the water pan and up the bank on the other side to where we had noticed the lion prints and the jawbone. It was likely it was the drag marks of the hyena pulling the carcass after the lions had finished. A recent footprint on the drag marks was from a young leopard.

The artificial waterhole that served as a campsite for the night was a pit sunk into the ground with a wide escape ramp for any animals that fell in. The pit was large enough to accommodate our 10 tents. Six water drums, an assortment of treats for the evening – including two bottles of wine – and our daypacks for the last day of the hike were concealed in a covered concrete hole.

On the Sunday before we started the hike, we each gave Bjinse a daypack for the last day. He placed them in the covered spot when he dropped off the water drums. I looked forward to hiking with just a daypack.

I was one of the first to use the shower erected by the guides with a leafy floor mat beneath a large tree. An African fish eagle circled high above me, whistling as I looked up. I was blessed by the distinctive wail, so symbolic of Africa, as I stood free yet vulnerable, naked and exposed, in the African wild. The eagle was too high for me to tell but I am convinced we made eye contact.

As the sun set, we cracked open the wine for sundowners. A 2014 Blue Crane Shiraz and a 2016 Laborie Merlot were perfect for the occasion. It was just as good, and in those circumstances even enhanced, by drinking the wine out of aluminium or plastic cups. Corrie did not have a cup because he does not drink tea or coffee, so, to our amusement, he enjoyed his ration of fine red wine out of his cooking pot.

After dinner, we sat on the ramp and chatted. I lay on my back, mesmerised by the vastness of the night sky and stars shimmering like diamonds. Two shooting stars flashed across the sky. I missed a few more the others pointed out. I don't know if the purity of the darkness made them more visible, or if we were just lucky, but the number of them was astonishing. An aeroplane flew high above us on a northeasterly heading. I calculated it was going to a south-east Asian destination from Johannesburg. The flashing strobe lights of the aircraft were clearly visible but it was so far away, there was no sound disturbing the peace of the wild.

A giant, spooky-looking hyena prowled hungrily around the pit, feigning disinterest as it sniffed the ground. We kept a wary eye on him. Lions roared nearby. No doubt still digesting their feast of zebra. I held my breath after a second closer roar could have meant the lions were closing in, but my fears were groundless. Nevertheless, Bjinse mounted a flashlight on his rifle. Jennifer was nervous and we had to calm her down, pointing out Bjinse was just being cautious. I teased Bjinse about our weak position relative to the lions and hyena. "Bjinse, when under attack, which part of taking the higher ground did you miss?" I asked.

As we turned in for the night, I had to urinate. I was not planning to climb out of my sleeping place during the night with the hyena prowling, lions roaring and a waterhole nearby. I scanned the bush with my headlamp and no eyes reflected. The hyena had moved on for now. On the way back to the pit, I examined the surrounding bush with the headlamp, and eyes reflected at the foot of a tree close to the pit. I guessed it was a nightjar or a francolin and approached for a closer look. It did not move as a bird might; the gleaming turquoise jewels remained fixed. I got to the tree and was still unable to identify it, even though I was standing right by it. I bent down for a closer look and was amazed at what looked like a baboon spider. I had no idea spider eyes were so large relative to their body size.

The next morning, a tickle of excitement permeated the preparations for the last day of Leg One, partly because of the literal weight off our shoulders, but also because after six days it would be good to return to our families and homes. We expected to hike through open savanna peppered with stunted mopane for the longest hike of the first Leg.

I felt like the weakest link as we packed up. Despite working as fast as I could, I was behind the rest of the group with everything from eating to packing up my tent. I wished I could better emulate Clifford's time management, which he explained as being, "...important for me to start each day feeling unrushed and never holding the group back when heading off".

He said, "Bjinse shared with me the art of packing up more than one thing at a time, effectively halving the time to dismantle the camp. It allowed me to sit each morning and contemplate where I was and life in general while others were packing up. This was a precious time for me. I don't recall a morning where I wasn't listening for the distant 'ooh-ooh-ooh' calls of the southern ground hornbill," he added, referring to his favourite bird. "And then, if I still had time, I would read the 'bush newspaper' around camp from the previous night's animal activity."

We carried the backpacks and empty water drums to conceal them beneath shady trees. Everyone had a daypack except for Corrie, who insisted on carrying his bulky backpack after emptying most of what he had into a plastic bag he left with the other backpacks.

We set off on a disused water management road. Four paws around a large pad signified the track of a big lion walking in the same direction as us. A male lion track is up to 14.5 centimetres long, with four distinct toes, a large central pad, and three lobes behind it. The track was windswept and the edges feathery, so it must have been about a day old. A fish eagle called, and even though we could not find it, we stopped to discuss the difference between the mellow male call and the shrill siren of the female. There is also the lower pitch of the hunter in flight versus the parent near the nest when it gives more of a 'quock' sound. Most missed the black-backed jackal I observed cross the path behind us as we chatted.

A peacefully grazing cluster of impala ran off when we spilled from the tree cover onto a grassy plain. I heard the 'keks' of a hamerkop, before I noticed it standing alone on one of the fever trees that dotted the open ground. It was odd, as they are normally silent when alone, though vocal in groups. The bird is called a hamerkop because of the shape of its head, curved bill and back crest, which resembles a hammer. Whenever I come across them, I feel as if I'm conveyed back to medieval times because their shape and dusky-brown feathers evoke superstition and tales of dark omens. I react similarly to crocodiles and their broad bodies covered in leathery plate-shaped scales, short legs and long, thick muscular tail.

A fish eagle perched on the highest branches of a tall, bare tree caught my attention before another flew to the same tree. When it landed, they called out in the high-pitched whistling sound generally recognised as the call of Africa.

We came to a waterhole that was a muddy slush. I guessed after another week in the baking sun it would become hard, dried mud. The corpse of a hyena lay on its side at the edge. Its head and half of its body in the muddy water, but I could not make out what had brought it down. It was still in one piece and I wondered if it had got stuck in the mud. On the opposite bank, a stiff and alert tsessebe watched us uneasily from the safety of the mopane. Only its dark head and horns were visible, with its chestnut brown body hidden by trees. This is supposed to be the fastest antelope in Africa, reaching up to 100 kilometres per hour. I hoped it would catch fright and give us a show, but it remained still, allowing us to pass.

As we hiked, Bjinse pointed out topographical changes. The interplay in vegetation and soils was stark, and Bjinse helped us to understand this. Where the mopane was tall, the terrain was sandy, with minimal ground cover because of the competition for nutrients. After we entered an area with sparse mopane and dominant grasses, it became easier to spot animals. Like clusters of giraffes, zebra and warthogs. We followed animal paths until the track went in the wrong direction for our needs. We hiked for long stretches through pathless, stony grasslands, guided by Bjinse and his GPS. The afternoon was sweltering, and I was thankful for the light daypack.

As we rounded a tree, the frantic flapping of wings frequently scared us, usually from a francolin flying out in alarm from the shade of the tree where it had been resting. I always took more fright from Jennifer's screams than from the bird.

We walked hard all day in the heat and I was feeling it. I was in my favourite place behind Pilot when I stepped aside to go to the back of the line for a change. As everyone filed past, I was shocked at the state of each group member. There were drooping heads and grim expressions. While I was somewhat relieved it was not just me taking strain, I sensed we were pushing too hard, and something or someone would eventually give. Worst of all was Corrie, right at the back, hunched and leaning far forward.

We stopped for water and a short break in the shade of a conspicuous tall mopane tree, with roots that had somehow broken through the shale. Our destination was in the distance on the other side of a gentle slope down to the green belt tracing the riverbed, about an hour's hike. The wind from behind betrayed our presence, and in the distance, elephants with young stampeded away. A few tall trees loomed above the mopane shrubveld, and a giraffe's tense, ruler-straight neck moved as it turned its head to watch from the surrounding trees. As the tallest land animal at up to 5.5 metres, plenty of animals rely on its ability to identify predators early.

We readied for the last push to the finish; waiting a few minutes more for Corrie. It was clear he was struggling, but he is a fighter and did his best not to slow the group. The mopane soon gave way to other vegetation including thick, long grasses we trudged through. We approached a craggy section of the river for a short, steep descent to cross over the jagged rocks to the opposite bank. I was behind Pilot and again, I pulled over to the side to let the group pass and catch my breath before taking on the crossing. Clifford was second-to-last in the line and in front of Corrie, who was at the back. Corrie was shuffling, hunched over and on the verge of collapse. I fell in behind Corrie and became more concerned. I thought about alerting the guides, who, because they were at the front had no idea how bad Corrie was looking. We were so close to the finish I thought Corrie could make it.

With everyone showing signs of exhaustion, the line had stretched out, and by the time I got to the river, Bjinse and Pilot had crossed over the rocks. They were waiting halfway up the opposite bank, pointing to a small bunch of waterbuck upriver. I tried to grab their attention by waving my arms and pointing at Corrie, who was falling and stumbling. The difficult crossing was too much for him and, as he reached the other side, he collapsed on the rocks with a thud.

Everyone rushed to his aid. We sat him up and took off his backpack. I could hear the generator near the Ranger's home at Vlakteplaas, where we would finish. We gave Corrie a few minutes to recover before helping him move to the top of the ridge for safety. The generator's noise was teasing, testing our patience; we knew refreshments were waiting for us at camp. I was unnerved by how Corrie had walked 87.7 kilometres over six days at a solid pace, including over 18 kilometres on this day, yet he had buckled within sight of the finish. We waited for him to recover before walking on. The last stretch to the Vlakteplaas compound was flat and easy through short, narrow-leaved turpentine grass. I smelt the eponymous oils in the grass, which is why it is not grazed when mature.

As we took pictures, shook hands and hugged, a vehicle pulled up with ice, beers and soft drinks for the trip back to Punda Maria. It drove into the compound through the open gate of a game-proof fence protecting the main house and satellite buildings. Corrie soon recovered and was back to his usual cheery self.

I travelled with Bjinse, Corrie, Clifford and Arie back to Pafuri to pick up Corrie's Freelander. From there, Bjinse and I rushed to pick up the backpacks we had left behind that morning and collect the empty water drums from three overnight camps. The gates at Punda Maria Rest Camp closed at 17:30, and we hurried. The noose of time was back and tightening its grip. True to form, Bjinse stopped the car to sweep the tyre tracks away when we left the pathway after collecting the backpacks. He also respected the speed limits and, with official SANParks staff magnetic stickers on the vehicle, he travelled 15 kilometres per hour faster than the public. We got to camp as the gates were closing.

We took a vote about dinner back at the camp, all choosing waiter service in the restaurant, except for Corrie, who wanted to braai. Pilot had to leave, so the rest of us had dinner in the Tindlovu Restaurant with Bjinse handing out T-shirts decorated with a map of the Kruger hike. Buffalo pie was a popular choice. We brushed aside derisory comments from the few weekend vegetarians who could not bring themselves to eat our recent acquaintances.

LEG TWO

Vlakteplaas Ranger's Post to Mopani Rest Camp
SPRING, SEPTEMBER 2019

South Africa's Springbok rugby team was playing its opening game against the New Zealand All Blacks in the Rugby World Cup final in Yokohama, Japan when Arie Fourie and I drove to Kruger for the second stage of our hike. South Africans are mad about rugby, and we listened on the car radio. The result was devastating. The All Blacks defeated the Springboks 23 to 13.

Our despair turned to glee weeks later when the Springboks, under the captaincy of Siya Kolisi, defeated England in an epic final that united South Africa. The *New York Times* summed up the jubilation of South Africans with a headline that read: "Rugby World Cup Final: South Africa Crushes England." The sub-head read: "The Springboks won the country's third World Championship, 32-12, extending the dominance of teams from the southern hemisphere."

But that news was to come. In between commenting on the game, Arie and I got to know each other. He had completed the three-night Lonely Bull and Olifants backpack trails in the Kruger and said, "I enjoyed those hikes but wished they lasted longer, so when I heard about The Kruger Trails hike, I wanted to do it."

Our group should have camped at Shingwedzi Rest Camp instead of Punda Maria, some 70 kilometres north, however, the camp was closed for the three-decade-old Baroque in the Bush musical extravaganza. This beloved event brings together 16 musicians, under the direction of veteran conductor Dr Richard Cock, to perform baroque ensembles over three days. The concert hall is a large, thatched veranda overlooking the seasonal Shingwedzi River. In September, the riverine surrounds dress for the concert in bright green spring foliage and an appreciative audience of elephants.

Arie and I pitched our tents at Punda Maria Rest Camp in the same spot I used for Leg One. Everyone else stayed at Mopani Rest Camp on Saturday night. We braaied meat for dinner and ate it on bread rolls.

Arrangements were made to meet at Mopani Rest Camp on Sunday morning to place food in trunks to be left with water containers at the expected overnight locations for the second and fourth nights. After some debate, Arie and I agreed to do the almost three-hour drive to Mopani Rest Camp, 60 kilometres south of the Shingwedzi Rest Camp, to save carrying all our food from the start. We left early on Sunday morning and arrived at Mopani, the newest lodge accommodation in the Kruger, in time for a late breakfast. On the way, we watched two cheetahs strolling down the road. It was hard to imagine the stately pair reaching 118 kilometres per hour in a sprint.

We met Lourens and Jennifer at their bungalows, and they introduced us to Raymond Brown and Jennifer's husband, Morné Bester, who took the places of Henk and Antoinette Jonker. The Jonkers had relocated to the Netherlands because of an employment opportunity. Ray was a friend of the Van Aardt family and shared the bungalow with Lourens. I was introduced to Arnold Bam and Warren Deyzel, our guides for Leg Two. They looked the part in their olive outfits, SANParks insignia and matching long beards. I suspected we were going to have fun with them. Arnold told us he is married and lives with his wife and two daughters in White River. Bachelor Warren lives in Benoni, a small town east of Johannesburg.

We waited for Corrie and his wife Maritha, who took up the place temporarily relinquished by Clifford, who was in the Kruger with his family for their annual vacation. I remained concerned about Corrie's collapse at the finish of the first Leg, but I knew he would come prepared for the longer distances and hotter weather of Leg Two. Maritha, a software consultant, had 18 months prior undergone knee replacement surgery. Over the next few days, I would see how strong and tenacious she was.

After the introductions, we prepared to head to Punda Maria for an early dinner in the camp restaurant. Arie, Morné and I climbed into the back of Arnold's double-cab, with Warren and Arnold in front. Sixteen polycans, each carrying 25 litres of water, and two metal trunks with food were loaded into the van and a trailer hitched to the back. We needed to make the drops at the planned stops for the second and fourth nights, before parking the trailer at Shingwedzi Rest Camp, where we would sleep at the end of the hike.

We had a long way to go, so Arnold drove as fast as we were allowed. Once we were off the tarred road, we transferred the water and the food trunk into the back of the van and concealed the trailer behind some trees. It allowed us to go faster, and Arnold handled the rocky and rutted sections of the little-used roads like a rally driver.

I was disappointed by the fourth night stop in the middle of a vast, flat expanse of mopane shrub at an unsightly radio repeater station used for internal radio traffic by rangers. We hid the water cans and the food trunk beneath the stilted structure.

Teasing between Arnold and Warren began, and time passed quickly as we drove on roads closed to the public. I interrupted their jesting to ask, "I've heard you talk about trail guides, field guides, rangers and more. I'm confused. What do you call yourselves?"

"Legends!" Warren shouted with pride. Now we knew.

My question induced reminiscing. Arnold spoke of his love for the wild. "It started from a very young age with my grandfather. He instilled a deep love of nature during numerous multiday hikes across South Africa. My grandfather is a humble man, sagacious, and with immense knowledge and understanding of nature.

"After I finished school, I completed a two-year diploma in nature conservation, but work in conservation was not easy to find. Fortunately, I was already a member of the Field Guides Association of Southern Africa. The Kruger has always been at the forefront of nature conservation and the knowledge and skills I obtained with the FGASA enabled me to guide The Kruger Trail."

Yet, he needed to glean more experience: "To me, the ultimate guiding job was always the unsupported backpack experience, so for a few years, I did that on the Olifants, Lonely Bull and Mphongolo trails. When the opportunity arose to participate in The Kruger Trail, I did not hesitate. TKT is a milestone in my guiding career. After experiencing what Louis achieved for nature conservation, it is an accomplishment to be a small part of such a wonderful project."

Warren chipped in. "I grew up on a smallholding in Johannesburg. Nature was in our back garden. I was introduced to the Kruger National Park by my mother, Elaine. She took me and my three older siblings to Kruger Park several times a year. As the years rolled by, my love and appreciation for this magnificent place grew stronger.

"I later studied engineering like my dad, but over the years, I realised I wanted to be a part of Kruger. This is where I need to be. One evening, I found myself praying for an opportunity to live in the Kruger Park, and a few days later, I received a job opportunity to manage a small private concession in Kruger Park. I sold my house, resigned from my job, got rid of all the anchors I had in Johannesburg, and headed to the Kruger to establish my new home.

"Within a year of living at Berg-en-Dal Rest Camp inside the Kruger Park, I knew it wasn't enough to just be in the Kruger, and my journey to become a Nature Guide began. I did the Special Knowledge and Skills in Dangerous Game qualification in fewer than six years; a certification that is usually achieved within 10 to 15 years.

"I was lucky enough to get involved with The Kruger Trail from the beginning and this is the highlight of my guiding experience so far. I've driven every single road, I've slept in every riverbed, I've walked north to south, and I've even flown it in fixed-wing aircraft and helicopters. The Kruger National Park is in my blood, it's in my heart," he said.

By the time we got to dinner on the deck outside the restaurant at Punda Maria Rest Camp, I felt I was among friends. The last thing I did that night was to phone my eldest daughter, Shelby, to wish her happy birthday for the next day.

I spent a night of relative luxury in a bungalow and woke early, feeling a frisson of nervous excitement. The distances for this hike were long and we anticipated more animal encounters than the first Leg. I could tell the other hikers shared my excitement. We squeezed ourselves and 10 backpacks into two vehicles and were ready to leave at 05:30.

Halfway to the starting point at Vlakteplaas Ranger's Post, we stopped to watch two lionesses stalking a tsessebe alongside a deserted road. I had dispensed with my watch and had no idea how long it took, but the trip seemed to drag until we left the tarred road and turned onto a gravel road with a 'No Entry' sign.

The vehicles were parked and I made final checks on my backpack while the guides attended to administrative matters. A squad of six uniformed men, the anti-poaching unit, were huddled in discussion nearby. Most elephant poaching occurs in the northern Kruger, while rhino poachers concentrate on the south. Organised crime syndicates poach for ivory and rhino horn, but many poachers come from impoverished communities along the Kruger's western 300 kilometre boundary. They use snares to entrap animals for consumption or to sell the meat. Even though Kruger Park is one of the major employers for communities along its border, most villagers are poor, with scant job opportunities. A lot of people depend on poachers for cheap meat. With some towns on the western boundary less than 100 kilometres from Mozambique, undocumented migrants add to the problem. Wildlife poachers are also involved with cattle theft, slaughtering the animals for their meat, or driving them through the Kruger into Mozambique.

Poachers use snares to trap animals and up to 200 snares can be found in a single area. The snares are placed on and around paths leading to water. These wire traps differ in size and can catch any animal, from buffalo and wildebeest to kudu, impala and smaller antelope. They are often tied to a tree and the wire makes a loop that tightens around the animal's neck and suffocates it. Trapped animals are slaughtered and the meat is smuggled out of the Kruger, where it is sold in informal markets. It is estimated only a few of the trapped animals end up in the pot, with countless carcasses left to rot.

In addition to the illicit trade in bush meat, traps are set for scavengers such as hyenas, jackals and birds, including vultures and marabou storks. Because these creatures feed on carrion, scavengers are regarded as the villains of the wild, making their body parts useful as muthi to sangomas: the herbalists and 'doctors' of traditional African medicine.

The Kruger has also had a puzzling increase in poisoned carcasses, a practice debilitating to vultures. In one incident where an elephant carcass was poisoned, two lions and more than 100 vultures died. Authorities have yet to divine what the purpose is behind this.

SANParks rangers use dogs in anti-poaching initiatives, with up to 90 percent of arrests made in the Kruger aided by breeds such as the bloodhound, Belgian shepherd and Malinois. They track poachers and detect firearms, ammunition and wildlife products, including rhino horn and ivory. Training each dog takes three months. It is then assigned to a handler with whom it stays for the rest of its life. Tracker dogs are deployed by helicopter or vehicle and operate throughout the Kruger. These remarkable dogs work for five to six hours before taking a rest and can follow a scent for up to 48 hours over impressive distances. Poachers are armed and dogs provide vital early warnings for rangers and handlers, thanks to their superior senses of smell, hearing and eyesight.

In addition to the increased use of rangers and the South African National Defence Force to combat poaching, efforts continue to find better solutions. The long-term aim is to engender a sense of buy-in from the communities bordering the Kruger and other national parks, though poverty trumps diplomacy and this has met with limited success.

Run!

Waving goodbye to the brave anti-poaching team, I shouldered my backpack and focused on the journey ahead. The thing that concerned me was the unseen danger: heat. I knew some groups endured temperatures close to 40 degrees Celsius on Leg Two, but a cold front blew in and a chilly southeasterly wind stayed with us all week.

The first animal sightings were of zebra and impala before we stopped to look at a large termite mound defaced by an aardvark hole. This nocturnal has a long pig-like snout to sniff out food and can locate larvae developing inside dung pellets buried 30 centimetres underground. They use their strong claws to dig through the hard crust of termite mounds, and their holes may host up to 17 different mammal species, including leopard, jackal, hyena, porcupine and warthog, as well as reptiles and birds, which use the abandoned burrows for refuge.

We stopped again around a scattering of two different piles of elephant dung. The smaller was compact and lighter in colour and when we broke it open, the vegetation inside was well chewed. From the longest piece of bark in the dung, the length of one-and-a-half matches, we estimated it was from an elephant around 25 years old and in its prime. The larger pile was loosely compacted and darker in colour, made up of whole leaves, bits of bark and small pieces of sticks and twigs. An elephant has a total of 26 teeth if you include the two tusks that are effectively upper incisors. They have only four molars, designed for grinding tough vegetation, at any given time. What we were looking at came from an elephant near the end of its life. Its final set of molars were so worn down it could not grind leaves, bark or other coarse vegetation. It would not be long before it succumbed to malnutrition and died, as the limiting factor for an elephant's life expectancy is the condition of its teeth and how that affects its ability to chew vegetation.

We hiked through mixed riverine forest following a dry, sandy riverbed marked by antelope and elephant tracks, until we moved away from the river into mopane shrubveld and had the first of many tense encounters with elephants. An elephant walked towards us and so we stopped at a safe distance in the shade of a tree. We were distracted watching the elephant go by when someone shouted a warning. A second elephant was just 30 metres away and heading for us. We huddled behind Arnold and Warren as they took up defensive positions, standing an arm's length apart with their rifles at the ready. Even with the elephant's poor eyesight, we were within its range of sight, which was confirmed by its raised trunk and flapping ears. When the elephant was about 20 metres away, Arnold shouted. The elephant shook its head vigorously, flapped its ears noisily, and moved away to our right. By then, the other elephant was out of sight.

Encounters with elephants, the heaviest land animal at 6,500 kilograms, dominated our first day. Thankfully, we were led by two experienced guides. Arnold had been forced to shoot an elephant a few months before when leading a group on Leg One. Louis Lemmer was the lead guide with that group, but he was not feeling well that day and put Arnold in charge. As the group was weaving its way through mopane shrubs, they encountered a breeding herd. Two of the elephant cows mock-charged the hikers before stopping. A third cow charged from behind the other two and halted before them in a cloud of dust.

As the air cleared, the two cows moved back to join the troop, but the third charged again. Arnold fired the first shot that stunned but did not kill the elephant. Louis fired the kill shot into the brain. The elephant collapsed three metres from where they were standing. One more shot was fired to ensure it was dead.

Such incidents are rare and are not taken lightly by the guides or hikers. Whenever it happens, there is much introspection. Could it have been avoided? Why did it happen? What can be done to avoid this happening again? The question of when to shoot is important with elephants because they mock-charge. Guides need to know the difference. Guides are under immense pressure in those situations; life or death is dependent on split-second decisions.

After calming down from our first close encounter with elephants, we continued through the mopaneveld. A green and shady riverine forest traced the dry riverbed in the distance to the east. We aimed to stop for breakfast when we reached the trees. The southeasterly wind strengthened and we headed directly into it. We kept walking into elephants hidden by the high mopane shrub and were forced to backtrack on countless occasions.

Tension rose when we heard a stampede of elephants. Or so we thought. The mopane was too high to see anything in the distance and, in every direction, we seemed to hear elephants. The stampede grew louder. It had been drummed into us to never run; it's the worst thing you can do, as you will never outrun an animal. I could not believe it when I heard Arnold scream, "Ruuuuun" as he disappeared behind the mopane.

I followed anxiously in the confusion, trundling under the weight of my backpack, and looking back for charging elephants as I ran to keep up with Arnold. The disciplined hiking line broke as we raced through mopane. It was every person for themselves until we regrouped, breathless around the guides, everyone peering east in the direction of the stampede. We couldn't run anymore and I feared we were about to be flattened.

The cacophony of the stampede stopped abruptly. Then it started and stopped again. It did not make sense. It could not be the sound of elephants running. Arnold then remembered the South African National Defence Force had been planning to run military exercises at the Langtoon Dam, some 16 kilometres to the east. They were burning the veld around the dam in preparation for the exercises, to prevent vegetation fires set off by incendiary devices and explosions. Because the Kruger borders Mozambique and Zimbabwe, there is a military base close to the Langtoon Dam. It is not unusual for military exercises to take place there. The sound we heard was artillery fire.

The elephants were as agitated by the noise as we were and Arnold took pains to explain we ran only to get away from an area where we thought elephants were stampeding. We were not in sight of any animals, so it was safe to run. Nothing was said about us being within range of artillery fire.

The breakfast stop was a chance to recover. Abundant butterflies, starlings and yellow-billed hornbills made me feel at peace after the recent chaos. The northern part of the Kruger is ideal for birding and I hoped to see some of the first migrant birds arrive from the northern hemisphere. I also wanted to become better acquainted with Little Brown Jobs, or LBJs as peepers call them; a term for the scores of brown passerine birds notoriously difficult to identify. Females tend to lack the colouring of male birds.

The Kruger is a tree lover's haven, and some of Kruger's most beautiful trees are found in the drainage lines and rivers of the north; giant jackalberry, nyala, tamboti and sycamore fig trees abound. The evergreen typical cluster fig (*Ficus sycomorus*), or sycamore fig, is my favourite tree because of its stand-out presence, thanks to its vast fluted, buttressed trunk and spreading crown. The leaves are nutritious and various birds, insects and animals eat the fruit. Several of our guides on later hikes told us more about the symbiotic relationship between the tree and the fig wasp that ensures its survival.

Following the Mphongolo River, we arrived at the Sirheni Dam, which was being deconstructed to allow the free flow of fish species. The Kruger harbours over 40 fish species, and the man-made dams are a hindrance to their migration and survival. Wheelbarrows and construction materials surrounded a group of workers dressed in bright yellow. A family of four warthogs ran off from a drinking hole when we approached. The hole had been scraped out in the riverbed, possibly by elephants.

We crossed the river and stopped for a welcome break in the shade of an enormous tree with a dense crown of dark green leaves on its drooping branches. It was an evergreen nyala tree (*Xanthocercis zambesiaca*), supported by fertile alluvial soil close to the waterline. Given the time of year, it was devoid of fruits or flowers.

Lunch was meant to be brief because we wanted to press on past the scheduled night stop and reach the hot, sulphury Matiovila spring, where we would find water. We were exhausted by the morning's events and most of the group, including Arnold, fell asleep. Warren took the opportunity to eat his three-bean salad without taunts from Arnold, who teased him about having to carry the heavy item.

After lunch, another brief stop had us tasting the salty leaves of a broadleaf mustard tree (*Salvadora persica*), its sprawling pale bluish-grey branches hanging to the ground. The sticks of this evergreen tree are traditionally used as toothbrushes.

My mind was on the hot spring we were headed for and its imagined pleasures. The Matiovila hot spring is one of three spring mire complexes in the Kruger. The sulphuric water originates from deep aquifers that discharge at geological faults, and we were warned it would not be pleasant to drink. We neared the spring on a well-worn animal path. It was hot and windy, and a gang of four buffalo bulls lay on the ground amid the mopane, seeking shelter from the sun and wind. Their comfort engendered envy. We heard the playful and angry trumpet of elephants at the spring and gave them a wide berth.

Warren followed Arnold as we descended into the riverine bush. He was the first to spot a leopard coming towards us from the spring. It took him a moment to react – he was frozen by not knowing whether to alert the group and scare away the leopard or keep silent and give everyone a chance to observe it. I was behind Warren and saw the lean, spotted haunches of the leopard as it turned and disappeared into the trees. Other than the two guides in front, only Jennifer and I were lucky enough to witness the beautiful spotted creature.

I spotted the small hot spring close to a flat, elevated stand of subtly fragrant tamboti trees where we would make camp for the night. It had been an eventful day and a hike of more than 20 kilometres. I was exhausted, probably more from the adrenaline thanks to the wild animal encounters, than from the distance. A number of elephants were in and around the small spring. It would be some time before it was safe for us to collect water, so we headed to the stand of tamboti trees to avoid them.

The sun was going down and I was keen to offload my backpack and make camp, but we did not get far. A procession of elephants on the path we were about to cross was heading to the spring. We retreated. A royal march of trumpeting and foraging bulls, cows and calves swayed down the path, but another parade behind them was also heading to the spring, so we were unable to advance. It was a long wait as we sheltered alongside a fallen tree trunk high enough to lean against.

A young male elephant left the spring, seemingly oblivious to our presence, and approached us. He was close enough to us when he raised his trunk to sniff the air. After a pause, he continued approaching anyway. The insolence of youth, I thought. We scrambled behind the fallen tree trunk as Arnold and Warren took up defensive positions. Arnold aimed his rifle and shouted at the elephant. It stopped, shook its head in annoyance and retreated.

I was getting over that adrenaline rush when a small elephant, little more than a calf, headed for us. Thankfully, it turned and went back before sensing the human intruders.

The sun was setting and we needed water before nightfall. The spring was the only source of water in the area, and we were stuck in the middle of a parade of elephants. No doubt, other animals needed to drink as well. I like watching the cats in the Kruger but right then, I felt no need. A gap opened on the path to the spring, so we moved swiftly to the flat ground in the stand of tamboti trees to set up camp.

I rested my backpack against a tamboti tree after checking I was not going to set up my tent on a thoroughfare to the spring. Tamboti trees (*Spirostachys africana*) are semi-deciduous to evergreen, with a straight trunk and narrow straggly canopy. Notwithstanding the proximity to water, the trees looked unharmed despite the fondness of porcupines for the dark, rectangular bark. They sometimes ring-bark the tree, killing it off. Other than kudu that browse on the leaves of saplings, only porcupines and black rhinos feed on the trees. A poisonous latex is exuded by the bark, which indigenous people use for arrowhead poison, and if the bark is burnt, it has a harsh odour that irritates human eyes and skin. Numerous campers in the South African bush have suffered the after-effects of using tamboti wood to braai. Using the wood to cook meat causes severe stomach cramps with diarrhoea and vomiting. It is better to use the beautiful, fragrant wood for luxury furniture.

I was still deciding where to set up my tent when the elephants left the spring. Everyone grabbed water bottles and bladders, and we hurried to the spring. I put a hand into the muddy water and wondered how much elephant urine had contributed to the warmth. I winced at the thought of cooking and drinking that water as I filled one of my two bladders. I knew the smell would stay in it for days, and I wanted to keep one of the bladders untainted.

As expected, it was not long before another herd descended the path to the spring. We didn't have all the water we needed, but were forced to hurry away to the other side of the muddy rivulet. We sat on the bank in silence and took photographs as the elephants drank and the calves rolled and submerged themselves in the spring. A couple of elephants milled about the tamboti trees where our backpacks were. Thankfully, nobody had citrus because if detected, the elephants would have ripped the backpack to pieces in search of the tasty fruit.

We sat on the bank and save for the occasional whisper, waited quietly. I was enthralled by the unfettered proximity to Africa's largest mammal. Herds of elephant arrived as others left. At times, there were more than 20 elephants of all sizes around the spring. Despite the impending darkness, I was not bothered until a departing herd of elephants headed in our direction. Following Arnold's curt instruction, everyone retreated. I was the last to go and only after I was deservedly scolded for taking a picture, still seated with my feet in the frame, to capture the proximity of the elephants. Their size masks the speed at which they move. I had left myself in danger and any elephant that may have attacked me.

We could get back to the campsite only by taking a detour. The same thing happened again at the fallen tree we had sheltered behind when we arrived. This time a bull elephant trundled in our direction. We scrambled behind the fallen tree trunk as the guides readied their weapons. Arnold shouted at the elephant and once more, the huge creature retreated. I was emotionally and physically drained from standing our ground against elephants. It was a matter of time before our luck ran out and I felt I couldn't take any more.

We finished setting up the tents as daylight faded. I laid out the small groundsheet I had added to my packing list for this Leg. There was another interval with no elephants at the spring, so we hurried with two collapsible buckets to collect more of the muddy, agitated water.

Back at camp, Arnold used a Sawyer mini water filter to do the arduous filtration work for most of us. Lourens used a different, larger type of filter for himself, Ray and Jennifer. I added purification drops. The water filters removed the sediment and particles but did little for the colour and nothing for the taste. The putrid smell of sulphur was intense. Looking on the bright side, I reasoned the sulphur obscured the taste of the elephant's waste matter. I transferred my remaining clean water into the untainted water bladder built into my backpack, and filled the other bladder with filtered water. I cooked instant noodles in the spring water; no salt or spices were necessary.

It would have made matters worse to wash using the sulphuric spring water, so nobody showered. It blew during the night with gusts threatening to lift the tents. Despite the wind, I heard the trumpeting of elephants at the spring, and I prayed that for the rest of the night the footsteps of giants led only into the unquiet darkness of Africa.

Before dawn, we awakened and packed up for an early start. This was different from how Bjinse ran the show on Leg One, when nobody left the tents before first light. The aim now was to cover a substantial part of the day's hike before breakfast for an early finish. The other change was that the lead for the day alternated between Arnold and Warren.

Soon after, we came across the Mfayeni mire and its thermal spring. The rich soil formed a dome of peat moss, crowning an oasis of wild palms and reeds in the dry riverbed. The tracks of a solitary, nocturnal African civet ran alongside the mound. We wove through mopane shrubveld for most of the morning, often skirting small gangs of buffalo or solitary buffalo bulls. A group of waterbuck grazed as we approached a baobab tree that had a hole gouged out of it, large enough to sit in. We dropped the backpacks and took pictures, posing in and around the hole. Baobabs are succulents and elephants break through the soft bark to reach the juicy sponge-like inner tree.

After the photo shoot, we continued until we reached the soft, sandy riverbed of the Phugwane River. Squirrels scurried into the riverine forest to escape us. Elephants stood on the sloping bank and picked leaves off the trees as we crossed. The wind was so chilly I rolled down my sleeves. We followed the riverbed until we stopped for breakfast at a fallen tree trunk long enough to seat all of us. To conserve my untainted water for drinking, I made coffee using the sulphuric water from the spring. It wasn't good, but it was hot and I needed that. I sipped my coffee as I watched a troop of baboons move briskly through the trees on the opposite bank. They seemed to take no interest in us, though I did wonder if they were moving so fast because of our presence.

While sipping brackish coffee, I asked Arnold about the Glock 22, with a numbered seal, he carried in a holster on his hip. Arnold carries the Glock for personal protection when he travels and, by law, it must always be on his person or in a safe. Unlike Bjinse and Pilot, who carried SANParks-issued .458 rifles on Leg One, Arnold and Warren were armed with their own rifles. Arnold's rifle was a Zastava, made in the Czech Republic, and fires .375 Holland & Holland magnum bullets he loads himself. The 350-gram monolithic grain bullet is fired at around 2,400 feet per second and is effective against a thick hide of an elephant. Arnold carries only six rounds on his hip belt, configured into two sets of three for quick, unsighted reloading. The other six rounds were in his bag.

Warren carried a South African-made Musgrave .375 which shoots the same H&H rounds as Arnold. He carried 10 additional rounds on a hip belt and two in his bag, adding another kilogram or so to the weight. Warren's rifle is a collector's item, series number 258, and the last one meticulously etched by the late Georgina Musgrave. She was the wife of Ben Musgrave, a Springbok target shooter who turned to rifle manufacturing before being bought out by Armscor, the South African state-owned armaments agency. It was part of an initiative to develop hunting rifle production. On Warren's rifle, the knurling design coincidentally forms a 'W'; which he is proud of.

The muzzles of the guides' rifles were taped to prevent dust and other particles from entering the barrels. The rifles are carried in stage two, a technical term, with three rounds in the magazine, nil in the chamber and the firing pin released for safety. While single-stage triggers are less than a millisecond faster and military specification, two-stage triggers are used in high-stress situations where accidental discharges or missing the target can have disastrous consequences.

We set off on a service road, through mopane woodland into a cold wind and a fine drizzle. A journey of young giraffe headed in the same direction and kept a mindful eye on us. An army of Matabele ants, named after the feared Ndebele tribe that swept through Africa in the 1800s, marched six rows wide across the track we followed. Such a formation could only have been on its way to forage for termites, which scout ants would have spotted earlier and then returned with the army to conduct a raid. We knelt with our ears as close to the column as we could before Arnold blew on the ants. The wind was too strong and noisy for us to hear, but if quieter, we would have heard the rattling and hissing the ants make when threatened.

We stopped again when we came across two different animal footprints; one from a cat and the other from a hooved animal. Warren took the opportunity to teach us about locomotion and the three types of mammalian stances. He started by planting a firm boot print in the sand alongside the two tracks. That served as the third imprint. The cat-like track, like the one we had seen at the Mfayeni hot spring, was from an African civet. Their track is a digitigrade, which is usually found with carnivores that walk on their toes; such as lions and leopards. They put the weight of the body on the ball of the foot with the heel raised. The other animal track, a split hoof typical of African antelope such as kudu, was from a nyala, an unguligrade associated with herbivores and large-hooved animals. We compared them to Warren's boot print, a plantigrade, common in apes and humans who walk with the entire sole on the ground.

As we reached a sandy riverbed for our camp, a large herd of zebra ran past in a dazzle of stripes. We had hiked a relatively short 15.7 kilometres and it was to be the only time on Leg Two we slept at the planned night stop. On Sunday, we had concealed six water drums with a food container to save us from carrying all the provisions from the start. After the difficulties of getting water the previous night and the terrible taste from the spring, it was a relief to have clean, potable water.

The wind blew strongly and, after some debate, we set up a bush shower. A cold shower had little appeal in the chilly wind and in the end, it was only Lourens and Ray who used it, watched by a curious giraffe. On the way back to the tents I stopped to admire another giraffe in the distance and noted how high above the trees the head of Earth's tallest land animal was. A giraffe's neck is made up of seven vertebrae; the same number of bones humans have in their necks. The five- to six-metre-tall and graceful *Camelopardalis* ruminants find eating economical and easy, but drinking and sleeping are a challenge. Drinking requires an awkward stoop for an animal that can weigh as much as 1,200 kilograms. It is also the time they are most vulnerable to attack. Though giraffes lie down, mostly at night, they usually sleep standing up and doze for as little as five hours in a 24-hour cycle. It seems good sleep is not as important to giraffes as it is to humans.

I went back to my tent to attend to more pressing matters. I took off my boots to inspect my feet. A large blister on the ball of my right foot ran up to the toes. A blood blister made it look like a bloated tick had attached itself to my big toe. Arnold laughed as he watched me fiddle with my lightweight medical kit and offered to have a look at the blisters. He took out a bottle of Merthiolate and a syringe from a medical kit befitting a war zone. Between the weapons, satellite phone, spade and medical kits, I wondered again how the guides managed to carry their own food and personal items, as well.

Arie is a seasoned hiker and warned me about the pain from the antiseptic as he took up a comfortable position to be entertained. Only the popcorn was missing. I tried not to flinch when the Merthiolate was injected into the blister but I could not help it, and a lot went to waste as my leg jerked and I fought not to scream. I declined a second injection. Arnold was kept busy, as after me, Ray and Morné also needed attention to their feet.

Lourens had packed a bottle of wine in the food trunk and shared it among the group. Red wine improves bland instant noodles. We were watched by a tower of giraffes, their long necks stiff as they looked inquisitively over the trees tracing the riverbed. We were no threat, but their height and good eyesight allows them to spot lions up to two kilometres away in open country.

I had a disturbed night with the high riverbank funnelling the wind over the tents. The pegs I used to secure my tent were pulled out of the sandy surface and it was only my bodyweight and heavy backpack that stopped the tent from blowing away.

Red Rocks

The next morning, a gusty wind and whispered greetings from early risers woke me. We packed up camp in the dark and were ready to go when an elephant strolled past. Warren was the lead again and we continued along the same management road we travelled the day before. Lion tracks headed in the same direction. The pride had stopped and rested; the imprint of a tail was visible where a lion had crouched.

Cold blasts of wind hurried us along. I picked out a wildebeest in the dry, leafless mopane they blend into. We stopped for breakfast in a level, open area shaded by a sparse assortment of large trees. Corrie and Maritha, with Corrie's blue and Maritha's pink 31-year-old Karrimor backpacks side by side, shared the trunk of a fallen tree next to me. A cluster of impala ran past as we boiled water for much-needed coffee. Morné was having problems with his boots and resorted to silver duct tape to hold them together. The obstinate little toe of his left foot bulged out the side.

We had stopped close to a secondary road used by tourists. As we set off, a vehicle stopped to observe two bull elephants. For the passengers, the more unusual sighting was people on foot in the Kruger, and they gave us big smiles. I doubt that *Homo sapiens* were on their game-viewing checklist.

In a chilly drizzle, we stopped to look at what was left of a recent kudu kill. The skull and jawbone were still attached to the bloody spine. Shivering from the cold, we descended through a ravine to the massive slab of Gubyane sandstone, known as Red Rocks, which has, over time, been exposed by the flow of the Shingwedzi River. The drizzle was now a light rain, and the smooth rocks pitted with potholes of varying sizes were slippery. Warren slipped and fell while putting more acrobatic effort into saving the rifle than himself. He was peeved Arnold's first reaction was to check on the rifle instead of his wellbeing. It was uncanny how it started raining as we reached the rocks and stopped as we finished the perilous traverse. I felt cheated as I watched every step on the slippery rocks rather than appreciating the magnificent surroundings. As we stepped off the rocks, a noisy troop of baboons disappeared into the trees.

Red Rocks is filled with history. From the American prospector, 'Texas Bill' Lusk, who panned there for alluvial gold in the early 1900s, to the narrow escape in the 1940s from prowling lions by the chairman, Alfred Trollip, and the secretary, HS van Graan, of the Kruger Board of Trustees. The group was taken to the river by an unarmed ranger and were at the water's edge when they heard lions grunting behind them. They raced back to the safety of their car, where there was a lion and three lionesses in the nearby bush.

Our attention shifted to a white carpet of bird droppings beneath a tree where a flock of red-billed quelea must have settled for some time. These birds feed on the seeds of grasses and owing to their large flocks and the extensive damage they cause to commercial and private cereal crops, they are considered by some to be Africa's feathered locust.

From there, we followed an animal path on the banks of a tributary of the Shingwedzi River. In places, it was a narrow passage, with the river on one side and a high ridge on the other. Along the ridge were man-sized, pyramidal termite mounds alternating with surly kudu. The scene looked choreographed and I had to remind myself I was not on a movie set. We made our way to the top of the ridge and stopped for a break beneath a shady nyala tree. As we were leaving, someone spotted what was left of a leopard kill suspended some five metres above ground on the river-facing side of the tree we used for shade. From the hooves and the coat that remained we concluded the victim was an impala ram. A leopard can carry an animal heavier than itself up a tree to be wedged in a fork metres above ground. In that way, the kill is protected from scavengers and is a larder from which the leopard can feed undisturbed over several days. Leopards, on average, need a kilogram of meat per day and make a big kill about once every two weeks. The leopard population in the Kruger is estimated at 1,000 to 1,500 and they are found in dense forests and the open savanna.

A herd of impala allowed us to get close before they ran off. We were distracted by the concertinaed skin of a puffadder shed near the trunk of the tree where the impala had sheltered. It had wedged itself between branches or rocks to rid itself of the outer layer of skin. These venomous snakes are found everywhere in Africa savanna. They cause numerous snakebite fatalities because of their wide distribution, aggressive disposition and occurrence in populated regions. While looking at the snakeskin, someone noted numerous stems of shrubs around us were cut at a 45° angle. We took turns to guess the animal that had eaten the shrubs until the guides said it had been a black rhino, thanks to the give-away angle the stem was cut.

The sun emerged from the clouds and I felt its warm and comforting energy for the first time in days. Nature was joyous. Birds chirped, colourful butterflies fluttered and animals moved with purpose and vitality. A journey of giraffe passed and I watched their unusual canter, noting how they moved both legs on one side of their body; then both legs on the other. Some used their versatile dark blue tongue, up to 45 centimetres long, to strip leaves from trees as they passed, with barely a pause. We crossed a hyena latrine with a dozen large white droppings. Hyenas use such sites for territorial marking, and sometimes social ranking or to indicate reproductive status.

A number of zebra grazed peacefully in an unusual rectangular clearing we broke into from moderately thick bush. The dazzle of black and white was pleasingly contrasted against the early spring greenery. An elephant tusk lay in the grass, and we picked it up to feel the texture and weight before leaving it where we found it. Elephants are not like deer that shed their antlers each year; but they can shed a tusk if needed owing to damage or infection.

More concerning is the rapid evolutionary development of tuskless elephants caused by warfare, poaching and culling. Heavy poaching by armed forces during the prolonged 1977 to 1992 Mozambican war of independence, meant elephant populations in Gorongosa National Park declined by 90 percent, according to research led by American evolutionary biologist, Shane C. Campbell-Staton. His Princeton team found after the war, many female elephants were born tuskless. They suggest this was, "...sex-linked and related to specific genes that generated a tuskless phenotype more likely to survive in the face of poaching". The multibillion-dollar illicit wildlife trade in tusks and horns adds to the vulnerability of this species.

A picturesque spot on a dry riverbed adorned with shady trees was an invitation to stop we could not resist. We were making good progress and debated breaking for lunch versus pressing on to a place where we could find water and make a night stop. To my delight, lunch and relaxation won.

It was still windy, but the sun was out and the sky clear. I found the perfect spot beneath the wide-spreading canopy of an irregularly shaped apple-leaf tree (*Philenoptera violacea*). Part of the bent trunk served as a seat and an oversized flat nodule as a table. The apple-leaf tree is known for artistic twists and bends, and I made the most of it. There were no signs of the aphids known to infect the tree with their secretions dripping down to form a wet patch on the ground. So much so, it is sometimes referred to as the rain tree. Gusts of wind blew away my plate and cup twice, forcing me to chase after them. I hurried through lunch to give myself time to lie down on the gentle slope for a nap. It didn't pan out; the wind gusts were so intense and noisy I couldn't sleep.

Mixed groups of buffalo and zebra slowed our hike in the afternoon. Then we began a slow descent to a lush, green corridor of evergreen trees tracing the banks of the river. Hippopotamus tracks marked a path strewn with the neat dung of a female hippo and nearby, the dispersed dung of the male. Males spin their tails as they defecate – as much as 150 kilograms per day – to mark their territory and possibly to impress females.

The remains of an elephant lay off the path. The tusks had been removed by, we guessed, Kruger staff after the elephant died from old age or disease, as the skull showed no signs of violent death. Way back in 1989, a worldwide ban on ivory sales began and slowed elephant poaching for many years. After an initial CITES-sanctioned sale in South Africa in 1999, a second sale was permitted in 2008, where 47 metric tons of ivory from the Kruger was auctioned, fetching just under US$7 million to fund anti-poaching measures. No good deed goes unpunished, it is said. Instead of crashing prices by flooding the market, the sale led to a widespread and long-standing increase in elephant poaching. At the 19th meeting of the Conference of the Parties to CITES held in November 2022 in Panama City, known as CoP19, the long-standing ban on ivory trading was upheld.

Today, we stood before a piece of thick grey hide, large enough to make a tent, among the large bones of the dead elephant. The bones were intact except for those crushed by hyenas. The area smelt putrid, and we estimated the carcass had lain there for about a week. There are long-standing beliefs this is an elephant graveyard and we were not far from the Sirheni Bushveld Camp, appropriately named after the Shangaan word for 'cemetery'.

The teasing between our guides lifted the toil of our hike. As we moved away from the grave site through an expanse of mopane shrubs, Warren asked me to lead the group, which I did with some apprehension.

I was bombarded with playful abuse and confusing instructions from Warren.

"Turn left. No, go right."

"Wait, let's go straight here."

"Where are you going?"

"Do you see what I have to go through the whole day?" Warren asked as he pointed mock-accusingly at Arnold. "That's what I have to live with," he joked.

The few minutes in front were enlightening. With no visible natural features ahead, just mopane as far as the eye could see, it was difficult to determine a direction. The scattered mopane makes it impossible to walk in a straight line for long. I now appreciated how our guides led us so proficiently and without always reaching for their GPS. Never mind the ever-present vulnerability with potential danger behind every scraggy bush, high in the branches of a tree, or a lazy snake or angry scorpion upon the path or in the long grass. The guides always managed to exude a quiet sense of security.

A curious giraffe paused its chewing to watch us as we made camp for the night on the east bank of the scenic Tshanga River. The day's hike had been 18.6 kilometres long. There was little shelter from the frigid blasts of a gusting wind blowing over our camp and across the khaki sand of the dry riverbed.

Elephants seeking clean drinking water had dug holes around isolated pools of mossy, stagnant water. They splash around and play in the pools, but will not drink cloudy still water if they can avoid it, and nor did we. Flat rocks that dotted the riverbed were used to hold up the sides of one of the deeper holes. Moments after Arnold scooped out the brackish water, a fresh, trickle seeped in and we used it to fill the foldable buckets. Some of us kept watch as four buffalo waded in the pools upstream. From downstream, a tense giraffe eyed us, no doubt wary of the presence of humans on foot and not inside rolling metal boxes.

Arie and I took pictures atop an enormous five-metre-high termite mound built around a long-dead tree, before we helped each other erect tents. Normally, this was a routine exercise but gusts from the temperamental wind challenged us. My attempt at a shower was futile. I stood downwind of the nozzle, but most of the water missed and the wind chill froze my skin.

As the sun set, a breeding herd of elephant came downriver in our direction. It seemed every cow had a calf or two in tow, and there were elephants of all sizes. The wind blew over us and across the river as we sat on the upper part of the sloping bank to watch, while the elephants stayed on the lower part of the two-tiered riverbed. The lead elephant, the matriarch, was across from us when she stopped. The wind carried our scent to her. Though she must have seen us sitting on the bank, until then, she probably did not know what we were because of an elephant's poor eyesight. Now she knew. She lifted her head and threw it down in an arc, her ears slapping like the crack of a whip against her body. She moved away from us and the others followed her up the opposite bank where they lingered, feeding off trees and bushes, confident in their might. A thorn thicket largely concealed the elephants from view. Three periscope-like trunks stuck out from behind the bush as they swivelled from side to side, testing the wind from our direction.

An elephant trunk is a remarkable organ, consisting of about 100,000 muscles and ending in two dexterous finger-like projections so sensitive it can pick up tiny objects with ease. Elephants arguably have the best sense of smell of any species and can detect water up to 19 kilometres away, further than from where we kicked off the hike that morning on the other side of Red Rocks.

Another troop approached us from the same direction but by then, it was dark and cold and we retreated to the safety of our zippered tents. Animals in the wild regard a tent as a significant obstacle, like a rock, which they ignore. Little creatures see no such deterrent and so on a hike, it is advisable to zip up the tent to prevent smaller creatures such as spiders, scorpions and even snakes from entering.

The wind blew all night drowning out the chorus of the dark.

I woke to the early-morning roar of a lion walking past our camp. Icy weather persisted and I pulled my night fleece over a clean hiking shirt. The first shafts of light pushed away the night and the mood was jovial as we huddled to hear the briefing. I watched waves of red-billed quelea fly above the riverbed, almost at eye level, while I listened. These bright and busy cousins of southern Africa's weaver bird are endemic to the savanna and fly in large flocks when the season is wetter than usual.

Arnold was to lead and we shouldered our backpacks ready to go. I regarded the two guides, armed and standing side-by-side in uniform and with their flowing beards, with amusement.

"Arnold and Warren are so similar in every respect. Except for one thing," I teased. The two looked at me enquiringly.

"Their footwear," I pointed out. "Warren looks dressed for the ball with boots and gaiters, but Arnold prefers sandals." Arnold wore the same handmade sandals that Bjinse wore on Leg One.

"Yes, but where Arnold comes from, that is dressed up," someone in the group quipped.

Arnold and Warren smiled. Warren turned our attention back to the briefing.

"The lion we heard early this morning is probably still in the area and heading the same way we are going," he said.

"The second roar was in that direction," he added, pointing south and into the wind. "When we see a lion, we are not going to have time to talk or give instructions. You must all know what to do," he said.

"We must not run," some chorused as we all nodded in nervous agreement.

"Exactly," Warren assured. "You all know that by now. But a lion will feign a charge a couple of times. It will charge, stop and turn around and then charge again. When it turns back is when we must retreat. Do not turn around and run. Never. Face the lion. Then, take one step to the right, one step back, then one step to the left," he demonstrated with exaggerated steps as he spoke. "Have you got it?"

I nodded, as did the others, with varying degrees of understanding and enthusiasm.

"You must not turn. You must not run. Step right, step back, step left," he repeated as he took big steps again to show us.

It wasn't making sense. "Why the big steps?" I blurted.

"So you don't stand in your own shit!" he replied to our relieved laughter.

As we set off, we discovered the distinctive tracks of a kori bustard; its long foot ends with three finger-like appendages. It is Africa's heaviest flying bird with males weighing up to 18 kilograms and females about half the size. The kori bustard is common in the Kruger but becoming scarce outside because of collisions with power lines and fences. We detected the kori in flight soon afterwards, as it took off from nearby bushes and into the wind for added lift.

A rufous, or reddish-brown, steenbok with long broad ears darted through the vegetation so quickly few in the group noticed it because they were watching a stately group of giraffes. The male steenbok has slender, upright horns above its eyes with a button nose and outsized ears giving them an endearing look, magnified by an air of sadness created by conspicuous black facial glands coursing from their large, dark eyes.

We stopped for breakfast in a waterless riverbed of coarse sand, sheltered from the wind by trees, dense bushes and a high bank. I sat next to a hardy, deciduous common spike-thorn (*Gymnosporia buxifolia*), and ate my apple and rusks while studying the tree's long, sharp and straight thorns that can be up to 100 millimetres long. On the other side was a tough, deciduous buffalo thorn (*Ziziphus mucronata*), which, in my view, is one of the most interesting of the many varieties of thorn trees in the Kruger. It grows three times as high as the spike-thorn and is more resistant to drought and frost than other thorn trees. The thorns grow in pairs, with one straight and pointing forward, while the other hooks backwards. Legends and superstitions about the tree abound across Africa. The Nguni people of southern Africa believe the thorns tell us to look to the future but never forget where we have come from. In Botswana, it is believed the tree protects from lightning, so when travelling in a vehicle, the Batswana place a branch of buffalo thorn on a seat for the journey.

As we climbed out of the dry riverbed, a pearl-spotted owlet never moved. Despite its proximity, this small, long-tailed owl was camouflaged by brown feathers streaked with small white spots. It took some time for everyone to find it in the dry branches. The owlet flew off when our conversation and pointing became too much.

Soon after, we disturbed a fiery-necked nightjar. At home, when I lived in the garden suburb of Walmer in Port Elizabeth, I heard them every night, and it was good to find one in the wild. They may perch in trees at night but prefer to roost on the ground under a bush. The two-note whistle and the broad white tips on the outer tail make the bird easy to identify, which I did as it flew away.

We arrived at the camping spot after weaving our way through mopane shrubveld for most of the morning. I was not looking forward to spending the night at the unsightly radio repeater station. Repeater stations extend the range of radio signals in the Kruger between bases and mobile units and are usually positioned out of the way of tourists. We took off our backpacks in a flat, grassless clearing some way from the station. Most of us helped Arnold and Warren collect the stowed water and food in the shade beneath the stilted structure.

The sun was high. We could not have chosen a less interesting place to spend half the day. We had covered just 12 kilometres and it didn't make sense to stop there. Arnold and Warren were open to suggestions to go further, so we decided to have lunch, rest awhile, and press on further south after filling up with water and restocking our food supplies.

Lourens and Corrie each had a bottle of red wine in the food trunk. Lourens was prepared to carry his to be enjoyed with dinner that night, knowing the empty glass bottle would have to be carried for another two days after that. Corrie decanted his wine into one of the empty plastic bottles he used for water rather than carry an empty wine bottle to the end of the hike.

I found a fallen tree trunk framed by the low branches of an apple-leaf tree that offered protection from the howling wind. I tended to isolate myself at lunch to catch up with my notes while I ate, and afterwards to have a nap. A pied crow, perched on a branch behind me, waiting in expectation of scraps. Somehow, a crow seemed out of place in the Kruger, and with the nearby repeater station, I believed they stained the surroundings with the menace of urbanisation. I was pained by my thoughts, as it did not seem right I felt that way about a bird in the Kruger. I was the intruder, not the crow.

Before I could rest, I needed to attend to the unbearable pain in my feet. I took off my boots to inspect the bulging blister on my right foot and hobbled up to Arnold for help. He laid out his groundsheet and readied his medical utensils, which included his last unused needle. I don't like needles at the best of times and looked away when I heard him unwrap it, bracing myself for my second injection of Merthiolate. I could tell Arie was looking forward to another round of entertainment as he prepared to film my trauma on his camera phone. After the initial agony and stifled scream, he asked if I had anything intelligent to say to the camera. A single, four-letter word was all I could muster.

We hiked further that afternoon. I liked being ahead in terms of position and distance covered, instead of the pressure of having to catch up. The wind and cooler weather were also advantages. We even had time to stop and appreciate the small treasures the Kruger has to offer. A neat, deep, cup-like nest of mossy camouflage, identifiable as that of an African paradise flycatcher, lay on the ground, apparently blown out of the large vine-clad tree above it by gusty winds. We also stopped to prod, discuss and admire the curious shape of a large amount of triangular warthog droppings.

I picked out eight zebra grazing some distance ahead on our path, and I wondered how close we could get before they ran off. When they noticed us, they turned their heads to stare as we approached. We were almost upon them, when the rush of a trio of doves taking flight from the long grass prompted the zebra to flee.

We entered a section of dense mopane shrub and common spike-thorn bushes that snagged my backpack, tore at my clothes, and scratched the skin on my arms and legs. It was the first time I observed moss growing on mopane shrubs; it was so thick sunlight couldn't reach the south-facing branches.

The last stretch was through flat grasslands with sparser mopane and other trees. This terrain is favoured by predators; the sun-bleached bones that dotted the landscape were evidence. The skeleton of a giraffe was unmistakable, as the long bones, large neck vertebrae, and even the jaw-bone cannot be confused with any other animal. In contrast, an almost complete spine had us guessing to which animal it belonged. We left with most of us believing it was from a buffalo. Out of place in the graveyard of giants lay the remains of a long-dead leopard tortoise; a handful of scutes were scattered around the crumbling skeleton.

We made camp on open ground at the source of the Tsendze River, setting up our tents with some difficulty in the strong wind. We had covered 17.4 kilometres, finishing the day closer to an average distance. As the sun set, elephants crossed the savanna upwind of our position. Many of them trumpeting in response to the unusual presence of humans in their neighbourhood.

After eating the evening meal with no logs or rocks to sit on, we clustered uncomfortably on cold ground and in the wind. Lourens graciously shared the wine he had carried since lunch. We played the teenage game of Spin the Bottle to resolve who was going to carry the empty bottle to Mopani Rest Camp. To ease the burden, we agreed to spin for each of the two days left. Lourens was exempt as he had carried the full bottle, and so he was given the fun task of spinning the bottle. Ray, Morné, Jennifer and I drank the wine and so it was on us. On the first spin, the bottle pointed to Jennifer. Lourens spun the bottle for the second time, and it pointed to Jennifer again. Chivalry was absent. None of the gentlemen offered to carry the bottle for Jennifer, even for one day.

Tropic of Capricorn

I felt cold during the night and arose before dawn to clear skies and copious dew on my tent, meaning it had been a clear, cloudless and windless night. We packed up by starlight and I borrowed Arnold's stool to tie my laces properly. I suspected the blister problem was because I tightened my boots sitting on the ground, and that reduced my ability to get leverage to tighten the laces properly. I was convinced by then that adding a small lightweight stool to my kit was a must for future Legs of the hike.

The morning briefing was more conversational than usual because it was still dark and the guides were stalling while dawn grudgingly revealed disorderly ranks of trees and thickets. The many francolins in the bush around us were noisy, probably in reaction to our activity. We cheerfully competed with the defensive chorus of 'ker-aak, aak' and the fading 'kara-kara-kara' of what I thought was the Coqui francolin.

We set off behind Warren as soon as there was enough light. It was a cool, crisp and quiet morning, save for the francolins, who no doubt believed they had chased the noisy humans away. My feet had recovered and felt snug in my boots, adding to the lightness of my step as I cherished this perfect moment in the wild. I told myself to never forget it. I know I won't.

In a grassy plain with scattered mopane, a couple of healthy eland bulls grazed peacefully. The largest of the Kruger antelope, the magnificent tawny eland adds elegance to the African bush. They ran off but not far away, for which I was grateful. Warren stopped for no other reason than to appreciate their gentle beauty. I felt like I was in paradise until the howl of a spotted hyena reminded me of where we were. While everyone was looking for the hyena, I focused on the glossy black feathers of a fork-tailed drongo that was doing its best to keep up with us by hopping from bush to bush. The grassy plain was busy with animals. A tranquil herd of impala moved away from us, more out of deference than fear, before continuing with the essential business of grazing.

The mopane was thick after we crossed the Shongololo Loop road. A protruding branch must have ripped Corrie's glasses from around his neck, but he only discovered this much later during a short stop. He had no clue where the mishap occurred, so we didn't go back to look for them. As we got going again, we alarmed a tribe of impala concealed by the mopane, and unlike the earlier sighting, these took fright and scattered. Shortly after, a solitary giraffe calf stepped inquisitively towards us, its long neck lowered and large eyes unblinking below long, thick eyelashes. It ran off only when the animal path we were on took us closer. Humans do not like surprises, and neither do wild animals.

A kettle of white-backed vultures flew in a tight circle some way off. The guides conferred, and after consulting the group, we veered off our heading to find what may have been a kill. Nobody minded the extra distance if there was even a small chance of lions still being busy.

After a brisk pace to get to the vicinity of the kill, we advanced cautiously to find a cackle of hyenas worrying the carcass of a buffalo. They slouched off like reluctant adolescents as we approached. Other than the four legs and the head that were mostly untouched, the spine and rib cage were all that was left of the buffalo. We estimated the kill had taken place two days earlier. The stench of death was so strong I could taste it. A fresh wind was blowing, so we stood upwind and ventured to the other side of the carcass to take pictures.

It is unlikely the kill was made by the hyenas. Buffalo is the favoured prey of lions and the stomach is their usual point of entry as was the case here. Lions quickly get to the most nutritious organs, such as the liver and kidneys. Despite popular belief, hyenas are not only scavengers, but they are also high-stamina hunters and, in the Kruger, they kill more than they scavenge. They work in a pack to isolate, chase and bring down their prey. Impala, kudu, waterbuck and wildebeest are their preferred catch. Lions are also effective scavengers. They like to hunt in prides, with a lioness usually initiating the kill in open terrain. In wooded areas, males are active hunters and, in the Kruger, up to half of lion kills are initiated by males.

Our group resumed a southerly course as three vultures, including a Cape vulture discernible by its large wingspan and pale colouring, flew over us heading for the kill. Cape vultures are endangered because of human encroachment. Poisoning has reduced rodent food supplies, and collisions with powerlines have been the death of many of these birds. A giraffe, accompanied by a solitary impala, sheltered from the sun beneath the dense canopy of an evergreen tree close to where we descended into a ravine for the breakfast stop.

The beat of the two-metre wingspan of a large Verreauxs' eagle thwacked the air in a mist of dust when we started crossing the almost dry Tsendze River. We were intruders and our fears suggested – perhaps with some exaggeration given the weapons our guides carried – if we were not careful, our carcasses would join the countless bones visible everywhere along the riverbank. Most were unidentifiable, yet the long leg bones of a giraffe were unmistakable. We were in the middle of a favoured hunting ground for predators.

I was surprised when we almost ran over a plump double-banded sandgrouse. Her streaked crown and barred lower breast and belly revealed her gender and, for some reason, she did not fly off until we were almost on top of her. There must have been a nest in the vicinity she was reluctant to leave. A gang of old buffalo bulls – or dagga boys as they are known from the Shangaan word for the mud in which old bulls like to wallow, either on their own or in small groups – grazed on a sloping grassy bank. For our safety, we made an abrupt turn away from them.

Our heading was southerly to a busy juncture where we intersected the Tsendze River on a wide, muddy bend. Zebras on a ridge above ran off in single file, while impala bounded across the dry cracked mud of the riverbed towards our bank. A breeding community of elephants dallied among the trees across the sandy expanse from us. They massed on the bank as they prepared to cross; then changed their plans. I presumed because of us. After a threatening display of trumpeting and flapping ears, they moved from the bank and stayed on their side of the river. From hyenas to elephants, I observed wild animals acknowledge the predatory nature of humankind.

We stopped for a break in the shade of a tall jackalberry tree (*Diospyros mespiliformis*) that had a view of the busy bend in the river. Jackalberry trees are evergreen and found largely in riverine habitats. Their rough, deeply grooved, burnt-looking black bark means they are known as the African ebony tree.

Dense, spiny tendrils of a woolly caper bush (*Capparis tomentosa*) entangled the Jackalberry tree in a symbiotic relationship and contributed to the shady canopy. The woolly caper bush has edible fruit and leaves used in rituals and as a traditional medicine across Africa.

Somebody remembered it was Corrie's 68th birthday and a round of birthday wishes ensued. I considered I would not mind being fit enough to be doing what he was at 68. To complete the festivity, a mongoose scurried up a large anthill next to us, and a lone elephant bull, left behind by the herd, loitered in the shade on the opposite bank. A large flock of chirpy red-billed queleas enriched the impromptu celebration with a well-timed flyby.

Usually, I was instinctively aware of the direction in which we were headed, made easy by the sun when it was not overcast. Sometime in the middle of the day, I realised we had veered off course and our heading was west into less dense mopane shrubveld. My suspicions were confirmed when Warren brought us to a halt.

"Can you see the sun is on our right shoulders, when we should be moving south?" Warren asked. "Arnold doesn't like the scratches on his skin and tugs on his clothes from the bushes, so we have to walk up here where there's less bush," he said with an accusing look at his fellow guide.

The look on Arnold's face was worth the extra distance and I chuckled at their never-ending banter as we moved through the mopane and abundant common spike-thorn.

Crossing the Tropic of Capricorn called for a photograph, and the guides ushered us into a straight line to take pictures. Not far from where we were, is an official signboard where tourists are allowed to exit their cars to take photographs marking the crossing. We debated making the detour, but there wasn't much enthusiasm for the extra distance, so we pressed on in search of a scenic place to have lunch and rest.

A large jackalberry tree on the bank of the Tsendze River provided plenty of shade, good for lunch and a nap beneath its dense, dark green canopy. I enjoyed my lunch in harmony with six eland grazing on the shady opposite bank. I appreciated the blessing of so many of the elegant antelope together in one place. A grassed terrace in the shade beckoned for an afternoon nap and I descended with my groundsheet. Warren and

Corrie sat together on the ridge above me, and did not look like they were going to do the same. I thought it opportune to enlist their help.

"If anything furry with four legs and a tail comes for me, please let me know," I said.

The light breeze was pleasant after the wind of the preceding days, and the sky had cleared. For the first time on this Leg, insects were active. I did not want to climb to fetch the insect repellent in my backpack, so my nap was not as peaceful as it could have been.

While we packed up, three elephant bulls on the opposite bank fed off the branches of an apple-leaf tree. Their fully stretched trunks reached the lowest branches, enough to pull off leafy shoots. When we left, I realised the three were part of a larger gathering at a water point further down on the river where buffalo jostled with elephants to reach the limited accessible water source. It seemed the elephants had the upper hand as many were glistening wet from the muddy water they had sprayed over themselves.

There were animals all around us and it felt perilous. My relief when we moved along was short-lived as buffalo soon blocked us. The guides conferred to decide which way to go to avoid their massive numbers. We headed away from the river and west into the sun to ensure the wind was behind us and our scent would not drift to the buffalo. If they became aware of our presence, their instinct would be to flee. Waterholes are always a risk to buffalo and other animals, and the most dangerous animal in Africa – at an average of 900 kilograms of solid muscle – would have run straight over us.

We tracked south until Arnold pointed out elephants to our right in the mopane. Despite their size, it took a trained eye to pick them out in the shrubbery. We were forced to zigzag, veering sharply to the east. I expected we would go around and pick up our heading southwards again. However, they were moving parallel to us, to the green belt of the Tsendze River in the distance. I wasn't too concerned, expecting we would soon follow the river downstream and head southwards again.

At the river, a large breeding herd of elephant drank and played in one of the few deep pools where we would have headed if we could have. A hippo grazed in the dry section of the riverbed, not wanting to compete with the elephants for water despite the sun burning down on it from the clear blue sky. The hippo looked pinker than usual, probably as result of the reddish fluid from mucus glands all over its body that protects it from the sun.

I scanned the length and breadth of the river, wondering how we were going to cross. Upstream, a smaller elephant troop stood in the riverbed. A giraffe hid ineffectively behind a large bush on the opposite bank; its neck and head sticking out as it watched. The direct route for us was to cross the river and head south, but the mopane was denser and it would not be safe with all the elephants. We couldn't backtrack to the sparser mopane where we had come from either, as elephants were heading for the water from that direction, too.

The elephants at the deep pool organised themselves and began heading south along the riverbed. We had no choice but to discreetly follow. Elephants walk far faster than humans, and we expected they would soon be out of sight and no danger to us. A crocodile slithered off the bank into the dark, deep pool as we rounded the waterhole where the elephants had been playing. A hippo on the other end of the water spied us, its eyes just breaking the surface. The pink hippo unexpectedly climbed the bank away from us rather than retreat to the water.

Pachyderms loitered on either side of the river. We had made the right decision to follow the indolent group in the riverbed, but anxiety nagged at me. There were elephants on all sides, the sun was going down fast and our water was running out. We stopped in the centre of the dry riverbed for a break and to regroup. A vocal blacksmith lapwing at a small pool did not help our cause, choosing to sound its 'tink, tink, tink' alarm call to an audience that didn't need any more warnings. The break gave the slow-moving group of elephant downriver a chance to put distance between us. More of them came out of the mopane to cross, but stopped when they saw us in the middle of the river. Thankfully, they moved further away to make the crossing. I felt drained of energy. We had nowhere else to go by that stage and were at the mercy of nature.

After the troop crossed ahead of us, we carried on down the riverbed. A black-backed jackal approached on the western bank and then skittishly crossed to climb up the opposite bank. An impala ram grazed nonchalantly on a grassy island in the middle of the river until it realised we were getting closer, then ran up the western bank into the fiery red of the sinking sun.

An African fish eagle flew into the sky when we stopped and dropped our backpacks on one of the sandbanks for a short rest.

We continued along the riverbed following lion tracks, but another group of elephant was at the riverbed ahead. We were forced to climb the bank to the west to skirt the elephants and continue our southerly course. The mopane gave way to riverine forest as we approached the Tsendze River again. Two crocodiles slithered into a large pool of dark water. After a while, they surfaced in unison, their eyes and snouts barely visible, before they submerged, again in unison. Other crocodiles basked in the dying sun and did not move.

It had been a long day and I was relieved when I heard we would make camp on the opposite bank. Jagged pieces of rock broke the surface of the water, and we used them as stepping stones to get to the other side of the river. We had covered 20.9 kilometres, and it wasn't just me who was feeling exhausted. I chose a site for my tent close to a fallen branch large enough to use as a bench.

Before pitching my tent, I went down to the river to collect water. Arnold was propping up the sides of an elephant-made drinking hole with flat stones. The initial flow of brown water was put aside for the shower. I filled my water bladders with water clear enough for drinking without needing arduous filtration, though I added purification drops to be safe. As the sun set on the last night in the bush on this Leg, we shared fantasies about hot juicy burgers. Jennifer was drooling at the thought of a toasted ham, cheese and tomato sandwich. The thought of an ice-cold beer in a glass added further appeal.

After my meal, I was ready to sleep. The absence of wind and our proximity to stagnant water meant mosquitoes were out in force. One whirred in my ear, and after a few well-timed swipes, I was certain I had solved the problem. Still, there was an incessant buzz, and I turned on my light to sort out the irritating pest. I was shocked to find a scourge of mosquitoes inside my tent. They were everywhere. I thought of opening the flap to shoo them out, then decided against that, as there was a chance even more would fly in. I set about swatting them one by one, and after a long time, I felt the job was done. Of course, I never considered what it must have looked like to someone, or something, looking at my glowing tent.

I fell asleep despite the protracted growl of a leopard. In the morning, we spoke about the mosquitoes. Arnold and Warren, whose tents were closest to mine, thought I was having a fit when they witnessed the frenetic movements in my tent, but were too afraid to ask.

The morning was sunny and tranquil. Even the usually reserved folk in our group were animated. Morné used my blue duct tape to replace the silver tape that had held his shoes together for the last few days. It was a colourful ending to shoes that needed to hold out to the end. Two jackals calling to each other saw us off for what we hoped would be a quick and easy 10 kilometre hike to the finish. Anyone not fit at the start was certainly in good shape by then, or so I thought.

Stepping onto a rocky ledge, we looked across a big, shady pool where three hippos sank into the dark water. Hippos can hold their breath underwater for up to six minutes, and we stayed long enough to watch the hippos break the surface for air, prompting a nomadic black-crowned night heron to fly off from behind the cover of foliage-laden rocks. I was close enough to inspect its distinctive black crown and back, in stark contrast to its grey wings and tail.

Despite the advantage of being in the front with the two guides, I missed a honey badger spotted by Jennifer. I looked to the wrong side and missed it scampering off into the mopane. While these ferocious small creatures are widespread across sub-Saharan Africa, they are seldom observed, even though they are unmistakable with their light grey to white top and black underparts. I put disappointment behind me when a common duiker, tinged grey in the soft early morning light, zigzagged before diving into bushes ahead of us. I understood then how it got its name from the Afrikaans word, duiker, meaning 'to dive'.

A fish eagle took off in a languorous, wide-winged flight from the trees as our route intersected with the winding river. The eagle had something in its claws but we were too far away to tell what it was. We headed into an expanse of stunted mopane struggling to grow in the shallow granite-layered sands. A small gang of buffalo loitered, so we stopped next to a large termite mound to wait for them to move. Buffaloes are known to be brave in a group and one approached us for a look. Arnold and Warren took up defensive positions as the rest of us scrambled up the termite mound. The brash buffalo never came too close, and then moved away, allowing us to continue along the river.

There was more water in this part of the river, so herons and African jacanas were plentiful in the reeds and shallows along the banks. The rich chestnut body of the jacanas stood out in beautiful contrast to the white neck, black-and-white head, and blue frontal shield, as they pranced upon floating green water lily pads.

Deep drag marks, etched in the mud, ran up the bank from the river. From the prints alongside the drag marks, we could tell they were formed by the tails of two large crocodiles. The tracks were fresh, and Arnold followed them into the thicker bush but returned without sighting anything of interest. Before moving on, we debated having breakfast on the tranquil riverside versus pushing through to Mopani Rest Camp, where we would have table service, a hot breakfast with fried eggs, and a cold beer. We did not have to think too hard about giving in to the primitive lust for hot food and were soon on our way again.

A nyala bull ambled past when Arnold stopped to pick up an animal's jawbone. The teeth had an intricate and distinctive pattern, and Arnold asked us to guess which animal it was from. Nobody knew until he explained it was from a warthog.

We laboured up the steep dirt road next to the electrified game-proof fence that encircles the rest camp. Corrie and Maritha slowed as we climbed, and a big gap opened between them and the rest of the group. Our usual discipline and attentiveness had waned, so close to the finish. We noticed their absence only when they were already stopped, their backpacks off, and Corrie had Maritha in his arms. Maritha had suffered a bad asthma attack and with Corrie's support, she was taking long, deep breaths to recover. Arnold and Warren rushed back to help the couple while the rest of us waited at the top of the hill.

Maritha slowly made her way up the hill to rejoin the group, with Arnold carrying her pink backpack. The parallel with what had happened with Corrie at the end of the first Leg was uncanny. Maritha handled everything well for six days, yet, within sight of the finish, she collapsed, in an incident like that which occurred with her husband.

The service gate was unlocked, so Corrie and Maritha took a shortcut to the restaurant while everyone else took the ring road to the rest camp entrance. We rounded the final bend and found the welcoming entrance to the rest camp at the top of a short but steep stretch of road. The jousting between our guides went to the wire as Arnold, burdened by his backpack as well as Maritha's, challenged Warren.

"Let's race to the gate," Arnold said.

It could not have been more than the length of a football field, but it was all uphill. Warren did not respond, feigning disinterest. Arnold fell for it, and Warren timed it perfectly. As Arnold looked away, Warren bolted up the hill. Arnold gave chase but Maritha's pink bobbing backpack proved too much of a handicap and he stalled halfway up the hill.

We took pictures at the gate at the end of a short 9.9 kilometres, before offloading the backpacks into our cars. The clean camp restrooms seemed luxurious – flush toilets!

Ice-cold beers were served on the deck before we moved to the restaurant. It isn't every day I have beer for breakfast, but the exception was warranted. I enjoyed my hot English breakfast, washed down by more beer than coffee, and questioned the three new hikers to our group.

"Now that we're done, would you do another Leg if there was an opening again?" I asked.

Maritha replied without pause, "No!" Her asthma attack too fresh for any other answer.

Morné said, "Maybe."

Ray said, "Yes."

Sadly, the world was about to be assailed by an event that would delay our next Leg by a year. And it would affect Ray in a way we could not have imagined.

We spoke at length about poaching, gaining insight from our guides into the onslaught on rhino and the war that wasn't being won. They noted Kruger was losing an average of 1.3 rhinos per day and unless brought down to less than one per day, the number of rhinos in the Kruger would continue to decline.

After what felt like an indulgent breakfast, we made our way to Shingwedzi Rest Camp where we would spend the night. Ray took a vehicle back to Vlakteplaas to pick up our luggage.

We sat on the esplanade overlooking the seasonal Shingwedzi River and to pass the time we played catch-up with the foibles of civilisation, consuming beers, hamburgers and waffles with ice cream. A plaque attached to a nearby tree on the bank was the subject of discussion. It is inscribed with, *Flood Level 20 Jan 2013*. Surely it could not be accurate, I argued, as the tree would have continued to grow.

Bjinse Visser, who had led us on Leg One, came over to say hello. He was at the camp on a working visit. We gave him a rundown of our experiences on the second Leg.

Later, after a lengthy shower where I watched a week of grime and dust run down my legs and into the drain, I was the last to arrive for dinner to a loud and animated discussion. We spoke about the highlights of Leg Two, and Arnold suggested we go around the table, and each discuss the moment we felt ready to give up. No-one admitted reaching that point though a few jabs were made at the snorers. We shared instead our scariest, or 'side-step moment', as Warren put it. Unsurprisingly, many of those had to do with elephants. The storytelling was interrupted by a honey badger scurrying past to the braai area where it knew it would find discarded morsels.

The next day, Arie and I left early for the drive back to the airport in Johannesburg. In addition to elephant, buffalo, giraffe, zebra and hyena, we also spotted three cheetahs chasing a pair of warthogs. I thought the cheetahs were playing rather than hunting, as the warthogs got away.

We spoke about how much more interesting the second Leg had been compared to the first. Not just because of the guides who were good friends, innately competitive and fun, but also because of the abundant animal populations. We had almost three times the number of animal sightings compared to the first Leg, thanks to elephants and buffalos. Yet, we had seen more warthogs and eagles on Leg One. The many tense encounters with elephants were well handled by Arnold and Warren, our safety was never in question, and we were thankful the guides on The Kruger Trail are so proficient.

LEG THREE

Mopani Rest Camp to Olifants Rest Camp
AUTUMN, APRIL 2021

Covid-19 scuppered the plans of every human on the planet and caused the deaths of 14.9 million people from January 2020 to December 2021. South Africa was badly hit. Our hiking group mourned the death of Ray, who succumbed to Covid complications. I remember him as a fit and energetic 60-year-old on Leg Two, who gave an enthusiastic affirmative response on the deck at Mopani Rest Camp when I asked if he would do another hike.

The Covid-19 pandemic also delayed our next hike by a year. There was a time at the peak of the pandemic when I feared we would never complete the hike, but my health was good and I kept fit by running, biking and swimming.

On many Friday evenings in Eswatini, the tiny kingdom where I now lived, I joined friends and their dogs to walk a brisk seven to 10 kilometres through the pineapple, macadamia nut and sugarcane fields of Malkerns. Once I knew the Kruger hike would resume, I walked in my hiking boots and with a heavy backpack.

Leg Three saw significant changes to our Kruger Trail hiking group, with only half of the original eight remaining. Besides Arie and me, only Lourens and Jennifer would stay the course. Henk and Antoinette Jonker relocated to the Netherlands to take up new work positions, and so did Jennifer and her family. Jennifer returned to South Africa to do Leg Three, while her husband, Morné, stayed home in Geldrop to look after their children. Corrie developed knee problems and could not continue.

Clifford was back after missing Leg Two, although he completed it later with another group. Arie filled one of the three vacant spots by bringing along his partner, Brigitte Ruprecht-Gersteroph, a South African Airways stewardess. Since meeting Arie, she had engaged in multiple outdoor adventures ranging from tandem skydives to obtaining an advanced scuba-diving certification. Brigitte met Arie through her brother who hiked the Andes with Arie. In addition to riding her BMW G 310 GS adventure motorcycle, she told us she was crazy about lions.

I invited Marie Dahl, a Danish hiking company owner I met on one of my training hikes in Malkerns, to take up one of the open places. We were unable to fill the last spot, and so there were only seven hikers on Leg Three.

Our two new guides were Louis Lemmer, the Honorary Ranger who conceived of The Kruger Trail, and Pete Wilson, a freelance hiking guide, who was born in Kenya and now lives in Barberton, South Africa.

The base camp for this Leg was the Letaba Rest Camp on the banks of the Letaba River in the centre of the park, near the junction of the main tar road that runs from north to south through the Kruger and the road to Phalaborwa gate. The Letaba River is a wide, shallow river, named for the Sesotho expression: 'river of sand'.

I stayed at this camp a few years earlier and was stung by a scorpion on the little toe of my right foot, during an after-dinner stroll while wearing flip-flops on the unlit walkway running along the riverside fence. I should have worn closed shoes. I learnt then lightning can strike in the same place twice. The following day, wearing only sliders owing to the swelling, I was bitten by a spider on the same little toe at a tourist viewpoint where visitors are allowed to alight from their vehicles. My partner rushed me back to Letaba Rest Camp where first aid was administered. By then, my right leg resembled that of a small elephant.

On the Sunday morning before the hike, Marie drove with me from Eswatini to Kruger. I woke up with a sore throat, and while I was a little anxious because my Covid test was just out-of-date, I knew as a South African citizen, I could do a rapid test at the Oshoek border post where we would enter South Africa. However, if I failed the test, I would not be allowed into South Africa and the Kruger hike would be over for me. I told Marie about the sore throat and my expired Covid-19 test results, but neglected to tell her I had the option of a rapid Covid test at the border post. It was a thoughtless omission. Instead of a jovial chat and sharing the excitement of the week ahead, there was tension and mostly silence.

We arrived at the Oshoek border post as it opened. The border health authorities glanced at my Covid test certificate and waved me through, so I avoided the hazard of a sometimes-unpredictable rapid test. Marie looked relieved, but confused.

Buying the food and equipment I needed in Nelspruit was challenging. The entrance to the only store that sold the camping food and equipment I needed, was blocked by a security roll-up gate because there was a power outage, and the gate could not be lifted. I looked for the right food and equipment at other shopping malls, but none stocked the camping food I required. I ended up eating instant noodles and packets of tuna for dinner all week. I also could not find gaiters and that would haunt me, too.

Marie and I had breakfast at a takeaway restaurant with individual salt and pepper sachets. I tipped the waitress extra to supply me with five each of them, in addition to 12 sugar sachets for my coffee. Marie had visited the Kruger for years and is an experienced hiker who knows careful preparation and planning is necessary for a six-day hike. I must have seemed like a blundering novice.

We drove north alongside Kruger Park and through Hazyview. On Marie's recommendation, I took the turn to Orpen Gate, despite it being a slower route than going up to Phalaborwa. We spotted a white rhino through the fence of the private Timbavati Game Reserve. The wet animal glistened in the sunlight as it laboured up a steep embankment. It appeared to be a good omen. Shortly after, we came across an elephant. This was a great start, spotting two of the Big 5 before arriving in Kruger.

Once we entered the Kruger, an abundance of zebra and blue wildebeest welcomed us. These antelope have a symbiotic relationship around their need for safety from predators. The excellent eyesight and hearing of zebras complement the wildebeest's strong sense of smell. Zebra feed on longer grasses, while wildebeest, being bulk grazers, prefer shorter grass. I stopped the car twice as we skirted Satara Rest Camp to enjoy sightings of the endangered ground hornbill.

I thought the day's challenges were over when we checked in at Letaba Rest Camp and I had the key to my bungalow.

Marie pitched a tent. She later chastised me for not informing her renting a bungalow was something I and some of the other hikers did. I also discovered I had the wrong refill for my gas stove. I rushed to the rest camp shop, but they didn't sell my nozzle-specific brand. I asked Clifford if I could share his gas stove as he made the same mistake on Leg One and I let him cook all his meals on mine. Luck was with me. Clifford arrived at Satara two days earlier and when he discovered they did not sell his type of refill, he asked on our group chat if someone could bring one for him. When I arrived for dinner, Clifford had two gas canisters on the table in front of him. He happily gave me the spare.

Marie had met Clifford, Lourens and Jennifer by the time I got to the restaurant patio overlooking the pools and sandy islets of the Letaba River. I introduced myself to Brigitte and put my hand out to introduce myself to the man sitting next to her. It was only when he burst out laughing and said my name, I realised the bearded explorer was Arie.

Louis Lemmer and Pete Wilson arrived together. I already knew Louis and was introduced to Pete, whose dashing looks – combined with his five o'clock shadow, ranger uniform and rifle – gave him the air of the archetypical African adventurer. After introductions, we settled down to dinner in the quiet restaurant, devoid of tourists because of pandemic restrictions. The Kruger Park felt deserted. Before Covid-19, almost one million people a year visited the Kruger, and it was only thanks to a cash infusion from the government the Kruger authorities were able to keep the gates open and sustain basic services during the pandemic and immediately thereafter. While the Kruger Park is one of the top international attractions in South Africa, three-quarters of visitors to the Kruger are locals.

Tripping Point

At daybreak we travelled the 50 kilometre tarred road to Mopani Rest Camp to leave the cars beneath the shade of abundant trees. We were not able to overnight at Mopani because it does not have camping facilities.

Louis warned it was going to be a long, tough day with a 21 kilometre hike when our backpacks were at their heaviest. His only instruction was to stay in single file and remain silent. As we left the gate, Louis paused to show us the bristly, long, brown and tangled awns of the perennial spear grass that grows in well-drained rocky soil. He put a leaf sheath in his mouth and we watched it twist from the moisture, which is how it burrows into the soil and uses dampness for germination. It was a benign start but once we got going, Louis set a brisk pace.

There was soon a marked change in the terrain from what we had been used to on prior Legs. We hiked through energy-sapping, waist-high turpentine grass on rocky ground. Often there were no animal paths to follow. I thought about how savanna looks serene and beautiful from inside a car, but now I wondered how animals run at high speed through these grasses without breaking limbs.

At first, we were diligent, even those at the back walking in the exact footsteps of the guides. But as the day wore on, those at the back took shortcuts around the trees. Almost everyone was struggling, either from a gap in fitness levels or with backpack or shoe problems. It did not bode well if this was how we looked hours into a six-day hike. Marie was probably the most experienced hiker in the group and I felt confident she would overcome challenges.

Sightings of interesting birds and animals distracted us from blisters or aching shoulders. A fork-tailed drongo dropped onto a mopane shrub and inclined its head, its eyes turned to these unusual bush creatures as we stopped for our first break. Louis explained we would have occasional five-minute breaks with our backpacks on. For longer 10-minute breaks, we could take off the backpacks. Breakfast stops would be around 30 minutes and the main lunch break, taken in the heat of day, would be around two hours. I had no watch. I took my cues from nature and those around me.

Watching an army of Matabele ants gave another welcome pause as we examined a battalion march between the twin trunks of a tree. Louis told us about the once-feared Nguni tribes the ants are named after and how they raided south and central Africa in destructive military campaigns from their home bases in what is now the country of Zimbabwe and the province of KwaZulu-Natal in South Africa. These warriors – one feared group led by a woman – carried large oval shields called *isihlangu* painted black, red, white or with spots, to designate the warrior unit. They wore an ostrich-feather headdress and an *ibheshu*, or apron, to cover their buttocks and genitals made of leopard or civet skins. Around their ankles were rings of copper or brass.

We covered a substantial distance without seeing any animals, though an abundance of hyena, giraffe and warthog tracks told a different story. Even birds were scarce, until we came across a chirpy foraging party of red-billed quelea hopping from tree to tree along a dry river tributary.

As we descended a gently sloping bank for a short break, Marie tripped, hitting her head on the sandy path, and grazing her chin, cheek and forehead. Marie later said, "…my heavy backpack pinned me to the ground. I couldn't move. My mouth, nose and right eye were pinned to the dirt. The thud of the fall alerted the guides, and everyone rushed over to me. Someone pulled me to a sitting position and asked if I was okay.

"I couldn't see straight, and I couldn't feel my face. I shook my head a few times and used my fingers to touch my face, check my teeth, my hands, my knees, elbows and everything else. The others kept asking if I was okay. I said that I thought so, but the ground was spinning before my eyes and my head was sore. Louis called a long break – backpacks off. I was grateful. Someone took my backpack and carried it to the riverbed where the others waited. Someone else supported my slow walk to join them. Another person offered a mirror, while yet another perturbed hiker produced some antiseptic. Everyone looked at me with concern. I found some sanitising wipes from my backpack and wiped the dirt off my face. When I looked in the mirror, my chin, bottom lip and forehead were bloody with superficial cuts, but my teeth and eyes were unharmed.

"I felt unsteady on my feet when we set off again. I tasted blood in my mouth from a gash on the inside of my lip. My head was pounding and my right cheekbone was throbbing. I worried about concussion. Should I tell the guides at the risk of being extracted only 2.5 hours into the hike, or should I risk it and hope I could walk it off?"

Marie's trauma was heightened by a recent experience. "Six months earlier, my mother took a bad fall and ended up with a severe concussion, so I knew it meant rest, rest, and nothing but rest. A multi-day hike was probably not the best idea if I had a concussion, but I always fear the worst.

"I took a similar fall nine years earlier when an ex-boyfriend and I were on our first backpack trail in the Limpopo Transfrontier Park. I fell on a downhill slope and was pinned under an even heavier backpack. He pulled me up and noticed I had cut my lip. He wiped off the blood and gently kissed it. He held me tight until I regained my strength. I remember how comforted I felt.

"Tears filled my eyes. I was afraid I might fall again. It wasn't that I was missing my ex but I felt alone. I needed a hug, a kind word, compassion or a hand to hold. I would love to tell you someone grabbed my hand, kissed me on the cheek and made it all better, but I was among strangers.

"Once my pity party was over, I realised either I would quit the hike and rest my poor battered head, or I would change my mind-set and make the most of the rest of the trail. I decided on the latter and it was like flipping a switch. I was back in Kruger, heart and soul immersed in the wilds of Africa."

Her's was the first of several falls and, by the end of the week, we had all tripped at least once; except for Louis. We hiked much of the trail in silence. Thoughts loud in our heads. Some people are good at disconnecting and savouring the moment. Others not.

After we got going again, we detoured around an untidy community spider web that most people erroneously refer to as nests. We paused to discuss its dynamics. The web, made up of tunnels and chambers, can house hundreds of small spiders in the collection of dried leaves and debris, which includes the uneaten remains of small creatures. These small brown-grey spiders combine their efforts to catch prey and maintain the web.

A family of warthog with a litter of young raced away from us in a zigzag when we stopped for breakfast on the banks of the Shabarumbe River. As we left, we alarmed some grazing impala. They leapt over fallen trees and other obstacles as they ran. Impala can jump three metres high. They, in turn, scared off a gathering of yellow-billed hornbills. There were many more of those on this Leg.

We headed west, away from the Tsendze River and through endless stretches of stunted mopane. Louis paused for us to examine jackal scat atop elephant droppings. Jackals defecate upon the faeces of larger animals to feel more powerful. My initial reaction, standing around nature's commode, was to be thankful humans and domestic animals have no such aspirations. But when we walked away, I thought of how humans display similar metaphorical behaviour. A manipulative partner at home perhaps, or in the workplace a bullying boss, or an ambitious co-worker. I thought about how statements such as, 'Don't shit on me', or 'Don't talk shit' are used in everyday life.

These thoughts took my mind off the long, hard pull to the high southwesterly bank of the Tsendze River. Louis went down the steep embankment to scout for a lunch spot but came back saying there was no shade. The slog continued until we found an opening with large shady trees where we stopped for the long-awaited break. I took off my shirt to cool down.

The grasses were in seed, and I spent a long time removing prickly shards from my socks as I rested in the shade. I regretted not buying gaiters and recalled they were recommended as much for protection from grass seeds as they are to guard against ticks. I fell asleep and awoke in the burning sun. My backpack was toasty, and the Lindt chocolate balls I had packed as my lunch and dinner treat had melted over my food.

A huge shrub of the indigenous perennial wild rosemary (*Salvia rosmarinus*) added colour to the otherwise khaki vegetation. I squashed the rosemary's fragrant pale blue flowers in my fingers to enjoy its warm and grassy smell.

A lone zebra got me thinking about how few animals there had been. That was about to change. As we prepared to cross a gulley through a gap in the thorn bush, Louis put up a hand for us to halt. Elephants, with calves, lingered in the trees. I peered around the thorn bush for a better look. I was next to Louis and pointed across the stream at the elephants.

"We were going that way, weren't we?" I asked teasingly.

"Yes, we were," he replied. The question simmered.

"And now?" I asked.

"We are going that way," Louis replied, as he pointed back over my shoulder. "What good is a mind if you can't change it?"

We returned to the Tsendze River to circle the elephants. The soft, uneven sandy riverbed had us dragging our footsteps and straining our calves. In places, we stepped through deep hippo and elephant footprints, made when the mud was wet. I was near the front when Louis ran at us waving his arms to get back quickly. I was watching my steps and missed what had transpired. Later I heard an elephant, with its back to us, was feeding in a concealed tree-filled cove when Louis came up behind it. We crossed hurriedly to the other side of the river, but the bank was too steep to climb. The lone elephant had moved up the bank by then, so we continued our slog downriver.

Now we were rewarded with a variety of creatures as we made our way down the river. Small, swift tilapia glided over the stones of the shallow rivulets we stepped over. A pied kingfisher hovered ahead of us and giraffes cantered downriver as we approached. After the long detour on the riverbed, to put distance between us and a group of breeding elephants, we scrabbled back up the bank to continue in the right direction. A small group of waterbuck crossed the river to circumvent a gathering of impala and zebra, intent on grazing amid a large flock of rowdy, yellow-billed hornbills. Waterbuck, with their large ears and shaggy taupe coats with white markings, have a gentle appearance. The combination of calm, grazing animals and vocal birds made the scene dreamlike and not wild and dangerous.

On the ground were two different columns of Matabele ants. Their disciplined formation and hurried pace indicated they were on their way to raid termite nests. When we stopped in the shade for a short rest, a spotted eagle owl flew out of the concealing canopy of riverine trees.

Louis gathered us around a plant with two upright green leaves edged in tinged yellow, called skoonma-se-tong, or mother-in-law's tongue (*Dracaena trifasciata*). It is also known as Saint George's sword or snake plant. In an emergency, the root can be used for water, and rope is made from the leaf. We stopped where an elephant had a dust bath in the sand. The almost square lines drawn with its feet made it look as if children had been playing hopscotch.

Through the trees was a large hippo in a shallow pond. I was disappointed when we didn't go closer, but we were reaching the end of a long day and Louis was eager to make camp. We had hiked 24 kilometres with our backpacks at their heaviest. I was relieved when we descended to the riverbed to make camp close to the confluence of the Tsendze and Kaleka rivers. We had gone so far only because we needed to get to where we could find water.

The sky was clear with a crescent moon. I was exhausted after the arduous day and was not keen to carry my cooking utensils anywhere to make dinner. Even if it was just a few steps. Marie and Clifford came over to prepare and eat dinner in front of my tent. Afterwards, we sat on the soft river sand while Louis shared his knowledge of astronomy. Pointing out the Southern Cross, Orion's Belt, and the Milky Way. He explained the reasons behind the different colours of the stars hanging as if on brilliant chains, undiminished by the pollution of city lights.

Lionel Richie's hit song, *Hello*, played by Louis was our wake-up call the next morning. I was reluctant to wake up after a fitful night with sore legs, thanks to a build-up of lactic acid from the previous day's effort.

Another long day lay ahead of us, with Pete as the lead. A lone impala stared from the opposite bank at our bustle before it snorted and ran off. Shortly after commencing our hike, we stopped at a termite mound so large some of us stood atop it. While the mound was as hard as cement on the outside and strong enough to take our weight; inside was a maze of tunnels and ventilation pipes built with sand, saliva and termite excrement, known as frass. The mounds house a complex colony of workers, soldiers and a queen, with each playing a vital role. Pete showed diggings from an aardvark and showed its droppings on the termite mound, which the animal tried to cover up. This was a male aardvark, identifiable thanks to the indentation made by its 'equipment', Pete wryly observed.

Walking on, Lourens kicked a fallen branch, lost his balance and fell heavily on rocks. He suffered cuts and grazes that needed attention at the next stop. We made a small detour followed by a climb, which took us to the top of a rocky outcrop. The sun rising over the eastern plains was glorious and we had a long break, while Jennifer lovingly attended to her father. Cleaning off blood and applying plasters.

I chatted to Pete about his work as one of about 70 freelance hiking guides working in the Kruger. I knew most of them were unemployed during the Covid-19 lockdowns. We also discussed how SANParks assists local communities. A lot of the 10,000 people employed by Kruger come from the surrounding area.

Jennifer's nursing took longer than expected. After admiring the serene beauty of the vast expanse of bushveld from our vantage point, I asked Pete about his weapon. He carries a .375 rifle that fires Holland & Holland Magnum bullets. He got the rifle from a conservationist who claimed it was used by South Africa's first democratic president, Nelson Mandela, to shoot a blesbok. Pete carried eight rounds on a hip belt, in addition to four in the magazine. His belt included a small bottle of baby powder, which he uses to tell wind direction when the breeze is too gentle to discern otherwise.

Where we rested, armoured bush crickets competed in number with yellow-billed hornbills. This was the case for the rest of the week, even though the grotesque crickets are a substantial snack for a multitude of creatures. Their defensive measures would not be out of place in a dark cult movie; the crickets have body spikes, squirt blood from seams in their exoskeletons, and vomit to deter predators.

Our rest over and backpacks in place, we set off hiking again. I detected movement on a rocky ridge to my right as we hiked through a flat sandy expanse. It was a perfect area for a stalking cat and, because I focused too long on a particular spot, I tripped on a fallen branch, landing on my left shoulder with a thud. That fall made it three down in two days.

Soon, we stopped for breakfast on a rocky outcrop and spread to individual nooks in sight of one another. Brigitte was in tears about the discomfort of her backpack. We helped her to put padding on it and plasters on her back to reduce chafing. I felt sorry for her and was relieved I had no such issues. The weight and long distances over challenging terrain was tough enough, without backpack problems.

It was a hot day and so we stopped at the Tsendze River to refill our water bladders. The imperious white head and breast of an African fish eagle stood out atop a tree in the distance. The beauty and elegance of its authentic supremacy reminded me it is one of the few creatures in the Kruger with no need for camouflage.

I went to the back of the line when the group got going again. With nobody behind me, at times, I let myself fall further back than I should have to be alone in the wild; even if for just an instant. I caught up with the group huddled around two pink speckled eggs in time to hear Pete explain the find.

"These are the eggs of the double-banded sandgrouse," he was saying. "They need to be near water. The male bird will fetch water, somehow holding it under its wings for the mother and chick."

Pete turned to Louis. "Nice to see the eggs of the double-banded sandgrouse. I've never encountered any before," he added.

There's always a smartass, and this time it was me. "If you've never seen them before, how do you know they are eggs of the double-banded sandgrouse?" I asked.

"Because I scared them off as we approached," Pete responded.

Louis wasn't going to miss the opportunity and jested: "If you look under the eggs, it says 'Made by the double-banded sandgrouse.'"

Laughter lifted our spirits while our quadriceps screamed during a brisk climb up a long, steep bank. Pete seemed to have little regard for those who were slower and, at the top, we waited and regrouped before continuing. We held the brisk pace for a long, hard session on a little-used management road until we stopped for lunch beneath a stand of mopane trees.

I put my backpack down and it was soon besieged by ants swarming over the remains of the previous day's melted chocolate. My mood was not helped when I took out my camera and found it wasn't working because of a shutter malfunction. It was an unusually busy lunch break, with some attending to wounds or making repairs. Brigitte's boots were too tight, and

Louis made space for her toes by cutting off the front end of the boots, then closing the opening with duct tape.

We reconnected with the winding Tsendze River as a dark-coloured giraffe bull loped by. Its long front legs and shorter rear legs moved in graceful unison along the edge of the riverbed, before turning up the opposite bank and disappearing into the trees. Being close to water all day was a major advantage and lessened the amount of water to be carried as we stopped again to refill. Marie said something had gotten into her pants and was tickling her. We laughed when it turned out to be nothing more than grass.

As a fresh wind cooled us, I chatted to Louis about the rifle he used to shoot an elephant on Leg One when he was leading another group. He carries a South African-made Vector .375, using Holland & Holland cartridges. Louis carries 10 rounds on the hip belt and three in the magazine. I leaned against a tree and was so engrossed in the conversation I never noticed I'd thrown an army of Matabele ants into disarray by standing in their path. They must have been returning to the nest from a raid as most were carrying pieces of dead termites.

Our hiking group was in fine humour. Jollity pervaded and we teasingly reached consensus Clifford was the best-dressed man on the hike. He stood out among our scraggly bunch with his olive trousers and a white long-sleeved shirt with the cuffs unbuttoned. Giving him an elegant, yet casual look. If he wore cufflinks instead of a backpack, he wouldn't have been out of place consulting with clients in a boardroom.

We descended to the dry riverbed of the Tsendze River for another long, tough stretch in soft sand. I felt the strain in my calf muscles, as I expected everyone else did. From there we climbed again and cut across the veld to connect with the wide sandy riverbed of the Letaba River; rivulets of water encircled flat island sandbanks. A lone buffalo bull lay on the bank facing the trees, not far from our descent to make camp. I mistook the buffalo for a rock until I noticed the tired flick of its tail. The old bull did not look like he was going to move anytime soon, and it wasn't safe to camp close to what some call the most dangerous animal in Africa. So we pressed on to the confluence with the Tsendze River. Three elephants splashed in the shallow water close to the bank on the opposite side, then disappeared into the trees. A group of waterbuck nonchalantly observed us as we approached, then also disappeared into groves of trees when we got close.

After a hike of 20.5 kilometres, we camped on a large half-moon-shaped sandbar on the northern bank of the river. It was too late to relocate when we found the carcass of a hippo in the trees behind us. Only the bones were left, and there was no smell and no inconvenience to us, so we decided to stay where we were. From the size of its jaw and coarse, razor-sharp tusks, it must have been an old hippo.

A lone bull elephant ambled from our side of the river to the opposite bank while I was setting up my tent. The elephant disappeared into the trees by the time I was done, and I used the last of the daylight to bathe in the cool water. Bathe may be too strong a word – it was more like a rinse from the elephant-made waterhole on the bank.

An impromptu bonfire built safely in the centre of the sandbank created a convivial atmosphere. We chatted as we cooked on our gas stoves around the fire. The stillness of the night was melodically interrupted by the precise five-second interval call of the small African scops owl. A lion roared behind us. A reply from the opposite bank escalated into a conversational rumble of lion roars. The half-moon allowed the stars to shine brightly, though the Milky Way was not as clear as the previous night.

Fish Ladder

Sleep was deep and restful, and I awoke to clouds that had moved in overnight. The still, cool morning inspired the noisy banter of francolins, the churring whistle of a fiery-necked nightjar, and a chorus of southern ground hornbill. I was sure I also heard the sharp, penetrating dog-like 'wak-wak-wak' of a Cape eagle owl – unusual so far east in southern Africa – adding to a morning symphony urging the sun to come out from behind the clouds.

Clifford and I were at the rear of our newly energised group. A small cooking pot in my backpack set up a rattle to rival the bird cacophony. The rhythmic clink and clank of the pot got to me, and I irritably stopped without thinking and ripped off my backpack to still its clamour. Clifford paused with me. I should have whistled for the group to stop. By the time we got going again, the group was out of sight. It was an unwelcome misdeed in that environment. We hurried to catch up with the group. They had realised our absence by then and stopped, everyone looking back in our direction. As we caught up, I joked about following a rare pangolin. Louis, who was leading, was not impressed. His cold stare was on a par with our first guide, Bjinse Visser, on those who step out of line in the wild and potentially endanger themselves and others.

At the confluence of the Tsendze and Letaba rivers, the sandy riverbed was filled with crocodile footprints and their tail drag marks. White-faced whistling ducks announced their presence with a distinctive three-note whistle. We turned to cross on the dry riverbed of the Tsendze River and followed a path up the long, steep embankment. Louis stopped at the top to let stragglers catch up and to allow everyone to look back and enjoy spectacular views of the Letaba River below. As we savoured the crisp view in the early morning light, he reminded us the hike was as much about the experience, the views, the sounds and sights, as looking for animals.

As if on cue, we spotted an insect with an unusually long abdomen and two pairs of wings. It was hanging on a blade of grass. Louis gave us a chance to identify it. I was surprised when Marie said it was an antlion. I always thought of antlions as predatory larvae in the sand. This was an adult and quite different from the larvae that dig funnel traps in the dirt to catch their prey. The antlion is made up of hundreds of different species.

"The antlion doesn't defecate, and their waste stays inside their bodies until they shed their skin. That's when they poo. Otherwise, ants, with their acute odour sensors, would not come into the trap," Louis told us.

Marie summed it up. "What you are saying, is that they are full of shit," she said gleefully.

Louis grinned and turned to lead us away, then paused and turned to face us.

"I have good news," he said. "Ahead of us, we have a long stretch of easy walking on a management road."

I was pleased to hear that, as since leaving the river, we had walked on an uphill sandy path. The road ran parallel to the Letaba River, but was high and so far back on the ridge we could not see the river. We had barely started on the road when Louis silently pointed his rifle to indicate where our gaze should follow. A family of elephants with calves was partly obscured in the stunted mopane but they were moving in the same direction as us. Louis gestured us to fall in behind him as he hurried into a grassy opening.

Instead of the easy road we had just been promised, we slogged through thick, waist-high turpentine grass. Pete stepped into an overgrown hole and fell into ample grass for a soft landing. We were still circling to avoid the elephants, when the quiet of nature was broken by a loud whistle, followed by a shrill female voice. It was the last thing I expected.

"Give it all you got, girl," was accompanied by a blast of loud music.

I spun around in disbelief.

Brigitte apologised as she searched for her cell phone. The intrusion was soon overlooked. We took a short break and the brief reminder of city hullabaloo was replaced with the raucous shrieks of a brown-headed parrot.

Louis pointed to a long funnel of whitish faeces and asked if we knew what it was. Most of us guessed it was from a hyena owing to the tell-tale white of calcium phosphates found in the bones hyenas eat. Louis said it could also be from a lion or even a leopard. We concluded it was from a lion because they were straighter than the ball-like droppings of the hyena.

I thought it was a good time for me to add to the body of wisdom on the matter at hand.

"Did you know the banana is the only food humans digest without changing its shape?" I asked.

There were some chuckles, but I could tell others were struggling to process the information. Their quizzical expressions turned to dirty looks as they processed the edgy quip.

After we reconnected with the management road, Louis pointed out the place where the group before us had fired a shot to warn off a threatening bull elephant. It was close to the H1-6 tarred road that connects the Olifants and Letaba rest camps.

As we crossed, a family of tourists drove slowly past. A woman wound down her window.

"Can I take your photo?" she asked cheerfully. We would have let her, but the driver did not stop.

The plan was to hike along the east bank of the Letaba River until we found a suitable location to make camp. I thought it would be an easy, scenic afternoon, but there were demanding sections with steep descents and inclines when we crossed the rivulets flowing into the river. Most were dry although some were muddy.

Female impala were coming into heat and ahead of us a couple of bachelors sparred with guttural, rutting sounds to establish who was the strongest to secure breeding rights. We learnt more from our guides about impala as we stopped to look at a pile of droppings. They were from a female because the droppings and urine were combined. If they were from a male, they would have been separated. Some impala dashed up an open bank in front of us and in a show of caution, hurried into the cover of trees. Implanted in deep muddy elephant tracks were small and large lion paw prints where lions had recently crossed.

The sun beat down as we meandered across a wide grassy bank to the water's edge for a breakfast break. There was no shade close to the water, so we retreated into the trees. I munched on a small red apple while others made coffee. It was a good time to sit back and observe. A hippo lumbered out of the water downriver and disappeared into the bush. A juvenile bateleur eagle circled low, probably looking for food. While adults are easily identified, juveniles can be confused with other brown eagles; but its pearl-grey face is a giveaway. I was lucky to get this close as the eagle's survival rate is low, with only a tiny percentage of chicks making it to adulthood. On a leadwood tree on the far opposite bank sat a large bird. I could tell from its posture it was also an eagle, but even with binoculars I couldn't identify the species. As we prepared to leave, a large cluster of impala drank on the opposite bank of the river alongside the leadwood tree with the eagle. There were a lot of impala in the area thanks to all the water.

I was disheartened by the amount of debris that blemished the river banks. There was everything from plastic bottles to condom wrappers. Floodwaters two months before contributed to this blight inside the Kruger, as waste from communities living upstream flowed into the Park. Rubbish from human settlements sullied the walk along two of the great rivers of the Kruger over four days of this Leg. Based on my experience of hiking for six days over each of the six Legs, I suspect more than one-tenth of the hike is stained by pollution. I would be happy to be proved wrong.

Louis cautioned we had a tough stretch ahead as we moved from the river up the embankment. The gradient was gentle, yet exhausting in the sweltering heat. It was worse when we had no animal path to follow and had to trudge through stony terrain partly obscured by savanna. I had no time or energy to give quarter to those behind me, even though I knew the gap widened at times to a dangerous point. My shirt was drenched in sweat as I struggled to keep up with the armed and uniformed guides ahead. My mind drifted to a comparable scenario, where there was once conflict not far from where we were. I grew up during the independence struggle in Rhodesia in the 1970s. It led to the Lancaster House Agreement in Britain and independence for Zimbabwe in 1980. As an adult, I met those from both sides of the conflict. From what I was told, my backpack at one-quarter of my body weight was nothing compared to the weight of backpacks in addition to ammunition and weapons carried by combatants. I felt relief we walked in peace and with a sense of caring for all around us.

Louis stopped under an unusually large mopane tree to speak to us. "Another element has come into play that we must take into account," he said. "The short shade break. Do not take off your backpacks."

We stood in the shade and drank water. I felt my breathing slow. Replenished, we soon resumed the hike until we found a small creature blocking our way with its architectural masterpiece. A massive spider web stretched across the stunted mopane. Spider silk is the toughest fibre in nature. Pound-for-pound, spider silk is stronger than steel and tougher than Kevlar. A large golden orb spider reigned from atop, deservedly so I thought, after I had a chance to examine the web's intricacy. The princely golden orb spider is so named because of the colour of its silk, which it adjusts through pigment to vary the intensity. Though big and scary looking, this spider is harmless to humans, and scores of small parasitic spiders busied themselves in the kingdom of her web.

After navigating around numerous webs, we exited the bush onto a dirt road. I was grateful for the reprieve from bush-bashing as we walked without hindrance, for a much-needed recovery treat. The road crossed a small river over a low bridge that formed a lake on the upstream side. A waterbuck splashed through a causeway as it dashed across the lake to escape our incursion.

The bridge would have made an ideal setting for the lunch break, but we had to walk further downstream to avoid the road used by tourists. Large mopane trees downstream provided the shade and concealment we needed, and we stopped for the promised long lunch break.

I took off my shirt and watched the playfulness of blue and red dragonflies flitting around me. The dragonflies contrasted with the variety, in colour and behaviour, of numerous serene butterflies. Enchanted by the natural entertainment; I dozed off.

Louis relaxed in the shade near me and after our nap, we spoke about the infamous elephant kill when Louis led one of the first groups on Leg One. I wanted to confirm what I had heard, namely that rangers found about 70 snares in the area when they descended on the site after the kill. This was true, Louis told me. Poachers set up snares in a wide area to catch antelope, to feed impoverished neighbouring communities. Sadly, endangered wild dogs are often caught, too, as well as other threatened species.

As we packed up, Lourens announced he was wearing his gaiters for the first time. I must have come across as jealous when I spoke of my annoyance at failing to buy gaiters because of my poor preparations for this Leg. Clifford said he had a pair he was not wearing owing to his long trousers and offered them to me.

"Thanks, Clifford. I will take them from you tomorrow. These socks I'm wearing are so messed up already; they can't get any worse," I said.

"Do you want to take the gaiters from me now?" he asked.

"What a stupid question," Clifford and I said at the same time, as we laughed at what the obvious answer from me should be. I took the gaiters.

Not long after we continued, a scattering of vulture feathers caught our attention. We gathered around them in a patch of flattened vegetation and speculated about what had happened. The mystery was solved when a stench led us to the carcass of a young giraffe in a bushy cove. The bloodied head was still attached to the spine and parts of the ribcage. From the stomach-turning maggots and flies, we guessed the kill was two to three days old. A nearby tree where vultures waited their turn, was coated in whitewash. Vultures excrete the acidic droppings over their legs to kill off bacteria and toxins after stepping on a carcass.

From a vantage point high on the bank of the river, it was easy to spot crocodiles lazing in the sun and hippos in the water. The peace was broken by a flock of noisy hadada ibis – or hadeda as these birds are generally known – with their eponymous croaks during the hunt for worms and slugs in suburban gardens. They flew over the crocodiles and crossed low over a family of hippos with their young at play in the water.

Densely woven invasive water hyacinth was everywhere. Large swathes of the river were covered by the oxygen-choking blooms. Water hyacinth (*Eichhornia crassipes*) is a free-floating aquatic plant with fleshy green leaves and mauve flowers and is an invasive from the Amazon basin in Brazil. By choking rivers and lakes, it destroys fish and aquatic life, including other indigenous water plants. How the plant invaded the Kruger and other natural wonderlands in Africa, including Lake Victoria, is uncertain. The flower is beautiful and the plant may have been imported as an ornament for garden ponds, and so began its steady invasion of Africa.

There were signs of leopard scat in the dense forest flanking the waterway. Food was plentiful for leopards here, evidenced by the numerous impala sightings along the river as we approached the large concrete weir of the Engelhard Dam. The dam is named after Charles Engelhard, an American millionaire and chairman of the Rand Mines Group, whose estate donated funds to the Kruger for the construction of the large reservoir. The dam – built near the confluence of the Letaba River and the Makhadzi watercourse on land occupied by Chief Hatlani a century before – has some of the best birding in the Kruger and is close to the Letaba Rest Camp.

I was surprised men were fishing below the wall. Our guides explained they were off-duty rangers and fishing is sanctioned by Kruger management if done with permits and in places not seen by tourists. Even that comes with risks for the experienced employees of the Kruger. Two years later, Kobus de Wet, a forensic expert and senior manager in the SANParks Environmental Crime Investigative Unit, was stormed by a hippo on a river used by Kruger staff for camping and recreational purposes. De Wet surprised the hippo in the reeds while looking for an ideal fishing spot and died within minutes of having a leg severed by the hippo and being bitten in the shoulder.

While the dam is beneficial to hippopotami and crocodiles, it is unnatural and prevented fish migration, until the construction of the concrete steps of the fish ladder we used to descend to the lower level. The dam was built in the 1970s; however, the inscription etched into the cement reads 12-10-2011, memorialising the completion of the fish ladder. Fish migrate for several reasons, including to spawn and to find food. These migrations are essential to genetic fitness. The year after construction, a study was undertaken which concluded the fish ladder was working as intended, with fish moving downstream and upstream.

After passing the dam we took a short break beneath the pale green leaves of an acacia, the symbolic tree of the African savanna. The old tree, probably in its third decade, gave us ample shelter while we watched a pod of snorting hippos. Some disappeared under the water and resurfaced nearby. They made me uneasy; yet, I knew we were safe if we didn't get closer. The acacia (*Vachellia xanthophloea*) is sometimes referred to as the fever tree as it grows in the same swampy areas where mosquitoes abound. European settlers associated the tree with illness. Some settlers even thought the tree was the cause of malaria. Research into the deaths of 3,000 antelope in northern game farms in 1989 by Wouter van Hoven, a Pretoria University zoologist, found the trees, when nibbled by antelope, emit sufficient toxic tannin to kill browsers. At the same time, they emit ethylene that travels almost 50 metres, warning other trees. These trees, in minutes, step up their own levels of toxic leaf tannin. Giraffes tend to browse on the trees, although they avoid those emitting ethylene. Van Hoven's research contributed to a new generation of scientists studying tree communication.

There was little daylight left and we struggled to find a place to camp. The riverbed was rocky with the waterline higher than usual and so the sandbanks were too small to accommodate all of us. The wide grassy bank could have worked, but the best places had hippo paths running through them and we could not risk getting run over by a three-ton hippo.

We took off our backpacks and waited as Pete and Louis scouted for a suitable site. Pete went up the steep bank and Louis continued further down the river. Pete returned, looking disappointed, so I was relieved when Louis came back with good news. He had found a place on the ridge above the riverbank. The camping spot overlooked Voorsitspruit, an Afrikaans word for 'ambush stream'. In the 1980s, there was a low-intensity war between Kruger rangers and Renamo insurgents, as well as soldiers from the Mozambican army who were involved in elephant poaching.

In one year alone, 180 elephants were killed between the Letaba and the Shingwedzi rivers. When rangers killed a poacher at the ambush spot our camp now overlooked, it was a major psychological victory for the anti-poaching rangers. Poaching slumped, but as prosperity rose in southeast Asia, especially China, the slaughter of elephants and rhinos increased for their horns, which are believed to combat erectile dysfunction. The slaughter of rhinos has left white and black rhinos critically endangered. According to TRAFFIC, the organisation that monitors the illegal trade in African products, 90 percent of elephant populations were decimated over the 20th century, until a global ivory ban in 1989. The 13 largest seizures of illegal ivory shipments in 2011 represented tusks taken from 2,500 slaughtered elephants.

My concern was to erect my tent before going to the river to bathe and collect water in the fading light. The water was slimy but we had no choice. There was no time to filter and all we could do was add purification drops. Clifford, Lourens and I walked upriver to bathe. I sat naked in a deep pool and watched the sun go down. After three days of hiking without a proper clean, it was invigorating to wash using biodegradable soap. After dinner, we sat on rocks under a half-moon overlooking the shimmering river. Pete told us about the stars, planets and galaxies, adding technical details about space exploration. My mind filled with wonder.

My body was aching after the 19.5 kilometre hike. I slept soundly despite being awakened at some point by the discordant cackle of hyenas. I struggled to fall asleep again, as their mocking shrieks had me thinking about how hyena body parts, from the tail and genitals to their lips and whiskers, fetch premium prices in the local muthi (traditional medicine) trade.

I woke up to *Morning has Broken* sung by Louis and backed by subdued lion roars from far beyond the tree line on the opposite bank. Hippos snorted their greeting, although I was unable to see them. When I looked down on the river in the pastel early morning light, there was only a lone buffalo.

We expected a shorter hike of about 16 kilometres, mostly along the river. I saved two kilograms of weight by beginning the day with only half of my water bladders filled. Pete led us to the river where a large pod of hippos greeted us. They were surrounded by waterbirds, some of which croaked warnings at our arrival. We stayed close to the water's edge and made occasional forays back up the bank only when we encountered obstacles such as rocks or deep water. During one of those forays on a high bank, we found an ancient dead leadwood tree with a hole in the trunk in the shape of a pod chair. I sank in for a moment's relief with my backpack on and my feet dangling above the ground. After I extricated myself, I caught up with the group who were waiting in the deep shade under the glossy green canopy of a Natal mahogany (*Trichilia emetica*). A flock of noisy Egyptian geese flying over the river tried, but failed to disturb the tranquillity.

I enjoyed walking on the high bank of the Letaba River. The elevation provided expansive views of the rugged veld and I picked out a waterbuck on a grassy island. Crocodiles hunt alone and because waterbuck seem to believe there will not be a reptilian ambush, these antelope feel safe resting and grazing on the islets. The waterbuck were spread out and some stood on the opposite bank with a saddle-billed stork as tall as the waterbuck. On our bank, a deciduous buffalo thorn tree looked regal yet menacing. Zulus traditionally use the thorns to carry the spirit of a deceased person from the place of death to the burial site. The leaves and younger shoots are edible and, while the fruit is not tasty, it can be used to make beer, and the seeds can be roasted and ground to make a hot coffee-like drink.

Back along the watercourse, the birdlife was rich. Colourful bee-eaters were abundant, chasing flying insects over the water. A lilac-breasted roller flew high above us before tipping forward into its rolling pattern in a territorial display. We moved up the bank where a troop of baboons had passed through; they had overturned rocks and even elephant droppings in their search for termites. We crept up on a lone, distracted impala, as it peered into a thicket. It wasn't aware of us until we were close and then ran off with a start. We could have been complimented for how silently we moved through the bush as a unit.

Louis and Pete acted with an abundance of caution. I presumed it had to do with the topography, proximity to water, and the higher number of animals compared to the northern parts of the Kruger. When we stopped to talk or look at something of interest, one of them moved ahead to keep watch. When crossing streams obscured by trees or bush, we crossed only after the lead guide went ahead to ensure it was safe.

Someone pointed out the oval-shaped nest of a blue waxbill, built from grass stems and hidden deep in a thorn bush. In summer, we would not have noticed it owing to leaf cover. The nests are often built near active wasp nests for additional protection, though there was no evidence of wasps. Along the same path, we stepped around the bleached skull of a buffalo that must have been there for some time. The keratin-rich horns were covered with eerie moth tubes where caterpillars fed.

The sun was high in the sky and breakfast was long overdue. I did not mind the scramble down the bank to eat next to the serene river. When we climbed up the bank later, a small band of impala scattered.

We hiked a long way without a break before coming to a distinctive, roughly manicured shepherd's tree (*Boscia albitrunca*) that would have been at home in the Kalahari. With backpacks off, we enjoyed a well-deserved break beneath the ample umbrella-like canopy formed by animals browsing the low-hanging leaves.

After the break, Pete led us along a scenic stretch with the Lebombo mountains on one side and the Letaba River on the other. We pushed through rocky sections with ups and downs, to cross the gullies feeding the river. At one of the crossings, a restive herd of waterbuck hung out in the shallows. Fresh leopard prints explained why they seemed anxious. They were being stalked and our arrival could not have helped their cause. A troop of baboons crossed the wide, rocky riverbed ahead of us. One stayed back and perched sentry-like on a tree stump to glare at us until the troop had all but disappeared into the trees.

By then, the heat was intense; Louis soaked his hat in water for relief. We all followed his example. Blacksmith lapwings, or plovers as they used to be called, made noisy defensive sorties over our heads. They were a distraction we did not need. We had to look down, focusing on protruding rocks to find a way through the marshy vegetation without falling.

Once we were through, the shade of a large tree on the bank, combined with a fresh wind, provided relief from the heat as we took a welcome break. Brigitte, who had at our urging taken to using a stick, looked much happier and thanked us for convincing her to use one. A couple of Egyptian geese flew low, honking over a pod of hippos. One of the hippos disappeared beneath the water to surface close to us for an inspection.

We continued along the bank of the river until we found a suitable place for a long lunch break. An apple-leaf tree, with a jackalberry tree behind it, provided good shade over a swathe of long grass that invited a nap. My shirt was wet with sweat and I was delighted when I heard Louis say we could swim in the river pools below us. After a quick lunch and a short nap, I walked down to the river I followed upstream on the neat, hippo-mowed grass bank. I couldn't have done a better job in my garden using a lawnmower. After making sure there were no crocodiles or hippos in sight, I swam naked in the cold and refreshing water, out of sight of the hiking group. I spent a few minutes in the refreshing bliss of the cool water before I realised I was in the running for a Darwin Award[2]. Isolating myself from the group and my protectors so I could swim naked in a river infested with hippos and

---

2 The Darwin Awards recognise individuals who have contributed to human evolution by selecting themselves out of the gene pool by dying or becoming sterilised via their own unwise actions.

crocodiles was not smart. To make matters worse, when I stood up, I heard a car stop on the opposite bank. I had not realised the S93 tourist dirt road was on the other side of the river. I prayed they didn't have binoculars.

Our brief respite was over, and Louis instructed us to stay close as we moved towards a scattering of waterbuck and hippos occupying a mix of rocky and grassy islands. An African fish eagle took off with a fish in its claws and alighted on a leadwood tree ahead of us. It was so engrossed in its meal it never moved, despite our proximity.

Louis was behind Pete when he stopped unexpectedly in an open section. Pete had walked past a leopard tortoise without noticing it, and when he realised we were not following, he sheepishly returned.

"I was looking out for elephants," he laughed.

During another break, while I kept an eye on a nearby crocodile, I watched a large breeding group of elephant move away from the river. A calf had fallen behind, trumpeting, until it reached the safety of the others. The baby elephant's tantrum prompted the crocodile to take refuge, and it slid off the rocks into the water.

In the heat of the day, there were fewer animal sightings, though we did get close to a lone female kudu cooling off in the shade. The lull in animal activity and slower pace gave us time to better observe the little inhabitants of the African bush, including a large and complex hamerkop nest that is used only once, and a dead insect-eating bat we briefly stopped to analyse. The only mammal capable of flight, there are myriad bat species. There are also bats in southern Africa, known as frugivorous, which eat fruit, pollen from flowers and seeds. They remain in areas close to fruit trees and are unlikely to be found in the Kruger.

An unnatural-looking, wide track with straight lines swept through a flat sandy plain. We didn't understand how it came about. Most of us guessed it was from a large snake and followed the track until we discovered it was an ant highway. The track came to an end next to a mound of shells from de-husked seeds. The transport phase that created the track was over and we watched worker ants bring waste material up from the nest below the ground. Thereafter, we took pictures beneath a baobab tree with fewer than usual branches, although the ones it had were exceptionally thick. Elephants had stripped the bark to an incredible height.

Starting down a steep descent to cross a rivulet, a large spotted-eagle owl flew out of a tree and Louis called to Jennifer, who lamented not spotting any owls, to follow him. The rest of us followed at a slower pace behind Pete until we grouped around a mass of quills that must have been the site of an attack on a porcupine. Louis and Jennifer returned soon afterwards and from the smile on Jennifer's face, I knew she had finally sighted an owl.

As we stepped onto a long causeway across the wide Letaba River, a crocodile slid silently into the water. A waterbuck stood alone on the sandy bank on the other side of the river, while the rest of them grazed on one of the larger grassy islets. We set up camp within sight of the causeway. The distance for the day was 19.1 kilometres. More than we had anticipated. There was a lot of space at the water's edge, but the tents had to be set up close together high on the bank to leave open a path for hippos and other animals to cross between us and the river. A large elephant bull and a giraffe browsed peacefully on the opposite bank as I pitched my tent. A divine reminder of where I was.

My mind was still in Nirvana when I went down to the water's edge to rinse and fill my water bladders for the next day. I preferred to take deeper water instead of the still water from the bank or around the rocks. After a quick look around, I knelt on a flat rock jutting into the flowing water.

"José, get away from there," Clifford shouted at me from the bank. "You won't see a crocodile coming up from the bottom."

He was right, of course; what I had done was reckless. Crocodiles are some of the stealthiest hunters on Earth, and even animals with all their senses attuned for survival are regularly caught out while drinking and dragged to their death. Crocodiles are known to breach the water's surface by a metre or more to take antelope grazing on the bank. Humans are at a natural disadvantage and if Clifford had not called out to me, the ending could have been very different, as evidenced by a similar incident involving Mark Montgomery, the most experienced guide on The Kruger Trail, not long after.

I met Mark when he guided us on Leg Four from Olifants Rest Camp to N'wanetsi Section Ranger's Post. By that time, Mark had walked 113 backpack trails in the Kruger and 30 Legs of The Kruger Trail. In 2022, he walked the length of the Kruger twice.

In April 2023, Mark and Pete Wilson were guiding a Leg Five group when Mark was attacked by a crocodile while filling his water bottle at a river.

Only his experience and size – 1.89 metres tall and 95 kilograms – helped him survive the attack.

Mark told me, "We had just passed the Harry Wolhuter Memorial, where we stopped and chatted about the lion attack Wolhuter survived in 1904. We then walked about 500 metres into the weir of the Metsi-Metsi River. There were some nice big trees with good shade. Though it was still early, we decided to get water and have lunch. The shallow water nearby was dirty and did not look good to drink, so we went to a place further on with more rocks, where it was easier to scoop out water.

"I began ladling. On the third scoop I saw a crocodile head under the surface. I hadn't noticed it during the first two scoops. There was no ripple, no movement or anything. I pulled my hand back, but the crocodile grabbed my wrist and fingers. From the time I spotted the head until I was grabbed and pulled into the water, was so quick I can't wrap my mind around it. I could hear the people behind me shouting. One brave guest jumped in and tried to grab me, but it happened so fast, the crocodile pulled me out from under the guest. Later they said they saw a bow wave from the back of my head, under the surface of the water. And then I disappeared. It's unbelievable how fast it happened.

"As the crocodile dragged me under, I put my other arm around its neck and tried to get at its eyes or mouth, anything that would deter it. I thought about pulling my hand out while I was fighting, while frantically kicking upwards to try and get to the surface. I was worried about being dragged to the bottom. The crocodile was trying to turn in the water, and I kept kicking to counter it, bruising my ribs. Just as I was thinking it might be a bad idea to pull my hand out, I felt the croc let go.

"Thousands of thoughts went through my head. I have a lot of experience with close encounters with dangerous animals and as a trail guide, you learn to keep your cool, which probably saved me. Or maybe the crocodile didn't like the taste of my hand, or maybe it cracked a tooth or something.

"It felt like a hard plank rather than a muscle letting go of me, and as soon as I felt the release, I lurched upward through the water. Luckily, when I broke the surface, I could still touch the ground. I was imagining the crocodile grabbing me from behind; so I lunged for the safety of the bank almost two metres away with everything I had. I propelled myself onto the roots of a stunted jackalberry tree, where I pulled myself up and out.

"Being dragged under took an instant. Fighting free felt like it took ages. Getting to the bank took forever.

"I managed to get out and could feel my right leg swaying backward when I stood up. I thought maybe the crocodile had bitten me again and perhaps taken my leg off. But I lunged so strongly trying to get out of the water, I tore my right hamstring and bruised the left one.

"I managed to get up the bank and back across the dirty shallows of the river where we had thought about getting water. I went to lie down in the shade of a tree. Luckily, there were capable first-aid responders in the group. They washed and cleaned my hand, while Pete used the satellite phone to call for assistance from Kruger Park officials. They sent a vehicle to pick me up and drive me to Skukuza. I told the group to continue the trail. We had a mishap, but that should not spoil their experience. The section ranger gave the go-ahead for them to continue with another guide. An ambulance took me to Mediclinic in Nelspruit.

"I've reflected on what happened. I haven't been put off going on trails again, as it is a passion, but I will be more wary of water in the future. Animals can be as unpredictable as humans; it is important to be vigilant and never drop your guard."

The crocodile was estimated to be about 3.5 metres in length. Mark underwent six surgeries, and pins and a plate saved his hand. Doctors are confident, in time, he will regain most of its use. Within a year, Mark was back on trail as a backup guide and was brave enough, after a careful check, to swim in one of the rivers in the Kruger. His trigger finger and thumb work well, and he can handle a rifle again.

For us, on our walk, thoughts of such trauma were distant, though I am thankful I took heed of Clifford's wise counsel. Most of us walked to the centre of the causeway to dangle our legs over the edge as we watched the sun sink below the horizon. The waterbuck grazed on the islet and it seemed they were going to spend the night there. Brigitte shared her tiny bottle of Amarula with the group as we sat joking, chatting and relaxing.

Fading light forced us back to camp. The rising moon was close to a waxing gibbous moon. Giving enough light to cook without headlamps. Fireflies danced over the water while we chatted on the bank long after finishing our meals.

Stormy Weather

The next morning, after what Louis must have thought were less than enthusiastic reviews of his singing abilities, he woke us up to the Genesis classic, *I Can't Dance*, playing on his cell phone. I was so tired I slept through noisy hippos during the night and roaring lions at dawn. There were fresh lion tracks at the water's edge where we had bathed and collected water before nightfall.

Louis called us together and sketched in the sand to explain the geology of the Kruger. He told us about the continental shifts that formed layers of basalt, granite and the silica-rich volcanic rhyolite that shapes the Kruger. Southern Africa is buttressed by one of the oldest rock formations on Earth, as continents formed by Gondwanaland heaved and split 180 million years ago. The Barberton Makhonjwa Mountain Land, south of the Kruger's southern boundary and a UNESCO World Heritage Site, contains the oldest unspoilt sequence of volcanic and sedimentary rocks on the planet.

While Louis talked, I watched an elephant and a single waterbuck on the opposite bank. It was unusual for a waterbuck to be on its own and I wondered if it was the same one on the bank when we arrived. A loner or an outcast? Before we got going, Louis promised us we would encounter a surprise.

Lourens was decorated with freshly applied plasters. He would not have been out of place alongside a mummy display at a museum exhibition of Egyptian antiquities. I was glad to be wearing Clifford's borrowed gaiters as we set off across the thick veld of seed-heavy grasses. The ears and tail of a scrub hare stuck out in the long grass as it bounded off when we stopped to look at a candelabra tree (*Euphorbia ingens*), or naboom, as it is known in South Africa. This tree, often grown as a pot plant, can grow to 15 metres in the wild. Its milky latex is an irritant to the skin if touched and is toxic if ingested, even causing blindness in some cases. *Euphorbia* was named after Euphorbus, a first-century physician to King Juba of Mauritania, while the species name, *ingens*, means huge. As the plant grows taller, it can develop a hot-air balloon shape.

We took the opportunity to hike on a dirt road to make faster progress and escape the itchy grasses. I watched an African harrier-hawk get mobbed by two blue-eared starlings that chased it away from their nest. The hawk is recognised as a raider by some other birds, which keep the predatory bird away with chirps and dive-bombs. The air show took place over a small female kudu that remained motionless, despite our proximity and the battle in the sky above it.

Eventually, we left the road to return to the river. We followed an animal track between the water and the inaccessible rocky bank, where a picturesque large-leaf fig tree flourished. Its exposed roots were visible at the bottom of the rocky outcrop. The hike along the river varied from marshy to rocky and in places we slogged through sandy stretches. A couple of hamerkops flew past heading upstream. Their deep wingbeats silhouetted against the rising sun.

During a short break, I asked Clifford if he preferred using one walking pole versus the two he always used. We had spoken about it at camp on Sunday when I convinced him to use just one. Clifford agreed one was better because it frees up the other hand. A waterbuck grazed on a grassy island in front of us while we rested. On the other side of the river, a large flock of cosmopolitan herons, better known as cattle egrets, hovered before dropping out of sight behind the reeds.

An animal track led us through a dense thicket that tore at my hat. I felt for my sunglasses I often left on the rim of my hat, but they weren't there. I felt behind my neck where I thought they may have fallen, and they weren't there either. I whistled to stop the group and went back a few steps to search the grass at the foot of the thorn bush.

Jennifer looked at me and asked, "Are you looking for your glasses?"

"Yes," I replied, looking down in the grass while she helped me search.

And then we realised I was wearing the sunglasses. For a while after that, Jennifer and I were deservedly known as *Dumb* and *Dumber*.

Laughing in embarrassment, we continued to walk in the heat on the west bank of the Letaba River. A Nile monitor, or leguaan, scampered to the safety of the water. We did the same, but for another reason; to fill our hats with water before putting them on our heads to fight the heat. In the process, Arie slipped and fell into the river with a splash. I resisted the temptation to feign a fall and take a dip, fully clothed, in the cool water. This was, of course, before knowing of Mark Montgomery's sobering experience.

We continued along the river until a monolith of smooth black basalt angled across the bank down to the water. It was so big there was no way around it. It was slippery and treacherous to walk on, and so we took our time to cross safely. It would have been impossible if it had been wet. While waiting for the others to cross, a young giraffe appeared at the water's edge ahead. It fled as we approached.

Three speckled, pink eggs lay on a sandy niche in an outcrop of rocks we were about to climb. "Are those from the same bird as the others? The double-banded sandgrouse?" I asked.

"Same species, not the same bird," Arie quipped.

From there, we faced a tough climb, scampering over rocks and around trees until we crested a ridge that looked down on a series of rapids on the Letaba River.

"Death by torture," Jennifer sighed as she reached the top.

I knew how she felt after the arduous ascent. "I had similar feelings when doing the Ironman triathlon on too little training. First, you fear you are going to die, then you fear you are not going to," I said.

I peered over the ridge and there were two uniformed men at the water's edge; each armed with a military-issue R1 automatic rifle. They walked along an animal path headed for us and I asked what they were doing. They said crocodiles were dying in unusual numbers, and they were trying to determine the cause. I thought that was said as a cover-up to not scare us, and that they were looking for poachers.

Later, however, I discovered pollution caused mass die-offs of crocodiles in the Letaba and Olifants Rivers in 2008 and again in 2019. In the winter of 2008, 20 plus crocodiles perished each week. SANParks Head of Scientific Services, Danie Pienaar, said pollution in the park's rivers ranges from "...acid mine drainage, [to] agricultural pesticides and fertiliser use, sewerage treatment and industrial and household sources of pollution". A multi-institutional research project investigated the situation and found, "Invertebrate species numbers have halved compared to 20 years ago. The river has changed from being a free-flowing river with diverse habitats, to a standing water body thanks to the back-flooding caused by the raised Massingir Dam wall in Mozambique".

We had a breathtaking view of the veld dominated by marula and acacia trees with the river below us, so we made it a long stop for lunch. A large pool flowed into rapids leading to a small waterfall. After a quick lunch, instead of the usual nap, I went down to the river where the rocks formed a natural bathtub. Some in our group were taking turns to lie in it but there was no visible flow of water in and out. I went further down and found Lourens and Arie in a rock cove next to the rapids. It was big enough for three, so I stripped to my underwear to join them. The cold water was refreshing in the baking sun. I wedged myself between the rocks with only my head out of the water and the rapids tugging at my legs. I closed my eyes to savour cooling off in the Letaba River rapids, as the hot African sun shone down, and soon fell asleep.

Waking, dragonflies, one red and one blue, flitted energetically, then stopped momentarily on the rocks to scrutinise me from different vantage points. Louis came down to join us but there was no space in the cove we were in, so he sat in a smaller pool behind us. Clifford arrived a little later. By then I was getting cold, so I climbed out to make space for him. Word of our find must have got back to the lunchtime camp above because Marie came down and the guys made space for her in the rock pool.

Back at the top of the ridge, Arie was walking around in his underpants.

"I eat and I drink when I'm hungry or thirsty. And I wear clothes when I'm cold," he said in response to our quizzical looks.

There was no arguing with that, given where we were. He went on to tell us he had done two naked skydives wearing just a helmet and boots. The first time was on his 100th skydive, as is tradition in South Africa, and then again with a shy friend who did not want to do it naked on his own.

"He couldn't have been that shy," I said.

Soon, we were fully clothed and leaning under the weight of our backpacks. The hard work was not over when we left the ridge. We climbed another steep incline to a little-used management road, which we stayed on for some time. A lone giraffe bull crossed the track and stopped in an open grassy patch to watch us. The track led in the direction of the giraffe and it moved further away to where it towered over the trees to observe us from a less exposed place.

I had been bragging about my Wolverine Black Cap boots, after easily negotiating the various steep ascents and descents, but I kicked a rock and the lip of the right sole came loose. We stopped in a clearing where I wrapped bright blue duct tape around the boot to hold the sole in place. When we set off again, some plump plains zebra left the river and crossed ahead of us. They were in no hurry and I had the time to compare their individual stripes, confirming they were as unique as human fingerprints. We made a beeline for the river from there and cut across another open grassy field. Long gourd vines on which the calabash grows (*Lagenaria siceraria*), were concealed in the long grass and were so hardy, they ripped off one of my gaiters. I had to go back some way to fetch it and felt guilty my equipment issues were slowing the group.

After a steep descent to the Letaba River, we found a flat sandy stretch on the bank to make camp for the night. We were not too far from the confluence of the Letaba and Olifants rivers, but were unable to see it as the river had a sharp bend cut into high cliffs. We had covered 14.8 kilometres and, despite our leisurely lunchbreak, there was still plenty of daylight left. Pete offered to take the group to the confluence. I jumped at the chance along with Jennifer, Marie, Cliff and Arie. Other than his hat and boots, Arie again wore only his underpants. I was relieved we weren't skydiving.

Pete warned it was a tough one kilometre hike to the confluence and that we should take something to drink. We got to the bend in the river, but there was no other way except through deep water. We backtracked to go up the steep bank instead. A grazing hippo watched us detour. Hippos are the deadliest large land animal and I was relieved when it disappeared into the water as we passed. Having traversed halfway through the Kruger by then, I realised at first light animals went about their business with an unhurried air of harmony. At the end of the day, I sensed less flexibility in the wildlife, even a filament of arrogance. To prove the point, a pair of hostile blacksmith plovers noisily pursued us.

At the top of the steep climb, we were rewarded with pebbles of amazing shapes and patterns spread over a large area. I took one shaped like an ark as a memento. It was bigger and heavier than I wanted, but I figured I only had to carry it for a day and it would be worth it. I use it now as a paperweight in my home office.

Clifford fell backwards on one of the tricky uphill sections, adding to the count of those who had fallen on this Leg. Jennifer stepped into a hole and lost her balance. She insisted we could not count it as a fall, but the consensus was it was. By that stage, we had all taken a tumble, except for Louis and Brigitte.

The confluence was spectacular and well worth the extra walk. Looking down from the top of the cliff, the Letaba River on our left flowed into the voluminous Olifants River with an easterly course into Mozambique. The combined river eventually joins the Limpopo River, which flows into the Indian Ocean near Xai-Xai.

We were at eye-level with an African fish eagle facing us on the cliff. I peered down at a pod of hippos in the water, alongside Egyptian geese and crocodiles on the bank. A crocodile swam upstream towards the meeting of the waters, making slow progress against the current. At times, it hardly moved, despite powerful sweeps of its tail.

We had time for a group photograph and returned to camp a different way. The route took us to the ridge almost directly above the camp and dominated by a baobab tree. Three metal cages, probably used for crocodile capture when they were dying at an abnormal rate, lay abandoned at the edge of the ridge. Pete said if he had been leading, he would have made camp there for safety reasons, despite the trek to the bottom for water. We were about to learn how wise that would have been.

Back at camp, I heard the cries of the fish eagle coming from the cliffs at the confluence. I interrupted putting up my tent to watch a klipspringer on the opposite side of the river. It was stationed on the rocks in a seemingly impossible position. Klipspringers balance themselves delicately on their small, blunt, rubbery hooves.

The last of the daylight faded and I began preparations for dinner. I did not know then I, and the others, would sleep on an empty stomach that night. I should have paid more attention to the rumbles in the sky, than those coming from my stomach. Jennifer offloaded her excess food, including biltong and droëwors. Louis offered me a generous portion of droëwors from his bag, half of which I ate immediately. I had already taken two packets of surplus tuna off Jennifer, so I was planning to go big that night, with a double portion of mash. The droëwors was a starter and I munched on it as I collected running water from a gurgling gulley in the river.

The sun was setting and heavy clouds massed above us. Thunder and lightning shook the skies. I had already removed my boots and changed into shorts and a T-shirt when Louis called for our attention.

"We need to get to the top of that ridge," he said, pointing to the steep rise.

"You mean, we leave our stuff here and we climb up until the storm is over?" I asked.

"No. Pack up everything. We need to move the camp to the top of the hill."

"You know Louis," I said, "today must be the-20-something of April, far away from April Fool's Day." I had missed the gravity of the situation.

"I'm serious," Louis said. "It's now dark. We need to move quickly. It will rain upstream and the river will come down in flood during the night when we won't have light. We will be unable to see anything, including animals. We can't take that chance."

It was the end of the conversation.

"Let's go," Louis said.

I pushed stuff into my backpack, including my boots. That was a mistake; I was only in my slipslops. I put my sleeping bag in, but not the thin camping mattress. I didn't feel like I was panicking. I was. I knew there was not sufficient light or time to dismantle the tent, so I decided to carry the assembled tent by the spine. I put on my backpack and pulled the belt extra tight. I folded the blow-up mattress and held it in my left hand together with my walking pole. With my right hand, I gripped the spine of the tent and headed up the hill.

The slip slops did not hold well on the steep, rocky climb and I couldn't use my hands or the pole for support. Barbs and small stones got under my feet. There was nothing I could do about that except grimace. It slowed me down and I fell behind. I was halfway up the slope when Pete came down to help. He took the tent from me, and with the pole for leverage in my right hand, I made quicker progress to the top.

The rain began as we drove the tent pegs into the ground. In the dark, and in my hurry, I hammered my finger while helping Marie secure her pegs. The storm mercifully shielded the ears of the innocent from my exclamations.

There was no protection from the gusting wind on top of the hill. I sheltered in my tent, my body weight working with the pegs to stop the tent from uprooting. Louis warned us not to cook in the tents, so I went to bed hungry, thankful for the droëwors I had snacked on.

I opened the front flap I had set up to face away from the pelting rain. The tents were in a circle and most were dark. From the light inside Clifford's tent, his silhouette struggled with seeping water. He was trying to lift the groundsheet. I didn't think his tent was going to hold in that wind. I called out to him, but he could not hear me in the storm. I closed the flap and tried to sleep, but it was a fruitless exercise on an empty stomach with lightning and thunder cracking open the skies.

The wind subsided and, in the lull, the rain stopped. Everyone, except for Arie and Brigitte, emerged. Gas stoves were set out to cook dinner, though I opted to stay inside my tent and cook on the groundsheet laid in front of the opening. Lourens boiled a big pot of water and offered me a choice of hot chocolate or instant soup. I chose the hot chocolate and Pete brought it to me. I savoured it inside my tent and watched the head-mounted lights and gas stoves add a neon-like glow to the impromptu carnival in the wild.

Without warning, a gust of wind brought heavy rain. Everyone scrambled to put out the gas stoves and rush back into the tents. I turned on my headlamp and it flickered before dying. After several attempts, I realised it was a battery-low warning. Why now, of all nights? I scratched around in the dark and found three spare batteries. With hindsight, I should have felt for the way the positive and negative nodes were positioned before I removed the used batteries. I didn't. It was impossible to align and replace the batteries without light. I called to Marie, whose tent was next to mine, and she did the battery replacement for me.

During the night, the rain and gusting wind woke me several times, though I did not hear the hyena calls the others had.

LEG THREE

We woke to a clear starry sky. The river was now in noisy flow and the pools where we had bathed and collected water, had disappeared below the torrent. Fresh hyena tracks pockmarked the rain-softened soil. Scattered drops fell as we decamped.

Lourens later told us, "Once the storm blew over, Jennifer kept telling me she could hear thumping sounds in or near our tent. I thought she was probably hearing water drip. The next morning while I was outside the tent packing up for the hike to Olifants camp, where we would finish Leg Three, Jennifer yelled to me from inside the tent."

'Dad, there is a frog in here.'

"I found a small frog almost as scared as Jennifer. I caught it and released it outside. Since then, Jennifer has not stopped reminding me: 'I told you I heard something hopping inside the tent the whole night, and you didn't believe me.'"

We set off into a cool wind for what was to be a short hike at only 13.7 kilometres. A warm sun cast long shadows ahead of us on the stony animal track that dipped into the green sun-kissed valley. A giraffe browsed in the trees, its neck and head lit by sunbeams shooting out over the Lebombo mountains behind us, while a kudu warmed itself in a sunny glen. Some impala ran off but one stayed behind, inquisitive until we got too close, and then it scrambled to join the others.

We took a break on a high ridge overlooking the Olifants River where crocodiles basked on the bank. I observed the Olifants Rest Camp in the distance, but there was a lot of ground to be covered to get there. Brigitte tripped and fell as we crossed a rocky section. Another steep, rocky path through close-knit bushes took us back to a stream. We helped each other down the slippery bank to cross at the bottom. While we regrouped, Louis pointed to an animal track through the trees.

"That way matches how everyone else would have gone. Then...," pointing to where we had crossed, "...we have Pete's way," he said.

We teased Pete, as the leader for the day, he was going for a big finish.

At the next stop, I used the short break to reapply duct tape to my shoe, while everyone else watched a crocodile on the bank eating a fish. Wet hippos in the water were barely distinguishable from rocks.

A steep, sloping basalt rock formation went to the water's edge below a tourist lookout point. For safety, we removed our backpacks and passed them along a human chain to flat ground. From there, the walk along the banks of the Olifants River was marred by domestic waste and plastic debris. It was worse than the Letaba River. The Honorary Rangers have done clean-ups on the Letaba and Olifants rivers, but it is not a regular occurrence. I tried to focus on the wildlife instead. A saddle-billed stork couple stood on the opposite bank, while a small crocodile held its head out of the water to let gravity help it swallow a fish.

A pod of snorting hippos occupied a large, still pool of water, while two crocodiles basked in the sun on one of the rock islets. While crocodiles and hippos are often together, unlike other pairings, it is not because of a symbiotic relationship between the two. Hippos are herbivores while crocodiles are carnivores; they eat fish and small herbivores. Hippos have no interest in crocodiles and while foolhardy crocodiles may attack a baby hippo, they are no match for an aggressive hippo.

The skull of a hippopotamus lay on the bank surrounded by its skeleton. The eye sockets, ear openings and nostrils are placed high on the skull, allowing the creature to remain submerged, yet alert, and to protect its delicate skin from sunburn. The jawbones were intact, and Pete lifted and dropped the top half to show how the top and bottom teeth rub together to make them razor-sharp. Hippo teeth are a hard type of ivory, though it is considered inferior to elephant ivory because of their smaller size and yellowish colour.

I used the short breakfast break to attend to my boots. The last of my bright blue duct tape had come off, so Louis used a pink adhesive fabric roll to tightly wrap the boot and sole. While we ate, Louis told us about the biological relationship between the large leaf rock fig and the wasp. Lured by the fragrance of the flower, the female wasp makes its way into the fig to lay its eggs. The larvae are born inside the flower and spread the pollen from the fig in a mutually beneficial pollination cycle.

Musing on the wonders of nature, we hiked up the bank and away from the river. At one of the larger tributaries, we waited in turn to slide down a steep muddy slope on our backsides to make the crossing at the bottom. Flotillas of red and blue dragonflies flitted on the stones and branches in the shallow water. Several mated on the wing.

We were keen to get to the finish by then, so we did a cheat stretch on a dirt road. A serrated hinged terrapin crossed where a stream flowed over the road and where we descended back to the river. A lone nyala, with its spiral horns found only on males, took shelter in the shade. Nyala are always near water and good cover.

Pete searched for a place to start the steep climb to Olifants Rest Camp. A large pod of hippos lounged on the riverbank and sandy islets. Most of the hippos took refuge in the water when we came close, forcing the oxpeckers to fly off their backs. I had my second fall on the smooth rocks as we turned from the river to climb. Sand clung to the bandage holding the sole in place, so the boot had no grip.

The service gate at the back of the rest camp was unlocked and we took a shortcut to the car park. Once our backpacks were in the vehicles and we were on our way to lunch in the restaurant, Lourens ceremoniously dropped his boots in a bin. He said his 'shoe issue' was caused by a thorn on the first day of Leg One. He later told me, "The thorn went through the sole of my boot and into my foot, and I decided to buy new boots. I walked Leg Two in them with no problems. I am a lucky person who hardly ever gets blisters on my feet.

"On day one of Leg Three, I could feel my feet were taking strain, but figured I would get used to it. By the second night, my boots felt way too tight. The next morning, I began what would become a daily routine, of borrowing Louis's Leatherman and cutting a piece out of the toe of the boots to give my feet some space. By then, my feet were swollen and kept swelling, so each day, I cut away more of the boots to make space for my feet. Now I was bumping my exposed toes against hidden rocks in the long grass, and my feet became even sorer. I compensated for that by altering my stride, which caused blood and water blisters under my feet.

"When I got home, my wife took one look at my feet and rushed me to the doctor. He put me on a course of penicillin and dewatering tablets for my swollen feet. The penicillin was for the cuts on my leg from the fall on the first day, which were now infected despite Jennifer's best efforts at nursing me."

This Leg took its toll on everyone, some more than others. Lourens was not his usual self. I had little idea he had come close to quitting. Brigitte started off badly and pushed through tears to finish strong. Every Panthera had tripped and fallen. The Japanese proverb, *Nana korobi, ya oki*, which means 'fall seven times, get up eight', applied to our group; we were resilient.

At Crooks' Corner before the start. Left to right: José Neves, Henk and Antoinette Jonker, Lourens van Aardt, Jennifer van Aardt-Bester, Clifford French, Pilot Nxumalo, Corrie Barnard, Arie Fourie and Bjinse Visser.

The Kruger Trail poster in a bird-hide near Letaba Rest Camp.

Pilot ready for the trail on Leg One.

First campsite in the wild.

Resting in the shade of a baobab tree.

A poacher's boot print.

'Morning newspaper' – tell-tale tracks of the night's activity.

Walking through the wide, open spaces of the Lindanda Plains.

The self-proclaimed 'Legends': Warren Deyzel and Arnold Bam.

Arnold helping with Maritha's backpack.

The camp set up in a disused artificial waterhole.

Elephants at the busy Matiovila Spring.

Splish splash, Lourens and Morné were takin' a bath.

Opposite page: Training in the farmlands of Malkerns, Eswatini for Leg Five. Front of group to back: Cooper the dog, Ian Salt, José Neves, Grant Goldstone, Zocks the dog.

Quiet before the storm on the Letaba River.

Louis Lemmer tending the short-lived fire on the Letaba riverbed.

José rushing to the top of the hill with his tent before the storm arrived.

A proper siesta beneath a baobab.

Enjoying the sunset on the Letaba River. Front to back: Pete Wilson, Marie, Clifford, Arie.

Dinner around the fire on the Mnondozi riverbank, while lions roared in the distance.

Bush shower with a leafy shower floor.

Clifford recovering under a tree.

Lourens's legs after the fall and cutting open his boots - socks poking out the side.

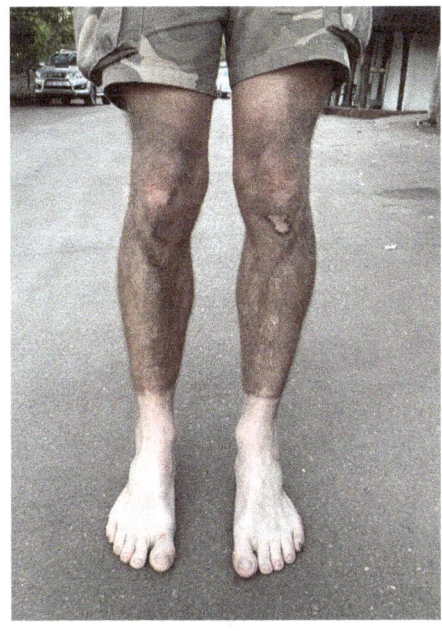
Arie's legs. It's not a tan.

Opposite page: Howard Spencer-Wilson and Pete Wilson digging for clean water.

Father and daughter on a break: Lourens and Jennifer.

Clifford collecting water from the Letaba River at dusk.

Morné's boots ready for the bin after Leg Two.

Opposite page: Mark Montgomery during a break on the Olifants River.

Ashraf Sayed looking for the elephants we could hear.

Early morning sun at the Mpondo Dam. Left to right: Jennifer, Lourens, Brigitte, Warren, Arie, Marie, José, Clifford, Alice.

Following tracks of a different kind on the dismantled Selati railway line.

Elephant rubbing post.

Denser bush in the south of the park.

José removing a thorn from his boot.

José and Marie in the prime seats for the final sunset on the trail.

Surprise lunch stop at Afsaal.

Alice making do without a table for lunch.

José making notes after a Merthiolate injection.

Clifford preparing his glühwein treat on the Mpondo Dam wall.

Ash celebrating atop Tlhalabye Hill.

José with his stone picked up at Crooks' Corner, for the cairn on Tlhalabye Hill.

A toast on the Mpondo Dam wall.

Arie, Jennifer, Lourens and José – the four who completed the hike from start to finish – at Malelane Rest Camp.

Celebrating in style with Cuban cigars and French Champagne at Lower Sabie Rest Camp. Left to right: José, Lourens, Clifford, Warren and Arie.

LEG FOUR

Olifants Rest Camp to N'wanetsi Section Ranger's Post
WINTER, JULY 2021

Covid-19 was rampant. We did not know if South African President Cyril Ramaphosa would ease restrictions in Gauteng where most of the Panthera lived, to allow the hike to continue. My youngest daughter, Georgia, was also leaving for the start of a three-year degree in Acting for Film with the New York Film Academy at their campus in Hollywood. I obtained a permit that allowed me to travel from my home in Eswatini to Pretoria to wish her well.

The lockdown was lifted on Sunday night and it was all systems go for the hike. Delaying the start by a day, instead of cancelling the hike, had paid off. I left early in the morning for the long drive to Satara Rest Camp and stopped to buy a bottle of whisky to make good on the Rand-Dollar exchange rate wager I lost to Clifford on the previous Leg. A road accident close to the top of the remote 11 kilometre Abel Erasmus Pass in the province of Limpopo between Tzaneen and Ohrigstad had traffic at a standstill. A truck laden with oranges had jack-knifed and spilled its load. It would take hours to clear. With no cell phone signal, I could not look for alternative routes on Google Maps. I backtracked down the pass and took a route past the private Timbavati Private Nature Reserve. Entering the Orpen gate of Kruger Park, my stress eased when I encountered elephants milling about the wildlife research station close to the gate. The drive was filled with antelope and birds, dwarf mongooses and more elephants. An extensive controlled burn had etched the grasslands in charcoal and green shoots were pushing through.

At Satara, I walked past Warren Deyzel, who I knew from Leg Two. He had shaved off his bushy beard and initially I did not recognise him. Warren introduced me to Paul Slyer, our new lead guide, and Mark Montgomery.

"Are we such a bad bunch we need three guides to look after us?" I joked.

The guides laughed, explaining Mark was the most experienced of the guides and the only one to have hiked all six Legs. Paul explained that as neither he nor Warren had hiked Leg Four, Mark would help navigate the route.

We met at Lourens's bungalow for drinks and an introduction to the new trail members, Donna van Schalkwyk and Annemarie de Lange. Donna wanted to complete the Leg as a tribute to her father, Ray Brown, who walked with us on Leg Two, but succumbed to Covid-19. She had his backpack and all his hiking gear except for her own walking pole and tent.

"Taking my dad's spot on the hike, which he had asked Uncle Lourens to hold for him, was something I realised I should do when it became apparent how important it was to him. I am terrified of the bush, and always told Jen and my dad they were crazy to walk in the wild," she said. "But I wrapped my head around the idea and became excited I could experience something that brought so much joy to my dad. He loved the wild, its tranquillity, beauty, the birds and the animals. After walking Leg Two, he came home with loads of stories. He was excited at the thought of joining another Leg. This is a chance to feel close to him again."

Donna worked hard to prepare: "I walked on the treadmill to improve my fitness, and over weekends, I did some 10 kilometre hikes and one hike of 21 kilometres. I could tell my preparations brought some joy to my mom. I think Jennifer and Uncle Lourens also felt comforted; they took dad's loss hard. I knew my grief was shared."

She paused and laughed, "Excitement turned to anxiety on the drive to the Kruger. I realised I had to walk in the wild. Terror! Now, after meeting everyone, I feel a little more at ease."

Clifford missed Leg Two and never met Ray, but was moved by Donna's account. He listened to her without comment and later told me, "I did not have the privilege of walking with Ray, yet I am moved by Donna's decision to hike in honour of her dad. I can't think of a better tribute to her father. I am sure he will be with her every step, siphon of water, kilogram of stuff carried, dehydrated morsel eaten, roar of lions, and sighting made."

Jennifer's husband, Morné, had done Leg Two with our group and travelled with her from the Netherlands to do another Leg with us. Arie was on his own. The other newbie was Annemarie, a friend of Jennifer's.

Kingdom of the Spiders

We left shortly after the gates opened for the 50 kilometre drive to Olifants Rest Camp. Paul, Warren and Lourens travelled with me. Everywhere were elephants, giraffes, zebra, guineafowl and francolins. A lone hyena patrolled outside the camp gates.

An overcast sky and a chilly seven degrees Celsius had us huddled around Paul for a briefing. In our hands were steaming mugs of coffee. Paul demonstrated signals he used to avoid scaring animals by speaking aloud during the hike.

After a short stretch on the tar, we made an abrupt turn into the bush near the river. I heard the common scimitarbill's harsh, chattering alarm call as we teetered down the steep, stony slope. At the bottom, we stopped around white, calcified balls of hyena scat. There were fresher, olive-green hyena droppings in the area, too. And so, we started with a lesson in scatology, the study of excrement, which conveys considerable biological information, including diet, health and diseases. Paul told us from carnivores, it is called scat; from humans and primates, it is faeces; from herbivores, it is dung; rodents, birds, and reptiles leave droppings. I later learnt from bats and seabirds, it is called guano, and the fine excrement from caterpillars and herbivorous insects is called frass.

A fork-tailed drongo hopped from bush to bush, as Paul told us how the red-eyed bird feeds on insects disturbed by passing creatures. Musing on his words, we had not gone far when Annemarie tripped on a small log and had a gentle landing in the grass. Falling early in the walk, it seemed, was a rite of passage.

There were numerous hippos in the Olifants River and our first break was under an apple-leaf tree in sight of the rest camp far above us. The leaves of the apple-leaf tree make a crunching sound when squeezed; like a bite into an apple. They also make perfect pot scourers.

We stepped over two different scouting parties of Matabele ants on the riverbank. Paul warned us to stay close because it was a cool, overcast morning. He was concerned we could get caught between hippos returning to the water after overnight grazing. About 500 people are killed by hippos in Africa every year, some in similar situations.

We cut away from the river to descend to a tributary that feeds into the Olifants River. Halfway down, we stopped to appreciate the operatic chorus of bird song from flocks of arrow-marked babblers, fork-tailed drongos and others. Jennifer pointed out some Verreaux's giant eagle owls, the largest owls in the region. Our presence scared them and they flew off. We continued the descent, watched by a lone impala. These antelope are sociable creatures and males of different ages stay together in bachelor herds. Still, some males remain solitary, re-joining the herd during mating season to contest for the right to mate with females.

Where we intersected with the Olifants River, an unusually flat example of the invasive cactus, the sour prickly pear (*Opuntia stricta*), sprawled on the sandy riverbank. It was first found in the Kruger in the 1950s; elephants and baboons eat the fruit and spread the seeds in their dung. Blacksmith lapwings, or plovers, flew in circles over the river. The pleasant ring of their alarm calls was drowned out by a large flock of Egyptian geese, which took off from the grassy centre island. I was beginning to dislike these geese.

The chill lifted and I rolled up my sleeves. The heat was getting to Paul, too, and he led us up the bank to shady bush. Two red-billed oxpeckers flew from the scrub and he decided to stay on the riverbank to detour around whatever animals may have been concealed under shady trees. The oxpeckers would not have been that deep in the bush unless they were feeding on the ticks of large animals like buffalo.

A white-fronted bee-eater flew over my head as we stopped for breakfast beside a huge basalt rock topped by a brown ivory tree (*Berchemia discolour*). Baboons, vervet monkeys and birds enjoy its fruits. Mark shimmied up the rock to sit in the ample shade of the tree, which atop a rock was safe from browsing game such as elephants, giraffes and antelopes. A distant giraffe watched as Paul handed everyone a leaf from the rough-leafed raisin bush (*Grewia flavescens*). Animals browse the leaves and birds love the tasty fruit, which is edible for humans. Paul demonstrated how the leaf can be used to brush teeth; something we all tried with favourable results.

Lifting our backpacks and heading off again, we strode past a large impala tribe and two giraffes at the water's edge. A crocodile sunned itself on an islet of sand, and a sizeable gathering of waterbuck grazed on the opposite bank of the wide river. An enormous pod of hippos forced us to back up to a dirt road, where we discovered big, knuckle-like baboon footprints in the sand. Two tourist cars drove up and one driver stopped and wound his window down. "Did your bus broke down?" he asked in his broken English.

A green and yellow water monitor basked on a man-made culvert and did not move when we walked past on the way to the river. Paul apologised to a motorist parked on the riverbank after we crossed the field of vision of his outsized zoom lens resting on the car door through an open window. A lone waterbuck, the subject of the photographer's attention, lifted its head to watch us from one of the grassy sandbanks. A lilac-breasted roller flew off in a flash of colour from a heap of dead branches. I had never been so close to one and was amazed by the brightness of its turquoise underside and tail in the morning sun; it is larger than I realised.

On the other side of the causeway, a hippo lay motionless among river reeds. It seemed oblivious to our presence, but it was so close I kept an eye on it for as long as I could. As we reached the end of the causeway, a grey go-away bird, or crested turaco, sounded a piercing alarm call.

We had to find a way to cross the Xipembane tributary, to follow the Olifants River westwards on the southern bank. As we searched for a crossing point, the distinctive sweet smell of buttered popcorn wafted over; it was the unmistakable smell of leopard urine. The tributary defied our attempts to find a crossing, so we backtracked to the causeway and jumped onto a sandbank and over pools to get to the southern bank of the Olifants River. The sun was high by then and hot, and we took a break beneath a clump of large trees on the bank to cool down and debate whether we should have lunch or go further. The consensus was to press on.

We followed the river, then spread out to pass through a large impala herd without causing a stampede. Even a group of waterbuck leaving the river at an easy trot did not disturb the peace. Paul stopped to point out the tracks of an African civet, and later paused around a partial leopard print. With the abundance of animals in the area and so close to the river, there were a lot of carnivores about. We soon gathered at a more distinct print made by a young male leopard and fresh enough to timestamp it to about a day old; heat loosens the sand granules and softens the print.

Paul noticed the group didn't seem impressed with all the stops. "Maybe we will come across a better print," he said.

"I want to spot the leopard, not just the print," I said, piling on the pressure.

"It's going that way," Lourens said, pointing back to where we had come from and adding, "We will wait for you."

Vultures groomed themselves on an exposed sandbank in the river. Paul told us they are clean birds, washing after attending to a carcass. Further along, we came to a pile of their messy droppings beneath a dying leadwood tree. A large, regurgitated owl pellet of mostly fur lay amid the scat. Paul pointed to a nearby fever tree's clean, smooth, pale green trunk as we left. "It is called a dead dog tree. It has no bark," he quipped.

We stopped for a long-awaited lunch break. I sat on sparse grass beneath a leafy leadwood and was entertained by a common chinspot batis chirping on a thorn bush. It is the only bird named after the female, which is distinguishable from the male by its mottled back, and a chestnut spot under the bill.

Walking along the riverbank after lunch, we heard the grunts of hippos. The large pod mostly concealed in the abundant reeds on the sandbank. Beyond them, an elephant troop descended the bank on the other side of the wide river. I was absorbed with watching the hippos and elephants when some waterbuck splashed through the river behind us. They gave us a wide berth as they trotted through the water. Once well past us, they turned abruptly to go up the bank and disappeared into the trees.

A bridge crossed the river in the distance. Paul brought us together around a fresh lion track while Mark took up a position as a lookout. He soon shouted a warning an elephant was approaching from the bridge. We scrambled to get out of the way. By the time I turned around to look, the elephant was alongside. I am always amazed at how quickly elephants cover ground; it's scary when you are on foot.

The adrenaline rush over and the elephant past, we took the management road parallel to the river to continue our westward journey. A shout from the back of the line brought us to a sudden stop. We had walked past a spotted hyena hidden in the thorn bushes. It crossed the road and then circled back in the trees to get behind us while we stood next to a large communal nest of Namaqua rock mice. They live in colonies of grassy nests stuffed into crevices in trees and rocks; though this nest was built around the foot of a tree.

When we crossed the tar road, Mark unearthed a wok concealed at the foot of a tree. He explained he had dropped it off there on Sunday to avoid carrying it from the start. Mark uses the pan to make fires at night when camping because it is safer and cleaner than making a fire on the ground. He carried the pan by hand because we were close to the finish point for the day. In the days to come, he hung it on the outside of his backpack. After limited fire-making on past Legs, I looked forward to having a fire every night.

On the other side of the tarred road, the terrain was grassy and stony. The purple-pod cluster-leaf (*Terminalia prunioides*) was now prevalent, taking the place of the mopane thickets in Olifant's rugged veld zone. I welcomed the short break and stretched out on a comfortable mattress of grass in the shade of a tree. An eagle flew high over the river. I struggled to identify it until I heard the African fish eagle's iconic cry.

The terrain was irregular as we wove around bushes and trees. I was behind the three guides when a thorn bush hooked on my backpack, forcing me to stop. Lourens disentangled me, and by the time it was done, we were out of sight of the guides. They noticed our absence and grumpily headed back. We got the inevitable talking to about procedures. I should have alerted them when I stopped. Not long after, Donna tripped on the rocky path to land on a soft patch of thick grass. She later said, "The first steps into the bush are calming. I felt peaceful, but nothing prepared me for the terrain. My lack of fitness caught me by surprise and I knew the rest of the week would be mind over matter."

I always found the first day the toughest and the backpack uncomfortable. I was not concerned because I knew my fitness and adaptability would improve daily. I was relieved when we descended the ridge to make camp on the sandy bed of the Timbavati River. Its name is a derivative of the Xitsonga, *ku bava*, or 'bitter water'. We had covered 18.8 kilometres.

Three elephants played in the water upriver, far enough away to not concern us. Another three passed on the opposite bank as we set up tents on a sandbank with cliffs behind and the river in front, giving the camp a feeling of safety. The pools were still.

Thanks to a gibbous moon and cloudless sky, there was enough natural light, although I had my headlamp with me when I sat at the fire to prepare my evening meal. While I waited for the water to boil, I panned my spotlight over the sandbank and the pools of water in the river behind me. I shuddered, and not from the cold.

The sandbank behind me and the river revealed the shimmering eyes of hundreds of creatures, which drew gasps from around the fire. I had seen those eyes before, on the first Leg, on a spider. This was an army of spiders. They came across the water and up the sand bank to the fire and swarmed around our bare feet. I had a chance to take a closer look at their flat, grey bodies and long legs. Although, with 152 species of spiders in the Kruger, I could not identify them. I was amazed a creature with such a small body had eyes that shone like those of something much bigger. We did our best to ignore them until they passed.

It was the coldest night on The Kruger Trail yet. I woke up freezing, so I put on socks and a warmer top. We were well past the winter solstice but the sun rose only 20 seconds earlier each day and set half a minute later. I kept waking from the cold to hear grunts, growls and wheezing from the hippos around us.

The sun was well up when Warren led the day's briefing for what was expected to be a 15 kilometre hike. The plan was to head west to a natural spring where we would refill with water, then head south to again connect with the Timbavati River.

The rising sun shared the sky with the moon when we left camp and headed west. The moon took much of my attention as I wanted to know how and when it would disappear. I might have asked the guides if we were allowed to talk, but I revel in the delight of discovery. The moon seemed to drop to the horizon as we walked and became fainter in the glare of sunlight.

The terrain flattened and impala scattered into the trees ahead of us. Trumpeting elephants saw us proceed with caution until we spotted a herd in the trees ahead. Warren pulled out a tiny bottle and sprinkled what I thought was baby powder to discern wind direction. Powder drifting behind us meant the elephants would not have detected us, and we might have surprised them, which is undesirable. Warren later told me the bottle in which he keeps wood ash was given to him by a section ranger's wife, the first family he befriended when he arrived to work in the Kruger.

We veered north to walk around the elephants and had not gone far when we heard the rumble of more ahead of us. Warren stopped to consider the options. He wanted to take us to the spring, but Mark disagreed, saying it would add too much danger to find a path around the elephants. The guides agreed to head south instead.

Walking in silence, filled with thoughts and keeping an eye on the moon, I forgot about the elephants, so it was unnerving when I heard them behind us.

"Why do the elephants sound so distressed?" Jennifer asked as we paused to take stock.

"They are in musth; it's either mating calls or they are chasing away predators," Warren replied unconvincingly, as he quickened the pace.

Musth in bull elephants is characterised by aggressive behaviour as their testosterone levels rise 60 times.

After a long brisk walk, we stopped for a much-needed break. Warren and Paul stepped away from the group to confer while Mark distracted us with facts about the sourveld topography. While he spoke, I watched Jennifer nibble on salami sticks. I told my sad tale of how they were sold out when I went shopping, which was enough for generous Jennifer to offer me what she had.

The moon was still visible when I rolled up my sleeves to stave off the heat. I had no idea of the time, but it felt late and my shadow on flat ground was as long as I was tall. I kept an eye on the moon despite the dangers of looking up in the bushy and uneven terrain. We headed east to follow the sloping topography downward and I lost sight of the moon. Even if the moon is in our sky during daylight hours, it may not be visible because of the Earth's atmosphere and the scattered light from the sun.

A high hill cast a long shadow across the animal path we followed. A neat row of four zebras, one behind the other, immobile, their heads held high, turned to face us. They never moved, even as the path took us closer. Not so for an equal number of kudu that sprinted away up the hill.

Trudging through long grass in stony terrain is difficult, so wherever possible, we followed animal paths. On one such path, we encountered a plate-sized fur ball thrown up by a hyena. We scratched it with our walking poles and found an undigested tooth and a hoof from an impala, although we already knew from the fur.

We stopped for breakfast when we intersected again with the Timbavati River. Three elephants and a buffalo stood on the riverbank, far below our elevated position on a ridge. The elephants were part of a much bigger herd. To avoid the steep descent to where everyone else had stopped and the return ascent later, I took off my backpack and sat alone in the copious shade of an apple-leaf tree after I let the guides know where I was. Being alone in the wild was unusual and I savoured every exquisite minute.

After eating my customary apple and two rusks, I sauntered down to the group. Morné, Jennifer and Donna sat in a row, airing bandaged feet. I was impressed by how well Donna was doing.

"I would join you but I don't have bandaged feet," I boasted.

"We can put some on for you," Jennifer replied.

My new boots were perfect, despite my fear they were a size too big. I should have tried them on when I bought them instead of relying on the size on the label. I was wearing two pairs of socks to fill them out.

I returned to my isolated spot at the top of the ridge and was making coffee when I heard Jennifer scream. After my foot drama with Merthiolate injections, I knew what was happening. I descended gingerly, carrying my hot coffee, to survey the battlefield.

Annemarie was applying bandages individually to each of her own toes. "No injection, Anna?" I asked.

"No. I'm tough," she replied.

While everyone else collected water from the river, I chatted to Paul. His Winchester Magnum CZ458 fires flat-nosed .458 rounds with the bullet design by Bjinse Visser who led us on Leg One. He said Mark was not armed because the established standard is one rifle for every four guests. Warren carried the same Musgrave .375 he had on Leg Two. In addition to being a freelance guide, Paul runs Maninghi Lodge in the Balule Nature Reserve within the greater Kruger National Park. He also has a safari company that operates in eastern and southern Africa.

Paul and I watched our group collecting water from the river. Behind them was an elephant, partly concealed by giant ferns on the opposite bank. No one at the river had noticed the elephant. They were more concerned by fresh lion tracks in the sand although they were in no danger, so Paul and I didn't warn them.

When everyone returned, we walked along the ridge extending along the river's eastern bank. We stopped to admire the elephant group, to which the three earlier elephants belonged. The lone buffalo was still there, watching us from the shade of a jackalberry while the herd disappeared into the trees higher up. A fork-tailed drongo perched on a branch next to us while we watched the elephants; the bird hoped we would disturb insects on which it could feast.

Further along the ridge, it looked like two men were seated on a fallen branch in the shade of a tree on the opposite bank. Warren pointed to them and Paul waved. There was no reaction, and someone said they must be from the anti-poaching team. It occurred to me they were poachers who stayed still, hoping we would not recognise them for what they were. We left, not sure if they were humans or if what we thought what we saw was no more than an illusion of light and shadow.

I noticed Paul and Mark often cleared the path of sticks and large stones without interrupting their stride. I had not seen such courtesy from the guides on prior legs of the hike, though in their defence, until now, the terrain had been sandier, with less grass and wider tracks rather than narrow animal paths. A massive jackalberry tree stood in the centre of a tidy clearing that wouldn't have been out of place as a village square. The copious shade around it must have been well used by animals and had a look of being swept.

Fresh elephant dung, wet and still warm on the outside, lay on our path. I broke open a pile, and it felt close to 37 degrees Celsius, the temperature at which it is excreted and the average body temperature for humans. Paul told us up to half a litre of water can be extracted from one dropping and he stepped on a pile of dung to show us water trickled out. He offered to do an extraction and filtration, but nobody admitted to being short of water.

A little sparrowhawk, identified by its white rump and bright yellow eyes, sat at the top of a big tree nearby. Though common, these secretive residents of forests and woodlands are not often observed. A lone kudu cow watched us from the dense mopane.

When we took a short break, I asked the guides about symbiotic relationships. They discussed commensalism, where one organism benefits and the other neither benefits nor is harmed, like orchids on trees. Warren explained the relationship between insects and animals is often amensalism, where one organism is unaffected, and the other is inhibited or destroyed. For example, a buffalo with an oxpecker on its back leaves the buffalo unaffected, and the tick consumed.

The conversation turned to group members. Arie had a headache, and Clifford, battling diarrhoea, sat alone and glum beneath the bent trunk of a fallen tree. On the way to Olifants Rest Camp the previous morning, he was so ill, he was forced to stop to let Morné drive. He was advised not to take anti-diarrheal remedies to avoid possible side effects, so Jennifer gave him tablets to reduce cramping.

Later, we stopped for lunch on a sandy riverbed in the shade of a black basalt cliff face. I tried instant soup instead of my usual crackers with cheese or tuna and soon regretted such a light meal. Before taking a nap, Warren showed me a knife made for him by his friend, Herby Symons, engraved with his name and four warthogs on the blade.

I laid my groundsheet and blow-up pillow in the shade for a post-lunch siesta, and most of the others did the same. The wind came up and the cold woke me, so I moved to an animal-formed hollow closer to the water and in the sun. When I awoke, everyone was done packing and I rushed to join them.

Despite the brisk pace and the need to make up time, we stopped for a short break on the high bank of the Shisakashanghondo stream. A small cluster of impala wandered along the dry bed below. We descended there after the break, and I felt tired as we zigzagged on the sand. I was relieved when we moved onto firmer ground to avoid two majestic kudu bulls. A male elephant moved away calmly as we stayed on our heading. Mark told us to collect firewood as we headed down the slope.

We found an idyllic place to make camp on a flat grassy stretch close to flowing water. But the bank was steep and narrow, and it meant there would be passing animal traffic around us during the night. To be safe, we crossed the stream to an elevated glade, where we set up camp.

We had hiked 19 kilometres; more than the 15 we expected. There was little daylight left, and two showers were set up. Night had fallen by the time I pitched my tent and joined the others around the fire to chat and eat.

Hippo Haven

In the dawn, we noted a shallow cave behind our campsite. Marks in the dust and the way leaves and sticks were scattered meant it had been used recently. We huddled around Paul for a briefing next to a fur-laden piece of lion scat. The plan was to make camp close to the Timbavati picnic spot, where Mark had arranged with the stall owner to wait past the usual closing time so we could buy cold drinks. The other big plus was using real toilets.

As we left camp, there was a variety of fresh animal prints on the path, including those from steenbok and hares to larger leopard and elephant tracks. Lourens quipped a steenbok is also known as a brick buck (*steen* is stone in Afrikaans). We collected water from a stream, and after leaving the river, we walked through a corridor of wild sage (*Salvia africana*), an aromatic shrub, the dried leaves of which can be burnt to keep mosquitoes away.

Hiking through the short, dry, grassy plain was easy as we transitioned from mopane to purple-pod cluster-leaf. A flock of about 10 white-crested helmet shrikes stayed ahead of us, foraging on the mopane and purple-pod cluster-leaf. I loved their beautiful bubbling chorus of clicks and chattering. A magpie shrike, or African long-tailed shrike, perched alone on a thorn bush. Usually, they move in pairs or small groups. The magpie was the favourite bird of the Zulu King Shaka; its traditional name, *isakabutle*, means 'the scatterer of enemies'.

The purple-pod cluster-leaf thinned until there were no more trees. While the endless flat plains might look uninteresting and devoid of game from a distance, there is always something going on. At one stage, a huge group of impala enveloped us. I heard the mournful, whistle of the black-crowned tchagra before one flew out of a bush near us. African violets (*Streptocarpus sect. Saintpaulia*) clustered in the shade where the bush was thicker.

Two kudu bulls stood on a slope in front of grazing zebra. Paul stopped to tell us about the length and width of the ample horns of kudu in the Kruger, versus the smaller horns of kudu in the Eastern Cape. He said the reason why the head and horns of the kudu are used as the symbol for SANParks is because the kudu is the only animal found in all of their parks.

Breakfast was atop a rocky outcrop on the banks of the Timbavati River. It was more social than usual, with everyone chatty. It was not often everyone participated in a group chat. Breakfast and lunch were often quiet, with most people eating alone or with one or two others. During a pause in the banter, Anna looked up the river. "I've got to go back to the office next week, but I know this spot will still look exactly like this," she said.

Everyone seemed to take more care than usual to ensure we left no trace of our stopover. While we packed, an enormous hippo emerged from the bush onto the sandy riverbed. Every time I come across a hippo when on foot, I'm convinced it is the largest hippo ever. It sauntered upriver through the sand and splashed through pools of water before going back up the opposite bank.

Three ground hornbills flew low. Despite their size, they nest in tall trees. They forage in thick short grass, where they feed on reptiles, insects and small animals up to the size of a hare. We continued along the ridge where there was a single bull elephant browsing with some zebra. The wind was behind us and when they caught a whiff of us, the elephant and the zebra scattered in different directions. A flock of brown-headed parrots flew overhead, and their raucous shrieks made us look up. In the distance perched two African fish eagles; one atop the rocks and the other on the bare branches of a dead tree.

The sky was bright and cloudless, with various birds of prey on the wing above a group of grazing impala. Walking through uneven terrain in long grass was not conducive to looking up. We paused to watch an eagle and heard the whistling day call of a pearl-spotted owlet. The bateleur eagle was easily identifiable by its white flight feathers and the broad terminal band on the trailing edge. Another three eagles appeared high in the sky. They were brown, so either tawny or Wahlberg's eagles, but we could not be sure even with binoculars. The grass was now short, with sparse purple-pod cluster-leaf trees and mopane shrubs. I had become used to brushing against the mopane and discovered I had to give the purple-pod cluster leaf a wider berth after I brushed against one, and it scratched my shoulder painfully, drawing a trickle of blood.

Paul wanted to stop for a short water break. Mark felt we should carry on until we were over the ridge. A tense discussion followed. Having a third wheel was unusual and occasionally there was tension, though always positive and well handled. It reminded me of Segal's law: a man with one watch always knows what time it is; a man with two watches is never quite sure. During the debate, I watched a charming family of three giraffes with their heads facing us. They were pleasingly arranged, from small to medium to large.

We climbed the ridge before stopping for a water break. After that, the topography changed and the going was not so easy. We hiked through vast expanses of metre-tall red grass suitable for grazing and indicates the sandveld is in good condition. Zebra and wildebeest roamed in abundance, but the sizeable white rhino could not be found. In the first six months of 2021, the Department of Environmental Affairs reported 249 rhinos were lost to poachers; more than half, were in the Kruger. The fight against poaching was being lost. Mark told us during full moons, up to 12 different groups of armed poachers are in Kruger taking advantage of the lunar light to massacre rhinos. It filled me with sadness, frustration and anger. If the political will and leadership were in place, rhino poaching could be controlled. The technology, with drones and thermal imaging is available and affordable compared to dehorning and dragging dirt roads nightly to detect poachers.

The sun was high by the time we reached the end of the taxing plains of long grass. The topography was now more interesting and dwarf mongooses scurried away on rocky ridges, while wildebeest grazed at the bottom of the slope. A dazzle of impala ran before us and regrouped close to an outcrop of trees. Stoic-looking wildebeest were not about to make space in the shade, so the impala moved on. We turned to head over the ridge and paused to watch a large group of waterbuck gallop by.

We had to work for our lunch, scrambling up a steep ascent to the top of the cliff in the heat. Halfway up, a cluster of the protected Lebombo aloe (*Aloe spicata*) was a good excuse for a short rest. The aloe was in flower and the serrated leaves varied from pale green to dull red.

At the top, we split into small groups to find shade. The Piet Grobler Dam on the Timbavati River was where we had a long lunch break. A crocodile floated motionless in the water and, behind it, impala grazed on the bank. Hippos snorted in the water far below. I found an apple-leaf tree on the cliff's edge, with a view of the dam wall and the last two bends in the river. Clifford and Arie joined me. Arie and I took off our shirts to dry after the sweat of the long, challenging climb in the heat of the day.

Lunchtime entertainment was provided by a dark-capped bulbul dallying on the leafless trees. A bloat of hippos sprawled out on a sand spit in the shallow water where a crocodile stealthily disappeared below the surface. A bigger pod of hippos on the river's next bend was tightly packed, with the fat, pink underside of most visible as they lay on their sides. A crocodile hid in the concealing shade of a tree at the water's edge, while another crocodile glided through the water towards the dam wall. A lone hippo moved out of its way.

After lunch, I spread out my groundsheet and pillow for a nap. The repeated calls of an African fish eagle roused me. I opened my eyes to two circling over the river. I put on my hat, grabbed my binoculars and sat on a rock at the cliff's edge.

A small waterbuck group, with an egret for company, stood on the opposite bank. I looked back to the river's first bend and counted seven crocodiles. While everything appeared sleepy and peaceful, on closer inspection it wasn't. Below me, a crocodile edged closer to two Egyptian geese. When I looked back to the sandbank at the first bend, it was now occupied by just two crocodiles. A sand spit formed the inlet to a small lake where four crocodiles, evenly spaced and sentry-like, faced upriver. Nothing was going in or out through that opening while they were there.

Flapping noises drew my attention to a hippo spraying its dung as it defecated noisily in the water. Hippos aid the health of rivers and lakes by moving silica-rich grass from land to water through excretion. However, the methane from the faeces also consumes the oxygen in the water. Fish die from a lack of oxygen, especially when water levels are low, so flowing water is essential.

Butterflies and birds added colour and serenity. One butterfly had all-white wings with orange tips and flew directly at my face, veering away at the last moment. A crested barbet, with its giveaway shaggy crest crowning its black, yellow and red plumage, dropped onto a branch in front of me. The bird was so close it looked big and imposing, even though it must have weighed less than 100 grams.

After a while, the heat from the sun was too much and I headed to the shade of the apple-leaf tree. On the way, I rubbed my itchy back up and down against a thorn bush like Baloo in *The Jungle Book*, one of my favourite childhood movies. Back in the protective shade and with the camp still at rest, I felt as lucky as Mowgli, the movie's orphan boy brought up by panthers in the jungles of India, who lived with the thrill of surviving the everyday dangers of life in the wild.

Once everyone woke from their siesta, we gingerly descended a steep, stony slope. After the treacherous descent, we had a short break where a buffalo came up from the river and scattered a herd of impala. Paul told us about the history of the Kruger and the Piet Grobler Dam, named after the great-grandnephew of Paul Kruger. Grobler was Minister of Lands and introduced laws to protect the area against powerful mining and agricultural interests. His work saw the Sabie and Shingwedzi reserves and the land between the two become the Kruger National Park on 31 May 1926.

Approaching the water, the guides were tense and cautious. A buffalo bull turned his head to watch us as we cut too close behind him. The impala ran from the water's edge, regrouped in front of us, and then dispersed as we approached. We spotted a hippo during the descent, but nobody knew where it went. To avoid being caught between the hippo and the water, Paul and Mark went to scout ahead and left Warren with the group. The guides never found the hippo and warned us to stay alert.

A wide sandy track leading away from the river was marked by a long stretch of zigzags, and Paul asked us to guess what it was. Most of us said it was from a giant python. We were wrong. It was from a lazy elephant dragging its trunk as it walked. The inevitable speculation about which trunk followed, until Paul made it clear it was from the one in the front. Nearby, the scattered feathers of a guineafowl suggested its demise.

Further along, a jackal ran across our path and stopped beneath a tree, where it turned to watch us. A bunch of wildebeest concealed in thick thorn bush didn't react to our proximity when Mark stopped to check through binoculars on movement ahead. It turned out to be harmless guineafowl.

Tamboti trees on the banks of the Timbavati River marked the spot for the night camp after a relatively short 14.8 kilometres. After off-loading our backpacks, it was a short walk to the Timbavati picnic site, where I looked forward to a sweet and fizzy cold drink after days of river water. We took turns to use the flush toilet while others bought the drinks. I downed an ice-cold Coca-Cola and took a ginger beer to enjoy with dinner. We were in no hurry to return to camp and sat at a picnic table next to a sign exhorting tourists not to feed the resident bushbuck, which lingered close to us with no apparent fear of humans. From its size, I guessed nobody was obeying the sign.

On the way back to camp we collected firewood. While setting up my tent, I watched an elephant through the trees on the river's opposite bank and almost missed one nearby. We were being watched, or smelt, to be precise. I could just make out the end of its trunk as it swivelled above a dense thorn bush. As night fell, I took advantage of being the last to shower and stayed under the spray until the water ran out.

We sat around the fire burning in Mark's wok; cooking and telling stories into the night. Mark stirred the fire regularly, adding dry sticks so it blazed with vigour. Warren told us how he won the *Pink Gown*, an annual award to the guide who does the silliest thing, with the proviso it did not endanger the lives of guests.

"I had just qualified as a Lead Trails Guide, and I led a group, with Heusten Mhlari as my backup, on one of the three-night Lonely Bull trails around the Letaba Rest Camp. The bush was thick with invasive plants. We were meant to hike along the north bank of the Letaba River, but because walking was difficult, I decided to head in a northwesterly direction to the Kushumba spring. We had an extraordinary leopard encounter, and all went well.

"We woke up on the last day, had coffee and packed. We planned to head southwest about four to five kilometres to our pick-up destination and to end my first successful trail as lead guide. After walking about two kilometres, I looked at my electronic GPS compass and it said we were bearing east, opposite to where we should have been heading. It was overcast, so I was unable to get orientation from the sun.

"I thought if the compass pointed east and I made a 90-degree turn to the left, we would head north. Then, we would head west if I made another 90-degree turn to the left again. I followed that principle, walked a bit, and took two turns. I looked at the compass, and it was still pointing east. I did it all again, and when I looked at the compass, it still pointed east.

"I heard someone at the back clicking their fingers. 'Warren, um, we've passed this tree before,' Jasmine said.

"That was not possible, I thought. How can this visitor from Germany, first time in Africa, identify a specific mopane tree? I explained to her because of genetics and the species of the mopane tree, they all look the same, and no one can identify an individual tree. She didn't seem convinced.

"We walked on, and I did the two 90-degree turns again and stopped to check the compass. Before I could do a reading, Jasmine started up again from the back of the line. Click, click, and click. 'Warren, this is the exact same tree. I told you it was the same tree, and we passed it back there, and these are our tracks going this way. What is going on?' Jasmine asked.

"'I'm sorry, I was temporarily disoriented. I'm trying to find my bearings. Let me reposition.' I told her we'll get out of it, don't stress.

"'Dude, sort your stuff out. What are you doing?' my backup whispered to me. 'You should be going west or southwest,' he said.

"'Yes, I know. But give me a minute to work it out,' I replied. The compass was still pointing east.

"We continued walking, and I did the two 90-degree turns again. We came back to the same mopane tree from a different direction. Click, click, click from the back again. Jasmine was furious by then. 'Warren, what the f...,' she said. 'This is the same tree. These are our tracks going this way. Those are our tracks going that way. And now we are going this way. What the hell is going on?' she protested in justifiable exasperation.

"'Put the compass down, Warren. This chick is going to kill you. Just walk,' Heusten whispered. He was right. Maybe it was a low-lying area where we were, or somehow the rocks around us were magnetised, but the compass was not working.

"'Guys, I'm going to try something different. Just bear with me,' I pleaded.

"I took out another compass, but Heusten convinced me to just walk in a straight line, and we did that for about one-and-a-half kilometres. I checked the compass later, and it pointed west, and from there, we got out safely.

"We had been lost for about one-and-a-half hours. But yes, I got lost on the trail with a compass and a GPS. I won the *Pink Gown Award*, and that was quite funny."

We laughed with him.

Warren scraped ash to drop into the tiny plastic bottle I had thought, until then, contained baby powder. Warren explained he uses ash only from wood burnt in the Kruger to check wind direction. There was a lot to be learnt from him. My thoughts were interrupted by Morné alerting us to a hyena. It was a safe distance away and scurried off.

Donna had gone to bed early, feeling flu-ish, but later revealed: "That night, in the shower, I had a good cry. I felt sore and somewhat wrecked. I told Anna my dad's body must have been broken in the end to have finally given in. I felt selfish for having prayed for him to fight through Covid."

The wind came up after I went to sleep, and the noisy gusts and the cold made for a restless night. It didn't help I could hear the cackling laughter of hyenas over the noise of the wind.

Into the Cold

A cold, southerly wind blew in a new day. I was freezing and annoyed with myself for changing into short sleeves and pants. Warren led us into basalt plains made up of sweet, nutritious grasslands, where trees and shrubs are found only on watercourses and rocky hills. On the savanna, grass is central to the food chain, with all animal species dependent on its nutrition.

A party of ground hornbills foraged and some took to the air as we stopped to analyse the track of a honey badger. The prints of the honey badger are like those of the weasel family. They have a fused proximal pad on the fore and hind feet, like the porcupine, which is a rodent. In a nearby dry waterhole lay the sun-bleached skull of a white rhino. The teeth were still attached to the lower jaw, and the sinuses below the frontal bone were intact; so it was unlikely to have been poached. Someone asked whether it was from a black or a white rhino. Lourens, who was living up to his new role of comic, suggested it was from a white rhino, because the bones were white.

Ground hornbills, although considered endangered in southern Africa, were plentiful. Their numbers have been decimated in recent decades owing to habitat destruction and other factors exacerbated by slow reproduction rates. On the path ahead, I cringed at what looked like a piece of plastic. Lourens turned it over with his walking stick and I was relieved to find it was a sun-bleached tortoise shell. A kudu cow looked vulnerable on its own in a grove of trees. Kudu bulls are often on their own, but not the females. I was wondering why it was alone when it ran off with a small group concealed in the trees.

During an early break, I looked for shelter from the incessant wind without success. The best I could do was lie low in the shade of a small bush until we got going again. Maybe because of Donna and her mission, I thought about my daughters a lot and how I would love them to join me on a hike through the Kruger.

Before we crossed a stream where a giraffe stood alone on the bank, Warren went forward to check whether it was safe for us to cross. He returned with a damaged boot. Paul borrowed Mark's Leatherman knife to make repairs. Safety and looking after the guests come first, and the three guides were exemplary in their teamwork.

The Lindanda Plains stretched before us and we walked long periods without spotting much. Paul thought he saw three cheetahs on a faraway plain, and we stopped to check through the binoculars. It turned out to be zebra. Nobody teased Paul about that. I chortled when I thought about the barbed comments that would have been generated if I, or one of us in the group, had made that mistake. We headed towards a tree with a giant, tawny eagle perched on one of its bare branches. The leafless tree, which looked dead to me, was the only feature as far as the horizon. Near to it, I called for a stop to attend to my foot. I found and removed the thorn fragment that had found its way past the gaiters and into my boot.

The red grass was thick and tall, making the hike challenging. In the distance, three rhinos lay in an almost dry waterhole with green tufts of grass on the creases of dried mud. The strong wind caused us to remain undetected. We slowly moved closer and, at about 30 metres away, still undetected, we stopped to enjoy the spectacle. Even at that range, with their poor eyesight, they would not have noticed us. Rhinos make up for poor eyesight with keen smell and hearing. The larger bull lay at one end of the mud pool facing northeast into the sun. The other rhino, perhaps the mother, lay further away alongside an adolescent rhino. As we inched even closer, Warren picked up a large stone in case we needed a non-deadly defence. Mark took out his phone to take a picture and inadvertently pressed a button that played music. The rhino cow stood up abruptly and looked in our direction. Moments later, the younger one stood up, and the two trotted up the slope away from us. The rhino bull did not move, but his ears perked up with one cocked forward and the other turned back, seeking out sounds. We stood still. Close enough for the rhino bull to detect us. He moved away to join the other two. The rhinos trotted up the slope while a black-shouldered kite hovered over them. Rhinos run with a deceptive high-step trot but at full gallop a rhino can run much faster than Usain Bolt, the greatest sprinter of all time.

I felt privileged to have been so close to a crash of three rhinos. They looked peaceful and still sported the horns that have brought death to so many of their kind. The kite left the rhinos and followed us, flying from the leafless branches of one tree to the next as it battled the wind. Next to the path was a rhino midden, or dung heap. Up to five rhinos can use one midden, though the dominant male will hold his territory. The smaller, submissive males stand outside, with the bigger, dominant bulls and females using the middle part of the pile.

We returned to trudging through thick grass on uneven ground. Morné sprained his ankle in a deep elephant footprint hidden by the long grass. Everyone agreed he should keep moving to keep circulation going. Far from help of any kind, he had no other options.

We were ready for breakfast but the wind picked up. This time, we were looking for shelter from the wind rather than the usual shade from the sun. An outcrop of bushes was the best we could find. Some wildebeest were downwind and our scent must have carried to them. They did not run off despite their visible agitation.

After breakfast, we crossed the H1-4 tarred road as we headed southeast. A bateleur eagle soared over a cluster of wildebeest and zebra on a ridge we were aiming for. My attention was on the eagle as we passed a thicket of thorn bush in the long grass. A rustle of leaves from it caught us unawares. Paul and I jumped away instinctively, but Warren kept his head and took aim with the rifle. A harmless duiker suddenly ran out.

We stopped at an artificial waterhole in a large grassless clearing. A kori bustard walked by at a leisurely gait. Males are arguably the heaviest living animal capable of flight, something they avoid, spending most of their time on the ground. Paul told us there are now only 80 artificial waterholes left in the Kruger, from almost 300 before the change in the water-management strategy that altered the availability of drinking water from every five kilometres to every 20 kilometres. A bateleur eagle I had watched in a tree while we chatted took off and circled above us.

The scenery changed as we approached the Mavumbye River, with abundant bush and leafy riverine trees in the distance. A buffalo moved slowly on its way to the river as we came up behind it. Warren seemed overly cautious and made us stop and wait until the buffalo was far away. I understood only when we moved ahead again. The buffalo was not alone as I had thought, but part of a massive herd that numbered in the hundreds.

The only two large trees in the area provided shade for the lunch break. I kept an eye on the buffaloes. A mantis sat on Jennifer's bag, while we had lunch and chatted. Jennifer took pictures of its prominent front legs bent in a prayer-like position, which she proudly showed everyone. These serene creatures are considered sacred by the Bushman or San. The wind died down and I tried to nap, but the animated chatter of the group kept me awake. I might have made a mistake by saying something about it when we packed up. The lunch breaks on the days that followed were extremely quiet.

After lunch, we followed the river on its easterly bank. A kite flew over us headed for a mixed bunch of zebra and wildebeest. The kite hovered in the fresh wind, probably in the expectation rodents would be exposed. Most of the zebra seemed unfazed by our presence. The wildebeest ran a short distance, taking a few edgy zebras with them near an elegant couple of secretary birds. Further along, zebra mingled with waterbuck and wildebeest. The sun was behind us and the wind into us, so animals could not smell us, and we got close before the startled animals ran off. A warthog trotting along the riverbank stopped to take stock of the commotion.

After 18.3 kilometres, we looked for a place to cross the Mavumbye River and make camp. We dropped stones into the shallow running water to make the crossing without getting our boots wet. A grassy area in a grove of apple-leaf trees provided shelter. The turpentine grass was thick and high, and I stomped on it to flatten before pitching my tent. We went back to the river as a group with one of the guides to collect water for the showers and cooking. The fierce wind meant there was a risk of the long, dry grass catching alight, so we didn't make a fire.

The sun set in a blaze of orange and red, a stunning backdrop to four giraffes, their necks stiff as they watched us. I had dinner when it was still light and used leaves from an apple-leaf tree to scour my cooking pot. Without a fire, we did not have the usual social get-together, and the camp was quiet by early evening.

Beads of Introspection

The yelps and groans of hyenas and my LED light turning on of its own accord, led to a restless night. I couldn't find a way to switch off the light or open the battery compartment to remove the batteries. Also, there was no place to put it where it did not light up my tent. I was relieved when I heard movement in the camp and knew it was time to pack up. Dawn's first rays highlighted an unkempt tawny eagle perched on a leafless tree. After my rough night, I suspected I looked no better.

Paul told us to expect a hot day of average distance before he led us back to the previous day's river crossing. Most of us set off with little or no water, and we soon arrived at the tree beneath which Mark had concealed two 25-litre water drums. While we took turns filling water bladders and bottles, I watched zebra, wildebeest and giraffe on the plains.

Fresh lion prints speckled the sandy road along the riverbank. The disturbed soil was still damp. Vultures congregated in a leafless tree, so Warren went downriver to find the kill he thought must be nearby because of vultures hanging about. We were downwind and Paul warned us to stay alert while we waited. Warren returned without having found anything. Further on, vultures perched on the highest branches of a dead tree. I noted given their diet, it made sense they prefer dead trees. They then took off and landed on the leafy top branches of another tree to prove me wrong.

A tawny eagle took off when we approached, followed the river for a short distance and landed on another tree further down. It did this a few times and I wondered if it was reacting to our presence or whether its movements were a coincidence. A tiny bushbuck stood alone in the shadows at the water's edge. I felt it was in peril, not only from the tawny eagle known to prey on small antelope, but also because of the fresh lion tracks on the path we were following.

We stopped for a break after a long haul through the featureless, flat, grassy plain. I lay in the grass against my backpack and followed an animated discussion between Warren and Paul about the grasses and animals we had seen. Wildebeest, they agreed, prefer shorter grasses, while zebra graze the longer varieties. But they could not agree on whether wildebeest are more selective while zebra are bulk feeders or the other way round. They decided to settle the matter by other means. An arm wrestle would have been an option if it was not for Paul's dislocated elbow, so they resorted to a round of good-natured rock-paper-scissors. I was amused among experts deep in the African wild, science was trumped by the games children play.

Donna said she had at last found serenity. "When we woke and started walking with the cool wind, I think I felt at peace for the first time in a long while," she said. "I embraced the tranquillity and it felt like the wind was pushing me along. Despite the thousands of tiny spiders, our camp among the apple-leaf trees was my favourite. It is as if we were on an island separated from the rest of the world. All the chaos, business responsibilities and everything else disappear long enough for me to gather my thoughts and face feelings I pushed aside. I slept like a rock. My body was sore, but my mind and soul were healing.

"The hike is one of the biggest challenges I have ever faced: physically, mentally and emotionally, and one of my most valued. Through this journey, I am growing. I have faced fears and found peace."

A bateleur eagle flew over us and we took it as a signal to get going. I looked forward to easy hiking in short grass with plenty of animal paths. Later, we tracked back to the Mavumbye River in an area with more trees and scrub. An impala grazed alone in short grass near fresh lion tracks. Things did not look good for the impala.

Ahead of us, three giraffes behaved differently, indicating their unpredictability and how they react to their safety zones. The smallest giraffe began running, then stopped to watch us. Another giraffe ran in starts, stopping often to check on us before scampering off again. The older giraffe continued to browse, unperturbed by our presence.

The rising sun shone behind waterbuck silhouetted with their large, round ears. A single giraffe calf stuck out above the waterbuck. The dense riverine tree line of mostly apple-leaf trees etched the horizon behind the back and head of a fleeing steenbok. At the confluence of the Mavumbye and Mapetane rivers, a solitary wildebeest grazed with a group of waterbuck.

On the other side, zebra and waterbuck mingled with a handful of wildebeest. Because of all the animals, we stopped in the shade of a leadwood tree for breakfast before crossing the waterless tributary. The Mavumbye River seemed to favour apple-leaf trees, while the banks of the Mapetane River were covered with hardy leadwood, some seemingly dead. The skeleton, or snag, of a dead leadwood can stand for up to 80 years because it is impervious to termites.

After breakfast, we crossed the dry Mapetane River. A lone wildebeest ran into the rising sun as it came up the bank. We walked close to a large dazzle of zebra and I took the time to count them as best I could while on the move. As a young auditor, I counted animal stock on farms in the Eastern Cape and know how error-prone the task is and why it is necessary to use a corral or chute system for an accurate count. Nevertheless, I counted at least 50. They were not alarmed by our presence and held their ground, though they all turned to look at us until startled francolins noisily flew off from the long grass. The zebra ran until they intersected our path and stopped. Paul did not want to disturb them again and changed course to hike around them. The detour took us past an impala and warthogs, which scattered. At the bottom of the ravine where the three had taken refuge, the warthogs disappeared into the long grass, but the impala sprinted up a slope. Francolins and guineafowl scurried ahead. We had noticed both species on the grassy plains throughout the day.

Moving on from all the animals, we took pictures of two clusters of the impala lily (*Adenium obesum*). They look like miniature baobab trees with their fleshy, swollen trunks. The white flower, with its delicate pink stripes and eye-catching red margins, belies its deadly poison. San bushmen use the sap of the impala lily to poison their arrows. We were mesmerised by the beauty of the plant and must have stayed too long. Warren called for the third time that day using his well-known refrain: "Let's go. This trail isn't going to walk itself."

The elevation on the eastern bank of the river gave us a good view of animal activity. Impala grazed higher up on the slope, while at the river, small groupings of impala congregated in the shade along the bank. It was a trade-off between safety in the sun or the cool shade, with a significant risk of attack by crocodiles or other predators. A lone buffalo looked down from higher up the slope as if looking for a spot in the shade to open. Chacma baboons barked from the riverine trees, although we couldn't place them.

The terrain changed, and the going was neither easy nor pleasant. I was tired. The ground was uneven and black from large expanses of a controlled burn. I noticed where the fires had been set, with burnt branches piled in places. I guessed it must have been part of the integrated fire management system. My mood lightened when giraffes appeared, journeying for the river where we were headed, which indicated the terrain would become more attractive. The flat plains were behind us and on the other side of the river, four giraffes stood at the top of a sharp ridge, giving them significant elevation and a long view. An African fish eagle must have found a thermal because it gained height without flapping its long, broad wings.

A waterbuck grazed alone. They are gregarious animals and a waterbuck on its own is unusual. The grass was long, so we followed an animal path into the riverine forest. We approached a large, leafy thorn bush and almost walked into a browsing giraffe. It was as surprised as we were, but stood its ground. After a brief face-off, it left in a slow, elegant gait. From there, we manoeuvred down a steep bank to reach the shallow river for lunch. A francolin took off noisily as Jennifer walked past.

"Heart-attack birds, one; Jennifer, nil," she said.

Paul and Anna dipped into the cold water, followed by Morné and Lourens. I shed my boots and walked about barefoot. While unpacking my backpack, two vultures landed on a tree nearby. I had no intention of sharing my lunch. But, to my detriment, I shared the shade of a sycamore fig with Warren and Paul, who brawled like spoiled schoolboys over Warren's barbecue sauce.

I asked Warren if it was a leadwood we were sitting under when I should have known better. A fig tree and a leadwood are vastly different. I got an honest talking to. Since then, I am convinced I can pick out the wood of a fig tree, even if it is in the casket of an Egyptian mummy.

It might have been a coincidence, but I wasn't sure my teasing about the noisy communal chat after lunch the previous day had gone down very well. There was absolute silence as we rested and I felt a little guilty. I consoled myself with the thought maybe everyone was exhausted and needed a nap.

We were soon on the go again despite the heat with sightings of large, mixed herds of zebra, wildebeest, waterbuck and the ubiquitous impala, which accompanied us to a wide, shallow ravine. The guides struggled to find a safe river crossing, so we used rocks to make stepping stones to help each other across. A small buck I was unable to identify scurried through the long, dry grass. Smaller antelope are difficult to tell apart when they are moving fast and partly concealed.

The river looped back, and we needed to cross again to the other side. I failed to understand why we had gone to so much trouble to build a 'bridge' when we would need to cross to the other side again so soon. We headed down to the river, to find a large group of impala and two waterbuck on the opposite bank. There was no safe place to cross, so we followed a jeep track, part of the private Mananga 4x4 adventure trail.

We left the track to rest in thick, long grass in the shade of leafy thorn bushes. If there had been more time, I would have napped. Five giraffes watched while we prepared to leave. They came closer as we put on our backpacks. I found their descending symmetry pleasing to the eye.

"It's a beautiful tower of giraffe," I remarked.

"I thought it was a journey of giraffe," Jennifer said.

"When on the move, the collective noun is a journey of giraffe, but if they are standing still, it is called a tower," I said as I put on my backpack to leave.

Warren was handing out sweets. Donna, mimicking his earlier instructions said, "Let's go. This trail isn't going to walk itself."

The giraffes came closer as we walked past. I was amazed at how comfortable animals in the wild can be with humans when they know they are not threatened.

We returned to the jeep trail and I was in the middle of the line when I stepped over a column of Matabele ants. I heard them hissing even from six feet above them. Someone ahead of me stepped on the column with fatal results for the ants. Initially, I felt terrible about our destruction, until I consoled myself with the thought there would have been several more casualties if we had been elephants.

The incident with the Matabele ants stayed on my mind for a long time. It's one of the benefits of hiking for days through the Kruger: the time to contemplate. I know some believe it is not suitable for humans to hike in protected areas like the Kruger, especially when the life of a protected animal is taken as a result of our presence. This does happen but on rare occasions. I was still wrestling with how hiking through the Kruger Park is in some respects detrimental to the animals we love, when a small group of impala scattered as we approached. They regrouped ahead of us, and when we moved again, they dispersed.

The shadows were lengthening when Paul and Warren went ahead to scout for a place to cross the river and make camp. They left Mark behind to look after the group. When they returned, they said the river was too deep and a lone hippo was in the water. It could have only been an ostracised male with a bad attitude and we did not intend to test his demeanour.

The sinking sun was on our backs as we followed an animal path. My thoughts moved to matters closer to my heart. I wondered if all had gone well with my daughter, Georgia, and her flight to Los Angeles. The United States was still closed to South African travellers because of Covid-19 and, despite her special student entry visa, I wanted to know if she was alright. My mind was everywhere, except in the wild when we came face to face with the king of the jungle.

The sweet tranquillity of the bush was shattered as we crossed a featureless, sandy expanse marked by a grassy patch with two thorn thickets.

"Lions," Morné shouted from behind me.

My first reaction was panic. The momentum carried me around the thorn bush before I could stop; there was a lion and a lioness metres away. The majestic male lion, his reddish-brown mane framing his half-open jaw and foreboding canines, took two steps at us. As the whole group came into his field of vision, he paused, taking stock of our increasing numbers, before he turned his head and looked back at the lioness, weighing up his options. Thankfully, he chose to go with the lioness instead of taking on the armed human invaders.

At the top of the slope in the direction we had come, another lion stood up. He looked at us with measured stillness before turning away and disappearing over the ridge.

The first lion ran up the slope with the female and stopped halfway between two leafy bushes. After an obedient pause, the lioness carried on alone and disappeared over the ridge. The lion turned and crouched between the two thorn bushes to observe us. He was not done yet.

We chatted in small groups about the encounter before we congregated around Paul, who told us more about lions and their behaviour. I wasn't paying attention. We were being watched and I was more interested in the lion on the slope, until one of the guides pointed out marks in the sand where the lion and lioness had been mating. The position of the female's front paws and back paws was visible. The enormous hind paws of the male straddled the female on either side. The earth was damp, with two wet drip points of semen in the sand. I felt uncomfortable as Paul pointed out the markings with his rifle. I turned to look back at the lion crouched on the slope, watching us gravely. A lion's eyesight is six times stronger than a human's and he stared as we prodded and violated his private place. I took out my binoculars to look at him on the slope. Contempt blazed in his golden eyes.

Our hike clocked up 19.6 kilometres and it was late, so we needed to make camp. I was still tense and hardly noticed the zebra, waterbuck and baboons around us. A rock formation on the riverbank and thick thorn bush provided a corridor of safety for our tents. I collected drinking water from the river and had a quick shower. Mark gathered wood and made a fire. We ate around it and chatted, interrupted only by the snorting of hippos.

I woke up with frozen fingers after a cold and uncomfortable night. My breath formed a small, misty cloud when I exhaled into the cold air outside my tent. The lions had been noisy, and we agreed it had probably been three different mating pairs we heard throughout the night.

We concealed the backpacks behind the rock formation we used for the shower. Before the hike, we had been advised to prepare a daypack for the last day. I did not have a small backpack and used the black cloth shopping bag in which I had kept my food for six days. I couldn't strap it over my shoulder and had to carry it by the handles. I endured taunts for the rest of the day about my 'handbag'. Warren took great delight in reminding me after every stop not to forget my fanny pouch.

Arie was holding nothing but his walking stick as we prepared to leave. I asked him about water, as we still had a hike of about 20 kilometres ahead. He said he was not taking water.

"If you don't push yourself to the limit, you won't know where the limit is," he said.

Warren led us through thick grass up the slope from where the lion had watched us the day before. A Burchell's coucal flew past and stopped on a shrub. I appreciated being so close to it, as they are shy birds. Further up the path, the grass was heavily trampled, and thick tufts of black and golden-brown lion fur were scattered in the grass. Someone suggested it was from a mating session, although it looked more like the scene of a brawl.

The rising sun silhouetted what appeared to be tree stumps with fresh shoots along the top of the ridge to the east. They looked unnatural, given how evenly spaced and straight they were. As the angle changed, I realised it was a row of waterbuck. Their bodies were below the ridgeline and I could only see the neck, head and horns as they watched us pass.

Thankfully, we were not carrying a heavy backpack as we trudged through energy-sapping, thick, waist-high grass. At the bottom of the slope, a male lion and a lioness sauntered across our intended path. They were challenging to find in tall, dry grass the identical colour of their fur. They stopped to look in our direction for a moment before disappearing into the grass. We continued on anyway. At the bottom of the slope, a hole and a fallen tree branch tripped Donna for her second soft landing.

The N'wanetsi River flowed strongly and our first attempt to cross it failed, so we backtracked a short distance. We had our first break in the abundant shade of a leadwood tree near the river. A defiant kudu roamed alone between us and the rest of the herd on higher ground. Before we set off, Arie accepted an offer to drink from a water bottle. He did throughout the day.

"Too hot and too long," he defended, his face streaked by rivulets of sweat.

An impala looked as if it was alone and vulnerable, and continued grazing despite us heading straight at it. I understood its confidence only when others appeared from behind a bush and they all ran off together. Further along, we came across a lone giraffe, which ran a short distance before stopping and watching us. It was still staring when we paused to look at an animal track in the sand.

"It's a fresh leopard track," Warren said.

"Not fresh enough," said Lourens. "I want to see the leopard."

The going was easier in the short, sparse grass and there was no need to stay on the animal paths. We stopped so Donna, Anna and the two guides could scrape scat off their boots. From the unpleasant smell, we already knew it was lion scat.

During a break on the bank of the N'wanetsi River, a black-chested snake eagle circled high above us. It had something in its talons and using binoculars we identified the prey as a bird. From there, we turned away from the river and trudged through long grass that came up to my armpits. Warren found an animal path through the grass to a high ridge. It was easier on the path and Warren bent over in a showy display of service to pick up a stick and throw it off the path. After what he had just led us through, he was not going to make up for it easily. We stopped for a rest and to cool off in the shade, and it was payback time for me after all his comments about my bag.

"Warren is such an operator. He takes us to places only the toughest of animals will go, then makes a show of bending over to move a little stick off the path," I said. "I'm not buying that con." I heard a few chuckles in agreement.

I lay on my back in the grass, admiring the clear blue sky and the still visible moon across which an eagle in flight was etched. I grabbed my binoculars. However, the eagle was too high to identify. I did not use the binoculars often and I wondered again if they were worth the extra weight. Few in the group carried them.

The last stretch to the top of the ridge was demanding. The long grass made it hard to avoid the stony ground. After going down the other side, we hiked an animal path parallel to the ridge. A kudu browsed on the leaves and shoots of an acacia tree, surrounded by a small cluster of grazing impala. They ran to the top of the ridge long before we were close.

Warren drew a line across the path with his boot to mark the completion of 100 kilometres on Leg Four. It was the first time the guides had marked that milestone. We stood in a line across the path to take photographs, as we had done when we crossed the Tropic of Capricorn.

My mind drifted to the bustle of life in the cities to which we would soon return. I thought about Georgia and wondered how she was spending her first Sunday in Hollywood. I loved every moment of the hike, but after six days in the wild and isolated from the world, I looked forward to catching up with family, friends and news.

The sun was scorching and I undid another button of my shirt as we took a break in the shade of a leadwood riven with deep scratches from a leopard. Or so we thought, as it could have been any of the big cats. Like domestic cats, leopards do this to keep their claws clean and sharp and to stretch the ligaments for maximum flexibility. It also serves to mark territory.

After a long time heading south, we turned east to follow the Shishangani River. I noticed what I thought was a lone elephant. Yet, as we approached, a large breeding group with calves became evident. They were spread out with no way for us to pass safely, so we stopped to allow them to move on. A tall leadwood with a small canopy provided the only relief from the baking sun, and we stood shoulder to shoulder in a line to take advantage of the shade. I felt the wind coming from behind us on to the elephants. Still, Warren sprayed ash from his bottle to confirm the wind direction. Our scent bore the whiff of danger to the elephants, which headed for the river and abundant trees. The calves had to run to keep up.

I unbuttoned my shirt in stages as the day got hotter. We crossed the river to take a break in a stand of young apple-leaf trees and by then, I was down to the last button. After a stop, long enough for a quick nap, we continued in the blistering heat and were told to expect one more stop.

A lone elephant bull forced us to reroute over a hill. As we began the climb up the steep and rocky hill, a lilac-breasted roller shimmering in hues of blue, turquoise and gold flew out of the cover of grass. It must have been cooler for the bird in the long, thick grass than any tree branch. My irritation, provoked by the discomfort of climbing in the heat, dissipated when we got to the top. A spectacular outcrop of the tallest candelabra trees, perhaps more than 10 metres high, made it worthwhile. The branches held clusters of eye-catching yellowish-green flowers.

We continued downhill. Some young zebra ran off. I was relieved to know we were close to the finish when we connected with the road leading to the N'wanetsi Section Ranger's post. It was a sweltering day and we were lucky we never had to carry backpacks. A southern red-billed hornbill, with its bright red, scimitar-like beak and white spots on dark feathers, foraged on the ground. They are smaller and less common than the yellow-billed hornbill found everywhere in the Kruger and loved by tourists.

We walked along the fence, and francolins had the last say. As Jennifer walked past, they flew out of the long grass with raucous 'keeeah' calls. Heart-attack birds 2: Jennifer 0.

Before entering the compound gate, we congratulated one another and took photographs. The women shed tears as they embraced Donna, acclaiming her dedication to the memory of her dad. The section ranger, Robbie Bryden, brought us a cooler box filled with soft drinks and ice-cold beers. The distance for the day was 17.5 kilometres, to close Leg Four with 108 kilometres, making it the second-longest Leg for the Panthera.

Lourens' pick-up truck was onsite while Arie and I had left our vehicles at Olifants Rest Camp. The plan was for Lourens to drive Arie and me to Olifants to pick up our vehicles, while the rest of the group would travel in a game-viewing vehicle back to Satara Rest Camp after collecting the backpacks. I went to the restroom and returned to find an anxious group.

Arie could not find the key to Lourens' pick-up. When we left the campsite that morning, Lourens reminded Arie and me to take our car keys to the finish and not leave them in our backpacks. I noticed Lourens hand his own key to Arie to put in a zipped pocket. I put my key in a zipped trouser pocket and, through the day, patted it regularly to check it was still there. After a frantic search, the key was nowhere to be found.

The new plan was for everyone to get into the game-viewing vehicle to fetch the backpacks and head back to Olifants Rest Camp to pick up Arie's and my vehicle. I climbed into the game-viewing vehicle and checked to ensure I had my key. The key was not in my pocket where it had been all day long. I checked my day bag and it wasn't there either. It felt surreal and I stood up to look at the seat. Nothing.

"My key is missing," I said, "I had it when we arrived because I checked."

"Didn't you use the bathroom?" someone asked hopefully.

"Yes, I did," I replied with cautious optimism.

The key wasn't there either. I returned to the vehicle to glares and checked everywhere. I looked under the seat where a canvas lay on the floor. The key was lying on top. The key must have slipped out of my pocket and landed silently on the canvas as I shuffled across the bench seat when I climbed in.

We made a detour to look for Lourens' missing key beneath the leadwood tree where we made the first stop. No luck. After that, we returned to where we had camped the night before. Nothing there either.

Arrangements were made for Anna's husband to drive from Johannesburg to Kruger the next day to bring the spare key for Lourens' vehicle. The mystery of the missing key was solved when Arie discovered a small hole in the zipped pocket of his shorts.

Dinner was on the restaurant veranda at the Satara Rest Camp. Jennifer made a short and touching speech to Ray and Donna.

"Through the camaraderie with everyone in the group, I was able to accomplish something great. In a strange way, it brought me closer to my dad. I felt as if I was walking alongside him," Donna said afterwards. There were moist eyes as we toasted with half-sized 'suitcases' – a shot drink made with whisky and passion fruit.

We took turns sharing memorable moments. The restaurant staff locked up, turned off the lights and left. We chatted late into the night in near darkness. A testament to the camaraderie.

I departed alone early in the morning for the drive back to Eswatini. Once out of the gate, I turned on the radio to listen to music and catch up with the news. I should have eased my way back into the real world, rather than letting the news swamp me with stories of corruption and ineptitude. I turned off the radio and instead let my mind revisit the wilds of Kruger. I turned to my playlist of 1,070 songs I always play on shuffle as I like the randomness of what the next song will be. My spirits lifted with *I Like to Move It* by The Madagascar Theme Players. The animated movie, *Madagascar*, centred on a group of animals who escape from the New York Zoo and have to adjust to life in the wild, after finding themselves stranded on the island of Madagascar.

I arrived home to excited dogs and, unexpectedly, to playful vervet monkeys in my garden.

LEG FIVE

N'wanetsi Section Ranger's Post to Lower Sabie Rest Camp
AUTUMN, MARCH 2022

We overnighted at Satara Rest Camp, before Leg Five started at N'wanetsi Section Ranger's Post on Monday morning. I felt flu-ish, without a fever. I convinced myself it was a common cold, yet congestion and discomfort stayed with me through most of Leg Five. It played on my mind I had recently spent time with a friend, Ian Salt, an avid 70-year-old walker, who was meant to fill a vacant space in our group, but pulled out at the last minute after testing positive for Covid-19. I invited Ian and another friend from Eswatini, 59-year-old Grant Goldstone, to fill two vacant spots on the hike. Marie Dahl, who completed Leg Three with us, joined for another Leg. It was too late to find a replacement for Ian, and so the group was down to seven hikers and two guides.

Grant and I left Eswatini early to enter the Kruger National Park at the Crocodile Bridge gate. Grant is the financial director of a food and milling company and was fit. He ran the 88 kilometre Comrades Marathon, South Africa's premier ultra-marathon, and participated in major cycling events. He had done a few day hikes, although he was anxious about camping in the wild. He agreed to it late one night after a few glasses of wine and trained hard to ensure he would not let the team down. He even practised bush ablutions by using his back garden as a toilet.

The Kruger was busy in this waning year of the Covid-era. Monday, the start of our hike, was also Human Rights Day, a public holiday in South Africa, and people took advantage of the long weekend. Marie celebrated her 40th birthday with Danish friends by doing the Lonely Bull Trail; one of three backpack trails in the Kruger, and met up with us at Satara.

Entering the Kruger, we saw a large herd of wildebeest, and turquoise and ochre European rollers all the way to Lower Sabie Rest Camp. The

European roller is a summer migrant to the region and is close to being classified as a threatened species. It lacks tail streamers, and with a bigger head and bill and a scruffy appearance, it appears larger than the indigenous lilac-breasted roller.

Grant and I arrived at Lower Sabie Rest Camp and met guide, Pete Wilson, whom I had not seen since he led our group on Leg Three the year before. He had just finished making a water drop for our third-night stop southeast of Muntshe Hill. I was delighted to have Pete as a guide again because of his knowledge of the African bush. Arie arrived with his head shaved and his beard braided. Clifford was there, too. Lourens and Jennifer joined us for lunch after driving from Satara Rest Camp, where they spent the night. Jennifer had again travelled to South Africa from the Netherlands.

The lead guide, Howard Spencer-Wilson, was making a water drop for the first night, and I met him in the evening when we all had dinner on the new outdoor deck of the Satara Rest Camp restaurant. A blood-red moon hung in the sky, silhouetting the trees and thorn bush as Howard told us about himself. He grew up in Johannesburg and studied nature conservation, before relocating to Hoedspruit, adjacent to the Kruger Park. He considered guiding backpack trails in the Kruger as the Holy Grail of guiding, saying, "As long as I can, I will." Married with two children, Howard runs a safari business when he is not riding adventure motorcycles, fishing or mountain biking.

The following day, the Swazi trio travelled with Clifford on the hour-long drive to N'wanetsi Section Ranger's Post. We turned onto the H6, Clifford's favourite road in the Kruger because of the open savanna and the large number of animals attracted by the grazing. Marula trees, knob-thorn and sickle-bush dotted the landscape. We passed lionesses and a drooling lion with a painful limp walking on the dirt road close to the Section Ranger's Post, where we would begin the hike.

The section ranger's wife, Julie Bryden, greeted us. I asked her about the battered lion, and she assured us he was well known and not as poorly as he looked. True to form, Jennifer handed out droëwors, the dried sausage loved by South Africans, before we even set off.

Howard delivered a short briefing before we exited the compound. Then we were off, leaping rocks straddling a stream spilling into an algae-filled pool. A crocodile glided past waterbirds while rasps of guineafowl romped in the surrounding grasses. The mournful whistle of a black-crowned tchagra resonated. Howard told us we would hear them often during the dawn hours.

Maybe because I wasn't feeling well, it was a tough start for me. A cool southeasterly wind blew as we trudged through redgrass on stony ground. Paths were scarce and golden orb spider webs linked bushes and trees. Impala spread out across a wide area, and Howard gave them no favour as he pressed on, sending the impala bounding in all directions.

I used my new tripod stool for the first time when we stopped for a break. Four hundred kilometres of traversing through the Kruger convinced me of the value of the nominal weight. I pulled the first of numerous ticks off my legs. The parasite was a repulsive nuisance for the first three days and a risk to debilitating tick-bite fever. Wearing long trousers, which everyone except for the guides, Lourens, and I wore, is the best defence against ticks and nobody was bitten during the hike. Howard had three ticks on his legs after we got going. He flicked them off when we stopped next to a flaky barked thorn (*Vachellia exuvialis*). The small shrub-like trees, germinate from seeds after a fire and were all the same height. Their peeling bark curls back in orange-brown, papery strips.

In the distance, two giraffes stopped when they saw us. Only their heads were visible above the bush and thickets. They resumed their slow lope until we turned in their direction, and then they paused again. I was so intent on watching them, I almost stepped on a large, fat millipede. The shiny black shongololo, as it is known locally, lived up to its proper name of giant African millipede. Jennifer insisted they were a sign of rain and there would be lots over the next few days, even after the clouds had cleared.

A steenbok, with its distinctive short, pointed horns and Y-shaped nose marking, bounded across our path near the galloping giraffes. The steenbok and the duiker, despite their diminutive size, are two antelope known to scavenge meat if they can, and are not absolute herbivores.

Lilac-breasted rollers with their gem-like flashes of colour in the morning sun distracted me from the difficult terrain, as did giraffes using their indigo prehensile tongues to pull leaves off the trees. We crossed a dirt road and Howard gave us a short, welcome breather by letting us walk on the road before heading back into the tall grass. If not for the rule of silence, I was ready to make the case a dirt road can be classified as a path. I did not think it would wash with Howard.

Our first breakfast was in the shade of a tree next to a trickling stream leading to a muddy pool. On the ridge above us, a giraffe grazed on thorn trees. As we left, zebra galloped away, their hooves a thunderous clatter on the stony ground. We headed at a giraffe standing with zebra; the group slowly parted, exposing a small herd of impala whose heads lifted above the sheltering high grass.

The grass became shorter and animal paths plentiful. The majestic horns of a kudu bull in the shade of a tree caught my eye as I stepped around a day-old rhino midden; the kudu ran off with a small pack of young kudu cows in tow.

During a break, someone saw vultures perched on the branches of a dead tree. Using binoculars, we identified them as the critically endangered white-headed vulture. Our conversation turned to water and Howard realised he had left the keys at Satara Rest Camp for the chain locks on the water containers he had dropped off for us to use that night.

Further on, another white-headed vulture circled low. Its distinctive wing pattern and angular white-head visible.

"Wow, three sightings of the white-headed vulture in one day," Howard exclaimed as the vulture flew over an impala in the shade. There must have been more impala in the surrounding bush but we couldn't find them.

A chattering, squawking, twittering tree full of birds drew our attention. One bird had brilliant dark salmon colouring with a long black tail feather. Howard suggested it was a southern carmine bee-eater and took out his binocs to confirm. He need not have bothered as it flew over us issuing a nasal 'gra-gra-gra'. The bird is a summer migrant to Kruger and we were lucky to spot it so late in the season.

Crossing a stream, we found a male kudu resting in the shade among a small harem of females. He sounded a loud alarm bark, prompting them to scatter up the embankment. They regrouped in the shade, but ran off again when we approached.

We stopped for lunch beneath the broad canopy of a Delagoa thorn (*Senegalia welwitschii*) with its paired and hooked prickles. Grant confirmed he was enjoying the hike and I was beginning to relax about the recruit. Grant loves the Kruger and is a regular visitor, although he is more comfortable staying in an air-conditioned vehicle and overnighting in a well-equipped bungalow.

Howard led us along the stream after lunch, until he made a sharp turn through a gap in the thick bush. Someone noticed Grant was missing and we stopped to look back. There was no sign of Grant. An elephant was on its way to the place where we had stopped for lunch. My heart stopped, until I noticed Grant walking briskly through the gap in the bushes with a grin. Oblivious to the elephant behind him.

"Grant where were you?" someone at the back of the line asked.

"Did you see the elephant behind you?" I asked.

"What elephant?" Grant replied, looking confused. "I went back to fetch my walking pole."

I was relieved Grant had escaped peril. If the elephant had been a fraction faster, Grant would have come face-to-face with it. "Grant, you should have shouted to tell us you were going back," I told him. "One of the guides would have gone with you."

An impala sprinted past in anxious leaps towards the river, making the point for constant vigilance.

A sizeable kettle of vultures circled, dark and sinister against the sunlit background. Vultures have the distasteful task of cleaning up the remains of the dead, playing a vital role in sanitation and disease control in the Kruger. Such a scene is frequently the indicator of a kill. The vultures flew high over two giraffes browsing on the shrubbery.

During a short break, Pete picked the ripe, small fruits of a velvet raisin bush and gave them to us to taste. They were a disappointing snack; all pip with orange skin on the outside. Large animals such as kudu and giraffe eat them, as do civets, monkeys and birds. A kori bustard took off with slow, heavy thrusts of its wings. Pete and I used the stop to clear ticks off our legs. I checked my legs for them at every opportunity.

A white-backed vulture, the most common in the savanna, did loops, while others circled over a reddish, sandy plain. More vultures were hunched on the ground below. A black-backed jackal ran across the clearing and the airborne vultures followed it. We understood their behaviour when we got to the place where the jackal had run from. A bloody impala leg lay on the sand with no other remains. So the kill hadn't happened there.

Beyond the sandy plain, an elephant wandered closer to us as it pulled at tufts of dry, brown grass. Another browsed on green leaves. A ridge to our right funnelled us to the first elephant which, up to that point, had looked relaxed. He either smelt or saw us and lifted his head with a jolt. The tension was palpable as he raised his trunk and flapped his ears. Howard made us backtrack quickly, while being careful not to run. We went over the ridge to pass at a safe distance and descended again to his level, as the ridge flattened out. The elephant resumed grazing until he looked up at the irritant that would not go away and approached us at a brisk pace. We bunched up in a defensive position behind the guides.

Howard shouted at the elephant.

To our relief, he turned away.

The going was easier in short grass with open sandy stretches. In the distance, a giraffe browsed on a small tree close to an impala standing in front of an animal that was large, dark and partly obscured by a bush. As we got closer, we realised it was a limping buffalo and we paused to let him get ahead. A white rhinoceros emerged from the bushes and walked towards the buffalo. The two hefty animals were on course for a head-on encounter. Either they had not seen each other, or neither was going to give way.

They stopped to face each other in a primal stand-off of ancient intensity. In the bushy thickets behind them, an elephant flapped his enormous ears. Three of the Big Five were framed in a tableau of wild splendour. The buffalo blinked first. He shook his head in reluctant deference to the rhino before hobbling uncomfortably around it to continue his journey to the Makongolweni River, where we were also going. In an act of defiance, the short-sighted rhino turned to drive off the buffalo. Only when the scene had cleared did I notice the rhino was dehorned. While the horn grows back after a few years, dehorning is one of the strategies to win the war against poaching.

A little further on, we took a break in a shady enclave on the bank of the Makongolweni River. Impala on the opposite bank so distracted us that nobody noticed the limping buffalo among the nearby pools of water in the riverbed. A dense thorn bush obstructed our view but once we were aware of the buffalo we kept an eye on him as we crossed the riverbed and headed south on the opposite bank. A mixed group of wildebeest and impala forced us to cross the river. We climbed the bank and, as we went around a large thorn thicket, Howard's voice rang out, "Get back. Behind me."

Everyone scrambled in panic, bunching up behind Howard. I had no clue what was happening until Howard pointed out an elephant he had almost walked into; partially hidden behind a large bush. The elephant ignored us and set off to cross the river and join the rest of the herd.

The easier terrain and the southeasterly wind helped counter the energy-sapping heat and we made good progress. We stopped to look at an unusual civet midden. The nocturnal mammal must have feasted on millipedes because there were numerous sun-bleached exoskeletons; it looked like a beach strewn with seashells. Some of the fresher civet droppings contained the whole orange fruit of the velvet raisin bush.

A sounder of warthog trotted by while we examined the midden. Their facial warts can grow up to 15 centimetres long. I reflected on the unfortunate naming of this wild member of the pig family. I enjoy the collective nouns for animals, though the reasoning behind the collective noun for warthogs, 'sounder', escapes me. Ants, for example, have four (army, colony, nest, swarm) and snakes have five (bed, den, knot, nest, pit).

We had covered 17.5 kilometres when Howard pointed out an area to pitch our tents. The space, between the Makongolweni River and the S37 dirt road, was open and flat, with small, bent trees on a grassy patch. We dropped our backpacks and most of the group followed Howard to a cluster of trees where he had concealed water drums. They were wrapped in a chain and secured with a padlock, which was a challenge because Howard had left behind the key. We tried different ways to break the padlock without success. There was no way I was going to rob a bank with that bunch. Eventually, Howard used the metal file on my Leatherman to saw through a link on the chain. I had carried the weighty multi-tool on my hip belt for over 400 kilometres and I was pleased it was being put to good use.

After laboriously moving one of the water containers to the campsite, I set about pitching my tent. I was still unpacking when Pete summoned us: "Bring a cup," he added.

Once we were congregated around Pete, he took out a thermos flask and poured the contents into the first cup proffered. I thought I heard the tinkle of ice. The thermos contained pre-mixed gin and tonic with ice. Pete even had a fresh lemon, which he sliced, and a spare bottle of tonic water. My initial reaction was to decline. As in addition to staying away from time and technology, I used the hike to detoxify from alcohol. It was the tinkle of ice in the heat, rather than the gin, that swayed me. The gin was bitterly refreshing and the moment so special, I felt justified.

I was using my headlamp in the gathering dusk when a vehicle passed by on the nearby dirt road. The rest camp gates were long closed and someone remarked whoever was still out there would be fined when they entered camp. Howard was arranging twigs for the fire close to my tent and I was preparing dinner when another vehicle drove by. That was unusual. I wondered what was going on.

I heard a dog bark. Can't be. I followed Howard onto the road.

Robbie Bryden, the armed and uniformed Section Ranger, came strolling over to us. Behind him scampered two barefoot boys and a German shepherd. I recognised Robbie from when we finished Leg Four at his home. We chatted while Robbie's boys played with the dog. Poachers had killed a rhino the previous night and Robbie told us about the tracking still in progress. He said the vehicle we had noticed earlier was dragging the dirt road using tyres weighed down with heavy railway tracks. The dirt roads in hotspot areas for rhino poaching are dragged every night and, at daybreak, two soldiers walk the length of the road looking for poacher tracks. The noisy dragging scares animals and they tend to stay away, even in daylight.

Lions!

Early the next morning, we followed Pete south on the way to the source of the Makongolweni River and the watershed that splits it from the Metsimetsi River. Two broad tracks in the sand, and signs of a powerful urine spray from its posterior-facing penis, marked the place where a territorial white rhino bull had spent the night.

A lone buffalo bull grazed on the riverbank in the rosy hue of dawn. Under a small bush, a handful of broken eggshells lay scattered inside a hollow formed in the ground. We guessed it once was the nest of a Swainson's spurfowl that was disturbed by a predator. While spurfowl lay eggs all year round, this was the peak of their egg-laying season.

Hiking was tough through long, thick grass on stony ground. Ticks kept attaching themselves to my bare legs. The little red bont tick is a vector for many diseases and infests cattle and domestic animals as well as wildlife. I did not want to think about that, especially as my nose was still running and I had a sore throat. A massive amount of red-billed quelea nests hung on the sagging branches of a swathe of thorn trees. The number of nests in larger trees can reach into the hundreds and even thousands. The red-billed quelea are the most prolific undomesticated birds on Earth and move in massive flocks, colonising large tracts of thorn trees by building nests.

Pete stopped to discuss the purple pan weed (*Sphaeranthus peduncularis*), which is found where there is underground water. We continued along the river basin, past a lone bull elephant in the shade of a large bushy tree on the other side of the dry riverbed. He blended into the shade so well, a casual viewer might have missed him. I was anxious walking between him and the elephants that roamed a ridge on our other side.

Far ahead, on the branches of a dead tree, a small, brown Wahlberg's eagle was distinguishable by its flat-topped head and short, spiky crest. It is an intra-African migrant and was alone. These monogamous birds form long-term pairing bonds and always return together to the same nesting site. Leaving the Makongolweni River, we hiked on the gently sloping grassy plains that form the watershed with the Metsimetsi River. A lone kudu browsed on the lower slopes of a hill where a small impala cluster ran in the direction of the rising sun.

A grove of trees stood out in the otherwise barren landscape and I took it for granted we would stop there for breakfast. I had not yet eaten anything as per my modified fasting plan for the hike and I was ready for breakfast. Since the previous Leg, I had started a 16:8 intermittent fasting plan, where I eat only from 12:00 noon each day until 20:00. I was disappointed when Pete walked past the trees without a hint of stopping. The plains ahead were vast and devoid of trees and shade as far as I could see. A while later, we stopped at a lone tree with scant foliage. Pete admitted it would not do, and we backtracked to the grove I had favoured earlier.

It was a sociable breakfast with lots of happy chat. We discussed the hundreds of nests of red-billed quelea from the morning. Our debate was whether the birds return to their own nest every time or take any nest. The consensus was they return to their previous nest or build a new nest.

Pete interrupted the conversation to ask, "Is everybody comfortable?" His sign we needed to get going. He teased us with that line for the rest of the hike.

We went over the watershed and paused at the top of a taxing rise as Pete contemplated whether we should circle west around a lone elephant or go east and closer to the river. East was the choice and we were rewarded with a wonderland of animals. We took it slow, stopping to admire a zebra with two impala in tow and wildebeest further down the slope. The zebra ran at the wildebeest, but stopped before they got to them, framing a lone elephant between them.

A dazzle of zebra grazed around the spring at the headwaters of the Metsimetsi River. We took a line south between them. The wildebeest ran down the slope. The zebra loped upward. At the river, yet another large group of zebra came into view. They sounded high-pitched alarm calls that could have been mistaken for a small yapping dog. A tiny zebra foal ran between its mother's legs, and I guessed it was the reason for the alarm calls. Some of them raced surprisingly close to us and circled back up the slope where they stopped and barked an alarm before running off.

On the other side of the river, kudu cows avoided the melee, lifting their heads only to observe. This was a good example of how the grasslands provide animals with safety in numbers and why the spacious eastern plains reveal some of the best sightings. All of which is why predators prevail, too. Grazing animals gather for security. The more sets of eyes, ears and nostrils there are, the lower the risk of being caught unawares.

At the bottom of the hill, we turned west. It was uncomfortable trudging through long, dense grass until we found an animal path that led back to the river. A small group of elephant soon forced us to abandon this route. Pete consoled us with a short break on the riverbank. I sat on my stool at eye-level on an animal path, with ticks hanging expectantly on the top blades of grass.

After the break, we continued along the riverbank past grazing zebra, while far on the other side of the river, a lone bull elephant stood between thickets. A kudu cow caught fright and, in a single leap, disappeared into the bush behind it. The zebra bolted when we got close, then stopped at a safe distance. They stood motionless except for the synchronised swivel of their heads as they watched us.

We made a small detour at the S35, a dirt road known as the Lindanda Road, to visit the Harry Wolhuter memorial, which commemorates one of Kruger's most enduring tales. A faded plaque dating back to 1903 marks the historical spot. A zebra pair sheltered in the shade of nearby bushes as Howard told the story.

"Wolhuter, one of the Park's first rangers, was far ahead of his travelling group. It was dusk and he was searching for a waterhole because the first hole they found was dry. He was alone on horseback on a trail he knew well when two lions attacked. The lions toppled him from his horse and dragged him almost 100 metres into the bushes. Wolhuter pulled a knife from the sheath on his belt and stabbed one of the lions. The mortally wounded creature dropped Wolhuter, who climbed a tree to escape the second lion. He listened to the dying groans of the first. A part of the tree still stands in the concrete column," Howard said. I looked at the dead branch protruding from the hole, with the plaque affixed to it and wondered if it was from the same tree.

"Wolhuter believed he was saved by his dog, Bull, whose persistent barking distracted the second lion until his assistants arrived and carried him away. It took four days to get him to Komatipoort for medical assistance for his wounds, which were by now septic. After which he spent several weeks in the Barberton Hospital.

"Wolhuter's knife, and the skin of the lion he killed, are on display in the Stevenson-Hamilton Library at the Skukuza Rest Camp," Howard added.

Wolhuter's brave dog, Bull, died sometime later in a fight with a baboon, which also perished.

By sheer coincidence, two months later, on my way to start Leg Six, I stayed at the Torburnlea homestead in Nelspruit. I learnt this was where Wolhuter was looked after while recovering from his injuries. The homestead, behind a superlative flamboyant tree, is now run as a boutique guesthouse.

That day, our heads filled with Wolhuter's fortunate escape, we headed for a nearby waterhole. Might this have been the one he searched for? Waterbuck fled before us. This too, had resonance with Wolhuter's tale, because when he first heard the lions, he thought they were waterbuck or reedbuck, as he called them.

Part of the waterhole lay in the shade of a sycamore fig, its branches and foliage leaning over the water. It was an ideal spot for a break, with fallen branches creating comfortable seating. A panicked Nile monitor, or leguaan, dove from a branch into the water. Leguaans are one of the largest lizards and, in addition to being fast runners, they are also good tree climbers.

Noisy blacksmith lapwings flew about the waterhole as we chatted. Their 'tink, tink, tink' alarm call meant we were probably close to their nest. They breed all year round, though we were still three months away from their peak breeding season. I sat on a fallen branch opposite Howard in the copious shade of the fig tree and asked about his rifle. It was a CZ550 bolt-action that fires hardnose .458 calibre Dzombo rounds with the bullet design by Bjinse Visser.

Our laidback mood changed to tense excitement when someone pointed to the top of the gently rising slope where lionesses ambled southwards in the direction we were headed. Everyone stood up for a better look. We watched in silence until the lionesses disappeared into the long grass. Pete cautioned us to move quietly as we left the shade of the fig tree and headed to where the two lionesses had been. The wind was in our faces and in the long grass, there was a chance of us stumbling upon them. They were some 50 metres ahead, stalking a bushy area at the bottom of the gradient.

Lionesses are the primary hunters in a pride. They work together, as their smaller and more agile bodies make them quicker and more effective in a chase than male lions. Their other key role is rearing cubs and teaching them survival skills.

A herd of zebra higher up the slope saw the lionesses, and stopped to watch with their heads held high and their ears pressed flat. A warthog ran out of the bush on the drainage line, the focus of the lionesses' attention. They did not react, even though warthogs are among their favourite prey. Lions are not as fast as the majority of their prey and so they count on surprise. Which is why impala are not particularly sought after by lions.

One of the lionesses walked past the bush where the warthog emerged and turned to look back in our direction. She must have noticed us for the first time as she immediately hunkered down in the long grass. We proceeded cautiously.

A long, tough stretch through high grass and few animal paths followed. I was thinking we had not observed any animals since the lioness encounter, when we came upon a flat, grassless expanse with four rhinos in a mud bath. One of the rhinos was dehorned. A warthog, pint-sized by comparison, bravely shared the mud bath with the rhinos.

A large sycamore fig on the other side of the Metsimetsi River looked so inviting we could not resist crossing the dry riverbed to stop for an early lunch beneath the tree's lush canopy. Pete told us to keep on our boots when we got there. A bull elephant was nearby and we had to be ready to go if necessary. The courteous elephant moved away soon afterwards, and I took my boots off while Howard radioed in our location on the satellite phone. One of the rhinos still had a horn that could be removed.

As we had lunch, a squirrel descended the tree trunk. It considered our colourful backpacks and other paraphernalia and, after a moment's consideration, scurried back into the leafy branches.

Marie and Pete chatted in the shade until a vervet monkey defecated onto Marie's head. Fortunately, she was wearing a hat, and although some believe if a bird defecates on your head, it will bring good luck and wealth, we were stumped as to what the same means from a monkey.

A zebra pair ventured nearer to our shady oasis as we packed up after lunch. I saw them before they knew about us and wasn't surprised when they veered away from our tree. They would have shared the shade with wildebeest, waterbuck or impala, but not humans.

After crossing the river, we returned to where we had watched the rhinos in the mud pool. To our disappointment, they had left. An elephant strolled down the gentle gradient to the river and we waited for it to cross. It stopped unexpectedly next to a bush and shook its head. Two rhinos were in the shade of the bush. The big calf suckled and had to lie on its side to reach the teat.

Another two bull elephants came down the slope. Howard kicked up a cloud of dust with his boot to confirm the wind was behind us and blowing at the elephants. We were so close they must have smelt us, but they did not react and continued on their way to the river. The first elephant to cross rubbed himself against a tree, near a lone impala, which darted up the slope past the unhurried elephants.

A grey foam-nest tree frog hopped across the path once we were off the busy plain. While the foam-nest tree frog is common in southern Africa, this was albino-like compared to the frogs to which I was accustomed. Their colouration adapts to maintain body temperature, and by then the day was hot. The frogs are lighter coloured on hot days as the pale colours reflect heat. Further down, two more elephants were on a dry riverbed. A young jackalberry tree grew parasitically from the trunk of an enormous, old sycamore fig. Jackalberry trees, also known as African ebony, are better known for curing parasites than being leeches.

An impala pair, camouflaged by the grass and a shady tree on the opposite bank, fled. It was a typical physiological response of fight or flight; though we would not have noticed them if they had stayed still.

From there, we followed a hippo path away from the river. They are wider than those of an elephant, because hippo feet are placed side by side as they walk and not one foot in front of the other like elephants. Two wide tracks on the path and a pile of dung with small twigs showed where a black rhino had marked its territory. I hoped to spot one, although the chances were not good. The black rhino population in the Kruger is small at less than ten percent of the white rhino population. Black rhinos became extinct in the Kruger Park by 1945. Eighty-one were re-introduced between 1971 and 1989, with some estimates putting the current population at around 300.

The World Wildlife Fund notes: "The number of black rhinos in Africa was estimated at 2,600 in 1997. Of these 1,080 occurred in South Africa and 686 in Namibia." The WWF adds that, "The Kruger National Park also houses a fast-growing population of about 3,000 white rhinos. This large population acts as an effective buffer against black rhino poaching as poachers are more likely to encounter the more numerous white rhinos than black ones. In the past 10 years, only one black rhino has been lost through poaching."

We reconnected with the Metsimetsi River and I was ready to call it a day. Pete went alone down a steep riverbank for a closer look at an elephant-dug hole next to a pool of slimy algae-filled water. A small group of impala clustered among thorn bushes on the bank. We needed water close to our campsite. However, a dejected Pete returned and said we should move on. Further along the riverbank, we found an open flat area surrounded by bushes and trees. After dropping our heavy backpacks, we made our way to the rocky, dry riverbed. None of the old elephant holes looked like they were going to yield water. Howard went alone to a distant pool, while we sat on the rocks. He came back looking as dejected as Pete had earlier.

"The water is too muddy," Howard said. "If elephants don't drink the water, then neither should we."

The sun would soon sink and Howard made up his mind. "Let's go back to that first elephant-made hole Pete looked at," he said.

Pete sounded cautiously optimistic. "I'll dig deeper into the hole and I think we will get to water. I'm sure the hole was lower than that pool of slimy water," he said.

"Guys, if that doesn't work, we will have to take water from the slimy pond. You must filter the water and use drops," Howard said. "I'm sorry, but it's getting late and we don't have time for anything else."

Back at the first hole, Pete burrowed into the cave-like waterhole on his stomach, as a leguaan would, except he was armed with a cup and a spade. Howard climbed the riverbank to scout for a campsite. He found a flat, grassy place between thorn bushes for the tents with a small clearing where we could make a safe fire.

After pitching my tent, I went to the river with my water bladders. By then, Pete was sitting inside the waterhole placing flat stones to hold up the sides. The water that trickled in was dark and muddy. Pete used a cup to scoop it out. In a miracle of nature, the water became clearer with every cupful as Pete scooped out the sediment. An elephant would have done the same thing, sucking up the dirty water with its trunk before blowing the water out over its back until it is clean enough to drink.

We filled the two shower bags first and by the time we started filling the water bladders, the water was crystal clear. When we were done, we must have extracted 80 litres of potable water. Most drank it as it was, noting how pure it tasted. I added purification drops to be sure. The waterhole was too close to the slimy pool for my comfort.

The sky was filled with stars, yet the moon hid. The fire crackled as we relaxed and chatted long after everyone had finished eating. After dinner, I washed my eating utensils and brushed my teeth before returning to the campfire. I wanted to socialise a little. Good thing I did because the night was far from over.

I'll let Marie tell it: "We had just finished dinner when someone heard rustling in the bushes behind Jennifer and José. 'Can someone please shine a torch,' Jennifer pleaded.

"A light was directed at the vegetation, lighting up a large hyena behind Jennifer, who yelped. The indifferent hyena walked off. All evening, we heard lions grunting in the nearby riverbed. Our two superb guides expertly deciphered the sounds around us.

"We were all a little uneasy after the hyena encounter and most of us began cleaning up. I was aware lions and hyenas were nearby and I asked Clifford if he could be on standby, while I went behind the tents. He was brushing his teeth and mumbled something I interpreted as agreement.

"I didn't venture far and shone my headlamp, checking for eye reflections. I've often thought that women are more at risk on these trails than men. I finished my evening routine and was ready for bed, but went back to the campfire to chat.

"Later, on my way to bed, I walked behind Arie. With my head torch, I anxiously scanned the area for eyes and then the massive body of a lioness emerged from behind Clifford's tent.

"'Lion,' I whispered, worried I might scare the animal or attract its attention.

"Time seemed to move in slow motion. I then yelled, 'Lion,' loud enough for the guides to hear. A second lioness appeared behind her. They didn't even look at us; they kept walking to Arie's tent.

"The guides rushed to our side as we watched the lionesses walk around the outskirts of our little campsite. An animated Clifford materialised from his tent when the coast was clear. He heard sounds. He however, thought it was me outside his tent. He called out asking if I had heard the lions grunting and thought it odd when I didn't answer. He was shocked when he heard me yell, 'Lion'.

"The two lionesses soon disappeared, but they left us excited to share what we had experienced. My heart was racing and I was sure I would never be able to sleep knowing two of the apex predators of the Kruger were prowling the perimeter of our little camp. Amazingly, I had the best night's sleep of the entire trail."

The next day was going to be hot, so Howard led us out of camp at first light. The rising sun over the Lebombo Mountains cast a golden haze over the animal paths through the short grass. The 800 kilometre-long Lebombo Mountains run in a north-south direction from Shingwedzi, form a border with Mozambique on the eastern side of the Kruger, and extend all the way to the Crocodile Bridge gate in the south. The range is a series of low, narrow hills of Jurassic-age volcanic rock.

The Kruger Park has billions-of-years-old granite foothills in the southwest and millions-of-years-old weathered basalt plains and rhyolitic Lebombo Mountains where we were hiking. The park also carries an extensive Stone Age to Iron Age history so prevalent that, in parts, Stone Age tools and Iron Age pottery shards scatter the ground. There is evidence, too, of early trade with Arab explorers and the University of Pretoria has long conducted excavations at some sites.

As we walked, lots of shongololos, mostly curled up tight, were not as big as the one from the first day. The loud, deep bark of a kudu made Howard stop. He said it could be because of the presence of lion or other predators, and we should be alert. I thought perhaps we were the cause of the alarm call.

A European roller sat on a branch; sunlight brightened its somewhat scruffy plumage. The annoyance of ticks continued and I probably spent more time looking for ticks on the guide's legs in front of me than I did enjoying the scenery.

A black-backed jackal ran out of the shade and up the slope near the Lebombo hills. We stopped to examine fresh lion tracks on the path and I looked back, wondering if I could still see the jackal. It had stopped halfway up the slope to watch us.

Two damaged dung balls, each the size of a tennis ball, lay on the path next to a hole in the ground. Howard explained, "The male dung beetle digs around the ball until it drops into a hole. After excavating further, the beetle returns to the surface to push other balls into the hole. The female lays eggs inside the ball, and the larvae feed from that." Dung beetles can bury faeces 250 times their own weight in a single night.

Someone pointed out that the dung balls had been disturbed.

"A mongoose, or other predator, attacked the nest and ate the larvae inside the dung-ball," Howard said. It could have been a honey badger, as they are superb at finding underground dung balls with larvae inside.

Later, we came across piles of dung rolled into balls by an army of dung beetles. Howard picked one up and we took turns to hold it to feel the beetle's remarkable strength. Dung beetles are found on every continent except Antarctica and live in habitats ranging from hot deserts to lush forests. Some say dung beetles in southern Africa use the Milky Way to orientate themselves. I quipped in addition to soil shaping and nutrient recycling, these armoured beetles entertain kids by making a living from pushing around a ball of poo.

A melody of doves, tchagra and other birds surrounded us. A large flock of red-billed quelea flew ahead, taking off and dropping down again from tree to tree. Their red bills were lit by the morning sun in contrast to their otherwise dull colouring. I estimated that more than a hundred birds flew along our path. Had we been there a few weeks earlier, we would have spotted far bigger flocks.

Our descent through a gorge to the Matilweni River did not disturb an impala group on the far bank of the wide river. We stopped for breakfast around a pond, half of which was covered by a mat of suspended algae blooms in the lee of a riverside cliff. I sat on a flat rock and tucked into an apple, while I made coffee to enjoy with my two muesli rusks.

I watched a kingfisher hover over the pond. Given how murky the water was, I was not surprised the kingfisher made no dives. The frog-like call of migrant European bee-eaters punctured the air. It was late March and because of how high they flew, I guessed they might have been on their way back north. A prehistoric-looking hamerkop flew downstream away from an African fish eagle couple perched on the dead branches of a distant tree.

After breakfast, we followed the river downstream. A regal kudu bull balanced awkwardly on the steep embankment. If it lost its footing, I didn't think it would survive the fall to the rocky river below. A small and stocky klipspringer scampered past the kudu, making the point about who belonged and who didn't.

Crossing the river, we leapt over rocks and clambered across sandbanks near another four kudu bulls. Perhaps the lone kudu was part of their group? The sun-bleached skull of an elephant lay on a small sandbank in the river. Judging by its size, it must have been from a bull, which appeared to have died of natural causes. When alive, the head alone – including the trunk and tusks – could have weighed up to 300 kilograms. The air cavities and honeycomb design reduce the weight of the skull without compromising the structural integrity. Only the lower jaw is solid bone.

Further along, Howard pointed to a pile of black rhino dung on the animal path.

"How do you know it's from a black rhino?" Clifford asked.

Before Howard could explain, I teased: "If you taste it, you will know."

Howard picked up a handful to remind us of the telling angle of the cut on stems and twigs eaten by black rhinos.

In the distance, a large troop of elephant romped in the wide river. The wind must have carried our scent to them because an elephant on the far bank swivelled its trunk in our direction. I was apprehensive as we boldly walked on the riverbank approaching them. By the time we got close, the elephants had wandered to the other side, or so we thought.

Circling a large dense bush, we confronted an elephant cow. Another reminder to never let your guard down in the wild. She took a step at us, raising her trunk and flapping her ears. We scrambled up the slope and bunched behind Howard and Pete, who raised their weapons. The elephant cow, satisfied she had chased away the intruders, crossed the river to join the others. We had a good view of the enormous breeding elephants of all sizes. The wind blew over us to the clustered pachyderms as they prepared to leave.

We began a slow descent into a narrow and lush valley. On one side, the cliff face was pock-marked with caves of the sort in which early humankind may have once sheltered to observe and hunt passing game. A kudu bull at the base of the cliff was startled by our arrival and scurried up the impossibly steep slope.

The cloudy sky made hiking easier. However, when the sun broke through, the heat seared. We took a break in the shade of a jackalberry tree during a hot spell and waited until the clouds obscured the sun, before we moved again. The bottom half of the tree trunk had a plastered appearance, where elephants a long time before scraped mud off their bodies. There was no visible source of water in the dry heat of the valley, which also explained why animals were scarce, despite the lush vegetation.

We were through the valley when a large bunch of impala ran up the slope. It was a good sign because impala are never too far from water. A giant plated lizard was sunning itself on a rock and slithered off as we approached.

It was time for lunch, so we stopped in a narrow gorge beneath a weeping boer bean tree (*Schotia brachypetala*). The tree has masses of deep-red flowers that produce large amounts of dripping nectar. After my lunch of crackers and cheese, I tried to sleep, but was unable to. I put my groundsheet in front of the huge web of a golden orb-web spider and watched the female host spider in the centre and a scattering of smaller males. Flies, bees, butterflies and other tiny creatures fluttered around this insect paradise. I hoped to watch a gladiatorial matinee for which I had a ringside seat. Somehow, the flying insects all missed the web, and the anticipated spectacle was a non-event. I should have slept.

Lunch was followed by another hard stretch through shoulder-high redgrass infested with ticks. A kudu scrambled up a steep embankment ahead of us, followed by an impala. Kudu are found in a wide range of habitats and are known for their remarkable ability to jump three-metre fences. I was amazed at how easily they took to extremely steep slopes, much like the klipspringer. There must have been water close by because there were impala, and rams that faced us until we got close.

A little further on, a group of six impala rams ran from the cover of long grass at the foot of a rocky ridge. A small, younger impala at the back paused to watch us. The rest of them had disappeared before it ran off. I wondered if its inquisitiveness would endanger it. After several near-death experiences in my own life and the scars to show for it, I know more about a rusty radar than I would like to.

Howard gave us another short break from the heat around a small, muddy waterhole before the long climb over the watershed between the Matilweni and the Mnondozi rivers. The gradient was moderate to steep. It was a long climb in extreme heat through tall grass sans animal paths. The vexing and dangerous ticks were back.

After what was one of the toughest slogs on the hike, we stopped at the top of the steep incline to look back to see how far and how high we had climbed; to admire our achievement. I was already on my last water bladder and I could feel it was near empty as I drank thirstily.

Descending was easier, with animal paths through the shorter grass. Our spirits were buoyed by knowing we would soon make camp. A kori bustard flew out of the long grass in fright. The kori bustard is the heaviest flying bird in Africa, and fly only when in danger. I sipped water, barely wetting my lips. I had no idea how much further we had to go.

After 19.2 kilometres over difficult terrain, we arrived at a large circular clearing in the catchment area of the Mnondozi River. I took a desperate sip from the water bladder as I unbuckled my backpack. It gurgled noisily as I sucked in air with the remaining drops of water. I had timed it to perfection, although I was not about to pat myself on the back. I had packed an irresponsible 3.5 litres and I could have done with more water. I should have started with the 4.5 litres I had space for; including the water bottle I used for mixing in a daily dose of electrolytes.

Pete had concealed water containers in the bush near the clearing over the weekend and we unlocked the chains to carry them closer. Thankfully, Pete had the key, as nobody was in the mood to saw through a chain again. I erected my tent between two thorn bushes, facing the centre where we would make a fire.

The shower was set up beneath tall trees on a nearby hillock. I walked there in my slipslops and ignored the pain from the bunion on the toe of my left foot. I was distracted by the beauty of the yellow and red hues of the setting sun. The shower was as invigorating as it was cleansing, and I enjoyed the moment so much I forgot to examine my foot.

I returned to camp and was dropping off my kit in the tent, when I heard Howard scream in pain. I knew that scream and hurried to watch Howard injecting himself with Merthiolate. It prompted me to take a closer look at my own feet. A blister had formed next to the bunion on my left foot. I could have left it, but we still had three days of hiking and decided to play safe. Arie used his phone camera as I reluctantly provided him with another agonising round of entertainment.

The wide grassless space allowed a fire that was bigger than usual. We chatted while sharing Marie's sugar-free chocolate. While not the best-tasting chocolate, Marie found it doesn't melt and is always a welcome treat in the bush. Over the dry crackle of the fire, we heard the distinctive call of a Shelley's francolin; a rhythmic, repeated call that sounds like, 'I'll drink your beer.' I was so absorbed in the post-dinner conversation, I didn't feel anything untoward until I gasped at a sharp pain in my crotch. I took advantage of the dark to discreetly slip a hand into my shorts to feel for what had bitten me. The offending creature was firmly attached and I couldn't remove it. I bid the group a hurried goodnight and rushed to my tent. Using my headlamp, I found the tick and pulled it out, squashing it in the dirt outside my tent.

Rhinos and Medicinal Trees

I was told leopard calls had filled the night when I awoke. Again, I slept through it all. We started early, packing in the dark to allow us to cover as much ground as we could before the heat of the day. I ensured I had 4.5 litres of water. We expected to camp close to a river that night; but there was no certainty it would be drinkable water. In these dry conditions, there was a chance we would have to filter and that was a laborious process. Howard and Pete spoke about Googled satellite images from the same month in prior years to show elephant paths, which are easier to follow and the most direct route to water.

A heavy morning mist cloaked the low-lying plains. At only 200 metres above sea level, there was no visibility to the east. Widely scattered pools of muddy water revealed we were at the source of the Mnondozi River. To the west, the grassy plains were dotted by the shrub-like rock albizia tree (*Albizia harveyi*) or the Persian silk tree, which some call false thorn. On two occasions, the early morning stillness was broken by the loud cough of a male leopard. I scanned the grassy plain, longing for a sighting.

Fresh tracks of the secretive African civet lay over a sandy part of the path where we could see a white rhino had spent the night. Pete pointed out the purple Wandering Jew (*Commelina livingstonei*), a perennial herb found in the Kruger grasslands. The sap can be used as eye drops and the rootstock for medicinal purposes. There are several plants known as the Wandering Jew, and the term refers to a myth about a man who taunted Jesus on the way to his crucifixion, and was then cursed to walk the Earth for eternity. As we chatted about the plant, I watched an enormous, distant bull elephant roam alone with the Muntshe Hill as a backdrop.

Pete stopped to let us feel the grey-tinged olive-green leaf of the woolly caper bush; its leaves are covered in fine hairs, giving it a velvety feel. Monkeys and birds love the fruit, which is toxic to humans. The root is a pharmacological cornucopia. The South African Biodiversity Institute lists its medicinal uses as useful, "...to cure HIV opportunistic infections, such as tuberculosis, Herpes zoster and Herpes simplex and chronic diarrhoea.

The roots are also used as an infusion to assist with sterility, threatened abortion, gonorrhoea, syphilis and to stop bleeding after childbirth." Small quantities also treat asthma and coughs. The plant is sometimes used for African magical rituals.

A while later, Pete showed us the short shrub-like African blackwood tree (*Dalbergia melanoxylon*) or zebrawood. It is hard and has been prized since ancient times as an excellent wood for carvings, wind-instruments and even violin parts. The sapwood is creamy white and contrasts with the black heartwood. While we were chatting around the tree, a white rhino cow and calf ran at high speed across the grassy plain. Despite the distance, we could tell it was a white and not a black rhino because the calf was running in front; with black rhinos, the calf runs behind the mother.

The scattered bushes in the long grass were an ideal resting place for francolins, which often took off noisily as we walked by. Jennifer had been near the front for some time and after another squawking lift-off from what she called the 'heart-attack bird', she dropped to the back of the line. A bull elephant ambled from the long Muntshe Hill on its way to the Mnondozi River where a rhino mother and calf lingered in the shade of a tree.

We intended to go past the southern point of the Muntshe Hill to camp on the banks of the Mnondozi River at a place where we could get water. Scant tree cover meant it was easy to see large game, and we spotted another two rhinos heading south between us and Muntshe Hill. Thanks to their poor eyesight and with the wind behind us, they were oblivious to our presence. We continued parallel to them until they turned. Our single-file line stopped to avoid a confrontation and they ran past some 40 metres away. Later, we caught up with the bull elephant from earlier and now he was closer, I realised he was accompanied by a small clump of zebra and, behind them, some wildebeest. Large congregations of wildebeest, buffalo and zebra are common on the plains in the autumn and early winter months.

Other than the guides, only Lourens and I were wearing short pants and gaiters. The ticks had disappeared. There were still harmless shongololos. The grass was wet from the overnight dew and had an ammonia smell, like urine. I spoke about it when we stopped for breakfast and found it odd nobody agreed with me. After the hike, I looked at websites looking for answers and discovered anaerobic bacteria in damp soil can create an ammonia odour.

We made our way for breakfast to one of just two trees in the vast expanse. The sun was still low, but so hot most of us lay in the shade of the sausage tree (*Kigelia pinnata*). In flowering season, the blood-red to maroon flowers hang in long panicles like German sausages. The fragrance is off-putting to most but attractive to the fruit bat, the tree's primary pollinator.

The sun was well up by the time we were done with breakfast. Before we left, I put on my hat for protection. Something was rattling in my backpack, so I brought the group to a halt next to a muddy pool of water. I took off the backpack to rearrange my utensils, then hauled the backpack onto my shoulders again. When I tried to tighten the waist belt, the strap was a whole hand too short. After an embarrassing eternity of fiddling with the strap, I took off the backpack to extend the waistband through the buckle to make it longer. It was bizarre the waist belt had shortened without me moving the strap. Someone suggested I shouldn't have eaten so much for breakfast.

Resuming our walk along an animal path past a cluster of stunted round-leaf teak (*Pterocarpus rotundifolius*) or round-leaf bloodwood, we noted how it was stripped by elephants. Pachyderms love the leaves of the round-leaf teak and when browsing, they can harm and even destroy the tree. The round-leaf teak is part of the legume family, the same family as peas, beans and lentils. I hoped the damage would not stop the tree from producing its showy bunches of yellow blooms that attract bees. Despite us standing on top of a small rise, the grass was so long only the head and horns of a wildebeest could be seen when it crossed ahead of us, heading for the river.

We continued. Clifford was at the back of the line when he shouted, "Eland."

Two large kudu ran across our heading. Clifford hid behind a broad smile. Although it would have been unusual to find eland this far south, they are among the most adaptable of the savanna animals with habitats from deserts to the tropics.

The sky was cloudless and blue. The rustle of boots broke the silence as we hiked through waist-high redgrass. Stopping for a long break beneath the rounded crown of a marula tree (*Sclerocarya birrea*) on the embankment of a stream, I looked for the edible fruit but could not find any. Stories of drunken elephants eating the fermented fallen fruit and become tipsy, abound. Scientists are sceptical such a large animal can eat enough of the fruit to have that effect.

A fresh breeze brought relief as I lazed beneath the tree. We got onto the subject of age and birthdays. I couldn't believe Howard, who looked so youthful, had a daughter of 18 and a son of 21. Howard had recently turned 50, and we realised he and Arie were born on the same day in 1972. The loud rasp of a bateleur eagle interrupted the conversation and we looked up to see a pair flying overhead. The older birds fly together over their territory, though juveniles wander widely on their own.

The path we followed from there was rocky, with steep ups and downs. We were not always able to see where we were going because of the long grass. Marie tripped, with a rolling fall like a pro, which protected her from injury on the hard surface. We continued through long grass on a flat, open section where our line stretched out, as it often did on straight, featureless stretches. Howard did a panicked pirouette when a snake crossed the path between him and Pete, who was leading. By the time we had all caught up, the snake was gone. Howard thought it was a Mozambican spitting cobra, though Pete said it was thick and golden-brown, so it might not have been.

Three large jackalberry trees stood like an oasis in the desert. There was ample shade and we offloaded the backpacks with a collective sigh of relief. Howard set up his stool so he could lean against a tree-trunk. I sat on my own stool facing Howard, and we were chatting when twigs cracked loudly on the branch above his head. A rock monitor rushed along the bare branch trying to reach the cover of leaves, but the branch was broken off, so it stopped above us. It was a sizeable specimen, easily as long as I was tall and I felt uncomfortable being so close to the heavy primeval creature.

I moved my stool.

Resuming our march of the curious, we continued along one of the tributaries that flow into the Mnondozi River. A kudu bull sheltering from the sun in the shade of the riverine trees, scampered away, weaving defensively from side to side up the steep gradient. Impala are not as adept as the much larger kudu at handling steep terrain, and a small group of impala fled up a gentle slope as we approached.

We stopped for lunch in the long grass, beneath the scant shade of a hardwood and termite-resistant knob-thorn tree (*Senegalia nigrescens*). It was not ideal, but we couldn't find any other open spaces with shade. An African fish eagle flew out of the trees and instead of soaring upwards as I expected, it stayed low over the river.

Finding drinkable water before nightfall preoccupied us. So, it was hot when we packed up, with no time for the usual lunchtime nap. Clouds were forming, although not enough to provide cover. The animals felt the heat, too, and we walked past two bull elephants pressed against each other, taking refuge in the limited shade of a large tree. My eyes burnt from sweat running into them, and I missed not having a sweatband.

Frequent short breaks were welcome in the heat of the day, and so we stopped at a small muddy waterhole for a break. A water monitor scrambled away through the water; its head up and turned to the side so it could keep an eye on us until it disappeared beneath the surface when it was far enough away.

We were past the southern tip of the Muntshe Hill when we intersected the Mnondozi River and followed it eastwards. A saddle-billed stork flew upriver above us. Its black and white wings making it easy to identify from a distance. The bird swooped into the shallows on the nearby riverbed as we stopped for a break beneath a shady tree close to the river. I asked Howard if I could walk to the elevated bank, less than 50 metres away, to see what was in the water below. He said no. I was disappointed and annoyed at myself for asking, because I thought it was close enough to be safe. The words of United States Naval Rear-Admiral Grace Hopper came to mind. She famously said it is easier to ask for forgiveness than to ask for permission. I have chosen that route several times. Although it is not wise to apply this in the Kruger. Pushing your luck where we were, meant there was no chance to ask for forgiveness. Grace Hopper did not get to be the oldest serving officer in the US Navy by abusing the principle.

Muntshe Hill was now far behind us and there was talk of making night camp around the tree we were seated under. Howard thought it too risky to collect water from a deep river. Crocodile attacks are never far from mind in African rivers. We agreed to hike to the confluence of the Mnondozi and the Mahoshanwembe rivers. After all the heavy plodding through long grass in the heat and nursing my water to ensure it did not run out, I felt a dehydration headache coming on. I had not yet run out of water, but it was close and I was annoyed with myself for being in this same situation.

We followed the river until the water dried up as the riverbed got visibly higher. Shadows were lengthening fast and the riverbed was dry for as far as I could judge. I applied my mind to how I was going to get through the night without water. I cut back on the frequency and amount

I sipped until we came to a green, slimy pond the size of a home swimming pool. Pete and Howard conferred and I was glad it wasn't my call as to what to do next. There was only rocks and sand.

With the fading light, we had run out of options after a 19.4 kilometre hike. Howard pointed to the bank where we would make camp. We climbed up the steep, gritty slope to find an open and flat clearing, ideal for camping. If we could find water, that is.

An old elephant-dug waterhole was an option. Although it was higher and far from the water. Pete and Howard teamed up to dig a new hole, barely a foot from the pool of slimy water. After the hole was reinforced with flat stones, the gap was too tight to scoop out water. So much for rushing. They began to make it bigger. Once the hard work was done, Marie and Clifford scooped out the dirty water until it was clear enough for showers. The water was never going to be as clear or taste as good as the water from the second night; but in our desperate situation, it would do. My water bladder had about a cup of water left and I drank it greedily, knowing we had found water. I was dehydrated and exhausted, so after waiting my turn to fill my water bladders, I excused myself from the water-mining activities and climbed the steep, slippery bank to pitch my tent and shower. I had a long wait for the purification drops to act on the harvested water before I could quench my thirst.

I heard a commotion in the scrub behind me while pitching my tent between two small thorn bushes. A rhino crashed through the bush and ran over a small hill. In the long grass we saw only the back of the animal, so we were unable to tell if it was a black or a white rhino.

Thunderous lion roars reached us from the direction of the confluence as we sat around the fire. A lion roar can be heard from six kilometres away. The confluence was closer than that. It brought no comfort when

Howard attached the light to his rifle as the roars got closer. A leopard added its voice to the chorus from behind the small hill the rhino had run over. Marie felt vulnerable with all the animal activity, so moved to sit between the two armed guides.

I awoke sometime during the night with the eerie noise of the wind in the riverine trees. Or, it could have been the crunch of paws on the hard sandy surface around my tent that woke me. I lay still as I heard an animal circle my tent. My heart pounded. I didn't think it was a hyena, as the footfalls were too delicate and measured. More like a cat. I wanted to open the flap to check. I also didn't want the animal to know there was something alive on the other side of the micron-thin nylon. I gave up because I was lying with my feet facing the opening, and I could not reach the zip without moving my body.

I heard the next day from Clifford, whose tent was close to mine, he had the same experience with paw steps around his tent during the windstorm. We looked for tracks but the red gritty sand revealed no secrets.

Showers and Lightning

A half-moon in an overcast sky greeted us when we rose on the fifth morning. The predawn was warm despite the wind. Everyone was up early, sparing Howard the chore of waking us up. I heard the pleasing grunts of the southern ground hornbill as I packed my tent. The squeaks and grunts of fighting hippos downriver carried. Their honking can reach 115 decibels, equivalent to booming thunder, and can be heard up to a mile away.

Lions roared as we left camp to head in their direction. Before we reached the confluence, we turned south away from the river, following a game trail through the long grass. Howard was leading and he stopped to take out his binocs to identify three birds he thought were raptors in a dead tree. As he put the binoculars to his eyes, we heard the boisterous call of the hadeda ibis.

"Damn, I take out the binocs for a hadeda," Howard said in dismay.

Jennifer thought she spotted an owl, her favourite bird, in a leafy faraway tree. Howard checked through the binocs and to Jennifer's disappointment, it was a vulture. Now seemed like a good time to downgrade expectations.

Arriving at the Mnondozi River, an African fish eagle flew out of the trees to land close by. It was barely worth the effort for such a large bird. The riverine bushes were dense and high, and the path we followed took us into the thick of it. Howard used a bullet to tap his rifle noisily as we trekked through the danger zone. Normally we walk in silence and making a noise to make ourselves known was an unusual thrill. Surprising a hippo or a buffalo, both of which favour riverine habitats, on a narrow path would not end well.

We entered a small clearing on the bank alongside a large pod of hippos in the water. All turned to face us with what felt like hostility. The high bank and dense riverine vegetation formed an amphitheatre. We looked down from our elevated position as if waiting to watch a gladiator spill the blood of a wild beast. Some of the hippos had their mouths wide open, baring long curved canines. Their eyes, nose and ears are all at the top of their brown, pinkish heads; not the prettiest of sights. We heard the grunting of a giant eagle owl but couldn't find it. As a consolation prize for Jennifer, a goliath heron flew downriver from the hippos, its wings beating slowly and deeply, while a loud, low-pitched 'kwaaark' issued from its large bill.

The midden of a white rhino blocked the path, though there were signs it had also been used by a black rhino. A collection of large and apparently deep pools along the Mnondozi River had no hippos. I thought it could only have been because the pools were too deep for hippos. They cannot float or swim. In one of the larger pools, a white-faced whistling duck splashed into the water, followed by a flotilla of juveniles with dirty-brown baby faces. Waterbuck ran from the long grass on the opposite bank. I guessed they had been sheltering from the sun because the bank was too steep for them to reach the water. The riverbed became drier and three saddle-billed storks took off in alarmed disarray from one of the few small ponds of water. Saddle-billed storks are usually solitary or in pairs, so it was unusual to spot three.

A couple of wildebeest walked parallel to us for some time, stopping for a careful look when they became aware of us. While descending into a dry ravine, a pack of wild dogs crossed the slope ahead; this was one of my most memorable sightings. The African wild dog survives only because they work in packs. They are an endangered species, with only four remaining populations in Africa. One of which is in Kruger, with just over 300 dogs. The increasing level of meat poaching by impoverished villagers means poachers set up strings of snares and a whole pack of wild dogs, in the wrong place at the wrong time, can be slaughtered. Breakfast beckoned in the shady ravine and the break allowed us to share our excitement at the rare sighting of African wild dogs.

After picking up our bags and heading off again into the warming day, the topography changed, with the russet bush-willow dominating vast plains of long redgrass. We were lucky to spot a delicate and shy Sharpe's grysbok. The Kruger is one of the few remaining sanctuaries for them. The antelope are nocturnal browsers and spend their days in the protective cover of long grass and thick bush.

The grysbok ran towards a rivulet where a black-and-white African hawk eagle rose. These eagles defend their territory and are voracious hunters.

Other birds, including guineafowl are their main prey. Although they also eat smaller mammals such as dassies and mongoose. I watched the hawk while Pete discussed the red bush willow (*Combretum apiculatum*) and its attractive burnt Sienna four-winged fruit that turns darker as it matures. The wood of the red bush willow is so strong, in the past it was used for struts in the mining industry. The leaves can be used to make tea to relieve stomach disorders. The tree canopy is irregular and, on some horizontal branches, a straight stem shoots up. This is used in the making of knobkerries, or *kierrieklappers* – like walking sticks but with a round knob at the top instead of a curved handle. Knobkerries are used for hunting or traditional fighting. I keep one next to my bed at home in case I need a handy weapon.

We examined an unusual single calcified hyena dropping on the game path. It led to a broader discussion about animal excrement. Grant, who is always at the ready with clever retorts, was impressed.

"Gee, you guys know your shit," he joked.

The landscape changed from the grassy plains we had been through for days. I was thinking the trees were taller when my observation was confirmed by the first sighting of a giraffe in four days. A second giraffe appeared from behind a tree where a small cluster of impala grazed. The impala moved away unhurriedly to continue grazing further up the slope where their safety zone was larger.

During a break on the rocky bank of the river, I cut the chinstrap off my wide-brimmed hat. The strap had annoyed me since the start of the hike and I never used it. I reasoned the strap was there for cowboys on horseback. Two tiny, iridescent bee-eaters darted about, catching flying insects in mid-air over the water.

Instead of following the river, the group opted for a long uphill slog to cut out the hairpin bend on the Mnondozi River. Despite the schlep, I knew we made the right decision. Once we reconnected with the river, the rocky gradient led to pools of water at different levels. A crocodile slid off the grassy bank of one and disappeared below the surface. At another deep pool, a hippo slept in the water with its back sticking out. Its nostrils broke the surface of the water momentarily for air. The eyes stayed closed, no humans disturbing its tranquil dreams.

The earthy water we had drawn from next to the slimy pool the night before tasted better as the day went by. We stopped for a quick lunch on the rocky bank of the river. We took off our backpacks only after Howard checked for hippos and crocodiles. Other than an impala that sprinted away, and the baboons on the other side of the river, we were alone. After we left, the baboons hurried over the rocks to take their place at the tree we sat under for lunch. From their aggressive stares, it felt we had made the regulars wait longer than they should have for a seat at the rocky table. Chacma baboons are the largest of the primates in southern Africa and can be intimidating in the open, despite posing no real threat to humans. They are always alert for predators, and one or two from the troop sit high in a tree to keep watch and sound an alarm, as they did with us.

The bush thickened along the river and we followed a narrow path that wound through high and dense shrubbery. Howard tapped his rifle noisily with a bullet to avoid surprising a hippo or buffalo. A large crocodile crashed into the water where the Mnondozi River turned sharply east against a high cliff face. The crocodile had been sleeping and panicked because we were so close. Otherwise, it would have slid in and disappeared beneath the surface as they usually do. Crocodiles spend more than half the day sleeping and with no natural predators as adults, they are generally relaxed.

Our route followed a line to the Sabie River where we planned to make camp for the last night. Impalas snorted as they scurried away. It was too early for rutting season and their raucous display was alarm at our presence.

The northern bank of the Sabie River was rugged and steep. The clearing where Howard said we would make camp was on a stony slope, out of sight of the river. There was no enthusiasm for the spot and Howard agreed to find a better one.

"You can take off your backpacks. Wait here while I look for a safe place to make camp and get water," Howard said.

"Can I go with you?" I asked.

I dropped my backpack and the two of us set off for the river. Without the usual burden on our backs, we easily descended the steep embankment to a sandy beach jutting out into the river alongside a thick bed of river reeds. On the opposite side of the fast-flowing river, a hippo, surrounded by reeds, faced away from us in the shallows.

"This is good," I said. "We can get water here and even get our feet wet."

"No," said Howard. "You won't see a crocodile in the water until it's too late. And we don't know what's in these reeds."

Further upriver, we considered an elevated rock with a flat top alongside churning rapids. A bucket could be dropped into the water with a rope. We headed up the steep bank to look for a camping spot. A gently sloping clearing with an old jackalberry tree at its centre looked ideal, so we went back to the group.

The campsite was close to the sandy beach we had first found. Howard agreed if we were all together for safety, it would be the best place to collect water. At the end of a 16.5 kilometre hike, Howard and I basked in the group's appreciation for a reconnaissance job well done.

"Get ready, and in a few minutes, we will all go down to the river together to wash and collect water. Bring everything you need because it's the only chance you will have, including water for tomorrow. We won't go down there again," he said.

Howard was cautious when we got to the river. He worried about a chance encounter with a hippo or an attack from a crocodile. He warned us not to get too close to the water. I had been looking forward to putting my feet in soothing cold water but was not allowed to. He didn't buy my argument we were on the outer bank where the water was flowing, and my belief there would be no crocodile lurking there. I have swum in the upper reaches of the Amazon River, deep in the jungle where piranhas and caiman, from the same family as alligators, are plentiful. In the Amazon River, it is safe to swim only on the outside bend of the river, where the water flows faster, and neither piranha nor caiman lie in wait for prey. But I wasn't the African expert, and this was not the Amazon, so I obeyed orders.

Howard threw the shower bag into the river beside the reed bed and dragged it back using a rope. We took turns to shower on the sandbank, sans soap, with Howard pouring water over our heads. Howard was deft at throwing the empty bag into the water and dragging it back full. The shower was as fun as it was refreshing, and almost everyone had more than one shower. Even Arie, who initially said no, ended up having three showers. It was the first time Arie had showered since we started The Kruger Trail, and I projected that by the end of Leg Six, Arie would be on track to average half a shower per Leg. Not bad if you believe in averages.

The wind picked up and dark clouds closed in as we prepared dinner. An African hawk eagle flew low over the tents, inspecting the new arrivals at what was probably its usual hunting area. As we ate, lightning and thunder raced across the skies. Despite Jennifer's prediction of rain because of all the shongololos, I hadn't seen it coming. We were still eating when rain began and we scrambled for cover. I tossed everything into my tent and finished eating inside.

The rain poured and the wind picked up. With gusts threatening to uproot the tents. I was glad I had hammered in all the tent pegs. Usually, I only put a peg at each corner. I slipped into my sleeping bag and fell asleep to a symphony of rain, flashes of lightning and thunder. I took misplaced comfort in the flawed calculation, that for every second I could count between the flash of lightning and hearing the thunder, it meant the lightning strike was 10 kilometres away. The truth is for every second between the flash of lightning and the sound of thunder, the lightning strike is just 300 metres away. A professional golfer can drive a golf ball almost that far.

I was worried we were too close to the towering jackalberry tree, and thunder followed some of the flashes almost immediately. Ignorance can sometimes be bliss, and that day it helped me to sleep. Sometime in the night, with heavy rain and the wind gusting, I woke up with someone calling outside my tent. I was bewildered and did not respond. Through the thin nylon of my tent, the sweep of torchlight moved away. A biting chill crept through the goose down of my sleeping bag. I feared that water had got in and I put my hand on the floor to feel. My hand stayed dry but I felt a river of water beneath my tent.

It was drizzling when we woke at first light. Hippos honked. They were on the ridge at our level, probably returning to the water after a night of grazing. We were all in good spirits despite the gloomy weather. Much of the banter was about the storm. The mystery of the shouts and roaming light in the middle of the night was solved when I heard that Pete had gone out during the storm to check everyone was okay.

I packed the wet, muddy gear and tent away without scruples; it was the last day. Luck was on our side because both the major storms we had endured on the hike were on the last night. I had misled everyone with my flawed formula about lightning. Friends and family know me as an ostrich, with an instinct to avoid unpleasant information and this time, it created inadvertent peace of mind for all.

"Clifford, how did you sleep?" Arie asked.

"I was worried about my tent blowing away," Clifford replied.

"It was either that or washed away," I said.

Lourens added, "At least you'd know where to find your tent. You would be in it."

We packed up quickly and because of the drizzle, nobody bothered with the usual early-morning coffee. An expected short hike of about 12 kilometres meant we could look forward to a decent coffee at the Lower Sabie Camp restaurant. I packed less than the usual four litres of water; though the saving in weight was nullified by the mud and water on my tent and groundsheet.

I was disappointed to hear we were planning to take a straight line to the rest camp instead of hugging the northern bank of the Sabie River. I was as keen as anyone to tuck into a hamburger and a beer. Yet I was also loath to miss the opportunity to hike on the banks of the animal-filled Sabie River. Which is why the guides wanted to avoid it. There was too much danger and it would slow us down. In addition, we would have had to make detours around impassable sections of the riverbank.

Even though we had not had ticks for the last two days, Grant decided to don his knee-length gaiters for the first time. He wouldn't have been out of place if he were wearing a skirt and high heels and on his way to a ball. I could not resist saying something.

We remain friends.

Shortly after Pete led us away from the campsite, Howard jumped to avoid a centipede. It seemed an extreme reaction until Howard explained, unlike harmless millipedes, centipedes deliver a painful bite. They are easily distinguishable from millipedes with longer legs that extend from the body.

At the first short break, an European bee-eater called while a flock of four young guineafowl ambled away. A small group of grazing impala viewed us impassively. The long grass was wet and I was almost envious of Grant's long gaiters. A little group of zebra crossed through the long grass ahead of us, before a lone buffalo bull appeared in the low thorn thickets. Closer than was comfortable.

Moving on, we stopped for breakfast beneath the shady canopy of a large tree. Only when we were seated did someone point out the heavy, ripe-looking pods on the sausage tree. The fruit weighs up to seven kilograms and can cause damage when they fall. So much so, Howard, Lourens and Jennifer moved into the open for safety. I stayed after checking there was no pod over my head.

Descending to a stream afterwards, we heard the grunt of hippos from the distant Sabie River. On the other side of a tributary, a warthog, so large at first sight it looked like a donkey, crossed a dry riverbed. We approached the stream lower down, where reeds concealed the flowing water. Pete hesitated as he reached what he thought would be a suitable crossing point. He realised too late it was too wide to jump across. The momentum, amplified by the weight of his backpack, carried him into the water. Howard followed him after a glance upstream, forgetting about looking for another crossing point. We took turns to cross, suffering the discomfort of wet socks. With his knee-high gaiters, Grant had the last laugh.

Howard looked miserable as we regrouped on the other side of the stream.

"Now my blisters are talking to me," he exclaimed in anguish.

"In Afrikaans?" Clifford asked. Those who know the language will appreciate how descriptive it is.

Howard had problems with his open-strap sandals from the first day. He wore the same type of sandals Bjinse Visser wore on Leg One. His regular supplier had closed shop, so Howard bought the pair he was wearing online. They looked the same onscreen, but when they were delivered, Howard realised the inner sole was boat-shaped and not flat. He made the mistake of walking in them for the first time on the hike and paid the price.

Oblivious to our small dramas, a crocodile basked alone on a sandbank in the middle of the Sabie River, soaking up the morning sun to warm its cold blood. Next to the crocodile, a pod of hippos stood motionless in the water. Just the flat top of their heads visible.

The path was clear and, in the distance, two vervet monkeys descended a tree with haste as we approached. Beneath another large, shady tree, the flat sandy clearing was littered with pieces of what I thought was a traditional cast-iron potjie or cauldron. We kicked the pieces around, wondering how they had got there. Someone suggested it was from poachers, or maybe hunters, or 19th-century trekboers, as the early European explorers and settlers were called. None of our theories could explain why the old pot was in pieces. Pete led us away from the river and our musings, and a huge pod of hippos, to a shortcut in the direction of the Lower Sabie Rest Camp. I made another futile plea to follow the river.

The last stop was on the path before we reached the tarred road. The ground was waterlogged and when I sat on my stool, it sank into the soft ground. Wide, muddy tracks from hippos walking to the grazing area and back in the rain criss-crossed the area.

We intersected the H10 tarred road leading to the low-level bridge that traversed the Sabie River. The bridge is visible from the restaurant deck at the rest camp and is a popular stop for tourists to look at birds, reptiles and animals in and around the water. There were no animals when we crossed, save for a water monitor that ambled across the rocks to the bridge and disappeared beneath it.

Once over the bridge, we walked in single file at a brisk pace on the Lower Sabie–Skukuza tarred road. Impala were the last animals we saw before we arrived at the rest camp. I had not known hours and minutes for a week and surrendered by asking the time. It was 10:00 and we had hiked 12.4 kilometres. Over soft drinks, beers and coffee with a hearty breakfast, Pete told us we had hiked 103.1 kilometres on Leg Five in 26 hours and 26 minutes of walking.

I was pensive, reflecting on what had been a relatively easy Leg. We had many rhino and lion sightings, though I had expected more animals. After toasting absent friends, Grant told me he was grateful for the opportunity and had enjoyed it, but he also said, "I won't do it again."

Pete, true to form, interrupted, "Is everybody comfortable?" We all laughed.

LEG SIX

Lower Sabie Rest Camp to Malelane Rest Camp
WINTER, JUNE 2022

Time passed quickly in the two months after Leg Five. I kept fit despite a lot of travel to neighbouring Mozambique. I either ran, cycled or swam almost every day. I was excited the end of a multi-year endeavour was near and I was sad; because the privileged behind-the-scenes access to the Kruger and its wonders would soon be over. I also enjoyed the adventures with my new friends from the hiking group.

Lourens set up a WhatsApp group for our Leg Six of The Kruger Trail, named 'TKT LEG 6, the end –'. Banter among the group was informative and entertaining. Clifford reflected: "There will be tears of pain and joy at the end of this Leg!"

"Pain because it will be the last Leg; the end of a wonderful experience," Lourens added.

For Leg Six, Lourens, Jennifer, Arie, Clifford and myself – who started this adventure at Crooks' Corner four years ago – were accompanied by Marie and Brigitte, fellow hikers from previous journeys. A new member, Alice du Plessis, joined us. Lourens had once worked with her husband and they were now friends. Alice was in her mid-fifties, hiked often, and was an active member of a fitness boot camp. Her training paid off, as often on the hike I had to work hard to keep up with her when she was ahead.

The guides were announced 10 days before the hike. Warren Deyzel, our support guide on Legs Two and Four, would lead and be assisted by Ashraf Sayed, a freelance guide who is passionate about the Kruger Park and the environment. Ashraf lives in Hoedspruit with his wife, Zahira, and seven-year-old twins. One twin, Imraan, is named after Ashraf's late brother, who was tragically killed in a vehicle accident Ashraf and his mother survived. Imaan, meaning faith in Arabic, has a name that endearingly rhymes with her twin brother. Ash says the Kruger Park and the wild are his calling.

LEG SIX

Inspired by Pete Wilson and his gin-and-tonic surprise on the first day of Leg Five, Lourens suggested we have a treat each night on Leg Six to celebrate our expedition. Everyone would have a turn to be host. A spirited debate ensued about the order for each of the five nights, as whatever the surprise was, it would have to be carried from the start and extra weight can become a significant burden. We agreed it would be women first and couples last as they could share the load. The rest of us would be in alphabetical order. I tried to convince Lourens in Portugal, where I was born, my name is spelt as aJosé. It was a cheeky try, nobody fell for it, and I was allocated night three.

I spent the week before Leg Six with friends at Mjejane, a private game reserve on the banks of the Crocodile River incorporated into the Kruger National Park. Many game lodges have been, to increase the range for animals and to improve tourist experiences. The first animal I noticed when I drove into the reserve, was a dehorned white rhino cow with a calf. They were unperturbed when I stopped my car near them.

I continued remote work at the beautiful location because I would be uncontactable the following week. I made time, nevertheless, for a bush walk in the Mjejane reserve, guided by Irving Knight and Richard Smit, who was nonchalant about losing a finger to a puffadder bite. We were rewarded with good sightings of elephants.

In preparation for my meeting with the Panthera, I travelled to Nelspruit to stock up on food and prepare for the hike. I arranged to pick up Warren at the Malelane Rest Camp on my way back and encountered Lourens, Clifford, Arie and Ashraf at Kruger's Malelane Gate. Ash drove with me and when we arrived at the nearby rest camp, Warren was parking his game-viewing vehicle and trailer. "I've just made the water drops for nights one, two and the last night," Warren said.

"What? Three water drops over five nights?" I asked, checking I had heard right. "We are getting soft."

I understood the need for replenishing water on the early Legs in the north, where water was scarce, but I did not expect to have water provided down south, where there were plenty of rivers and waterholes.

To make up time, we arranged an exit pass at Malelane Gate. Warren, Ash and I drove outside the Kruger on the faster national road to re-enter the Kruger at Crocodile Bridge Gate in Komatipoort. Ash's friendly nature is infectious and travelling with him enabled me to get to know him. Ash said the Kruger is his favourite place in the world. "Whenever I drive through these gates, I am grateful to my parents for bringing me here and for instilling in me the love of nature in the dark days before democracy in our country," he said. "It is where I form the closest connection to my Creator. When I'm here, everything around me reminds me of Him. It brings me closer to God."

We arrived at Lower Sabie with 10 minutes to spare. The camp was full of South African tourists. It was good to witness tourism returning after the pandemic, although foreign tourists were still rare.

The group met for an early dinner in the restaurant overlooking the Sabie River. Warren suggested we drink as much water as possible in the morning while still in camp, allowing for less weighty water to be carried. I was not convinced, especially after the last Leg, when I suffered from carrying too little water.

Selati

The road was damp from rain when I drove away from the bungalow at first light. I parked my car beneath a leafy tree and walked to the group gathered around Warren and Ash for a briefing. I heard something new that hit home. Ash told us not to cut corners around bushes and trees if at the back of the line when the guides change direction. Snakes and other creatures could have moved into the shrubbery for cover. I had been doing that since the beginning, and more so when I was tired and the day wore on.

The morning was cool as we headed into a brisk, southerly wind. The sky was clear, but to the south there was a build-up of thunderclouds. The Panthera walked with energy and excitement out of the rest camp gates, across the tarred Lower Sabie–Skukuza road and into the wild behind Sunset Dam. There were lots of doves and fork-tailed drongos that looked like giant black specks on distant bushes. The terrain sloped upward, accommodating small groupings of impala. Most paid us no mind while the alert sentinels regarded us stiffly. Impala are the drama queens of the bushveld, so I was surprised they remained silent. None barked in alarm.

An early stop for a bathroom break saw Jennifer leap from behind a bush, panicked by the snorting and grunting of nearby impala. A sprawling and dense thicket was nearby and we suspected a predator, perhaps a lion or leopard, was hiding. The impala stood near the thicket, snorting in alarm, as we put on our backpacks and made a hopeful detour to see if we could spot the predator.

A large herd of impala, darkly silhouetted against the rising sun, were so focused on peering into the perilous thicket they either didn't notice or just ignored us. They skittered away only when we stopped close to the animals. A pearl-spotted owlet's rising and descending whistles broke our reverie as we continued past a single wildebeest with another group of agitated impala. The wildebeest lacked the agility of the smaller antelope. It looked like a geriatric adult at a kid's party, unable to keep up with the antics of the chaotic impala that ran in all directions, back and forth, undecided as to which direction to flee.

The wet grass was thick but not high, so it was unnecessary to stay on animal paths. After a small buck darted before us, we stopped to examine a fresh aardvark hole covered with warthog tracks. We found a fresh lion track on one of the muddy paths nearby. All the small animal activity made this a prime predator location. Lions hunt primarily at night because their vision gives them a significant advantage over prey. They also take advantage of rain and wind because it makes it harder for their prey to see or hear them.

We stopped for a break in the open grassland, long enough to remove our backpacks. I made a snide comment about the lack of shade, I would soon regret. Warren defended his choice of location. By the time we got going, I was freezing, even though I was in the sun. The cool of the rain had not yet lifted from the soil, and the weak rays of the early sun offered no warmth.

After the break, the change in terrain was stark yet welcome. We hiked away from the grasslands into a long, narrow strip of wooded savanna over shale and sandstone that runs from Satara Rest Camp all the way to the Crocodile River. Around 200 impala browsed at the edge of the tree line. We were lucky to come across courting kori bustards as they pecked between the impala. I hoped the male would enact his spectacular display of bristling the long feathers of his neck. However, he was distracted by the bountiful insects disturbed by the impala and his mind was not on courtship.

The impalas ran off, exposing a large flock of helmeted guineafowl that scampered away, their polka dot bodies vivid below their red wattles and blue necklace. They waddled with all the determination of shoppers heading to a sale. The abundant wildlife meant predators might lurk among the bushes and trees, such as the thick and untidy-looking Delagoa thorn (*Acacia welwitschii delagoensis*), a favourite for browsers, as a giraffe and a feeding kudu revealed. The giraffe stopped browsing to look at us before it ran a short distance. Then, in typical giraffe manner, stopped, looked back and disappeared into the trees.

Jennifer, near the back of the line, clicked her fingers loudly. Warren and Ash ran back towards Jennifer, rifles at the ready. Everyone except Jennifer missed the elephant facing us through the trees; however, it was a relaxed browser not interested in us. The sighting made me realise how tough being a guide in that terrain was; searching for threats and dangerous animals while also looking out for holes, sticks and other obstacles on the ground, and the wellness of everyone in the group.

Another massive dazzle of impala ran off as we approached them. By then, I understood the guides do not detour or pause for herds other than elephants and buffaloes. A few straggling impala rams sprinted from the bushes to follow the rest of them. A large flock of white-crested helmet shrike foraged in the trees and on the ground as they do in winter. They were close to the waterhole where Warren wanted us to stop for breakfast, except a hippo dominated the pool like an unsympathetic bouncer at an invitation-only rock concert. He was not letting in any gate-crashers. I was ready for my apple, rusks and coffee. That would have to wait. The hippo stood guard in the centre of the waterhole with a cluster of cute terrapins clinging to his back, basking in the sunshine. We walked gingerly past the shallow waterhole. The bulky hippo turned his head to watch us leave. Solitary, he exuded a bad attitude.

The bush was now dense and jungle-like. Lion and leopard tracks marked the wet paths. A pair of hooded vultures perched on a dead tree while we gathered around a fresh set of lion tracks for a lesson from Warren. He showed us the difference between the front and back paws and, because male and female footprints are of similar size, how the slender toes of the female identify her gender,

Breaking into a clearing, we disturbed a group of impala and two nyala, which looked up and held their ground. Once the others in our line emerged from the trees, they ran off. The grass was now thicker and longer, making the going tougher. We didn't spot any animals for a long time, other than a smaller-than-usual group of impala that scarpered before stopping to watch us from a safe distance.

The wind blew in enough cloud to create a dense violet canopy over our heads. We made a stop beneath a leafy forest fever-berry tree (*Croton sylvaticus*), that is less common in the south than in the northern parts of the Kruger. Warren illustrated the difference between white and black rhino tracks on the path. The tracks are similar with three distinctive toes, but the outside toe of the black rhino is smaller, narrower and slightly lower from the middle toe than the white rhino's. After the lesson, we ambled westward through thick, short, wet grass.

I looked at the west side of Muntshe Hill, which we had hiked past on Leg Five. A hooded vulture glared from the branches of a leafless tree as our boots became caked with mud. A group of impala mingled with a magnificent kudu bull, majestically standing before his harem of kudu cows. Once we were close, the impala scampered off while the kudu nonchalantly strolled away. A stray warthog scurried for cover behind a bush.

A brisk wind blew when we stopped for lunch and set out groundsheets in the sun. I wanted to take shelter from the cold wind and sunned myself behind a fallen tree trunk. I joined the rest of the group with my coffee after eating my lunch. As we packed up, an inquisitive warthog approached us from the bushes. It was unable to smell us with the strong wind and its poor eyesight didn't help. As it got closer, its courage and curiosity failed, and it turned and ran off. The group chuckled as we watched the little man trot away, his tail held high.

A path took us down a gentle gradient to the catchment area of the Lubyelubye River. Ahead was what I thought to be a lone giraffe; until we got closer and nine giraffes appeared. They loped on, except for one of the dark, older giraffes that hung back to watch us. Warren led us behind a bush, where he could take close-up pictures of the skittish giraffe without frightening it.

We examined an unusual pink wild hibiscus (*Hibiscus engleri*). These beautiful wildflowers are usually yellow with five large petals. Warren noted later we should have taken pictures and even marked its location because a pink wild hibiscus is a rare and treasured find.

The first day was always the most physically challenging for me and, to my relief, when I was struggling to keep up, we followed a management road, which made the going easier. Walking on the road made it possible to look up instead of persistent eyes-downward vigilance for stones or twigs that could trip you up. I noticed a group of zebra in the trees that, for safety, mingled around a browsing herd of giraffe.

A dust bowl on the road had two ruler-length indentations in the centre. Warren pointed out the two lines, noting they were from a zebra and asked us to tell him how he knew.

We were stumped. He said it was from the stripes on the zebra and laughed at his own joke.

Right after that, we stopped at pieces of black, elongated dung. An impromptu quiz followed. Marie answered correctly that it was from a porcupine. Warren also pointed out the more common yellow variant of the wild hibiscus nearby.

The shallow Lubyelubye River flowed strongly and we couldn't cross without getting our boots wet. Ash threw down rocks to make stepping stones, so almost everyone followed his lead. Warren went further upstream with Jennifer in tow and returned on the other side of the river. The river meandered through wet and marshy woods and we soon crossed the river again to continue south. The wind that had blown all day was dying, but a large Verreaux's eagle owl took advantage of the light breeze for extra lift and flew over our heads. These large birds can weigh up to three kilograms.

After a moderate 17.2 kilometres, we made camp on the drainage line feeding into the Lubyelubye River. When I pitched my tent, Jennifer noticed it was orange; different from the red tent I had carried since Crooks' Corner. In a stroke of good fortune, a month before the hike, I had spent a Friday night camping at Mlilwane Wildlife Sanctuary near my home in Eswatini. When I pitched the tent I used on the Kruger hike, the elastic cord in one of the lightweight aluminium poles broke. If I had not camped that night in Mlilwane, I would have discovered the problem on the first night of the hike, which would have been a disaster. I bought the orange tent from Grant Goldstone who used it during Leg Five.

Warren made a fire on the grassless patch beside my tent and the others brought their gas stoves and utensils to cook and chat around it. I prepared dinner at my door flap.

Jennifer hobbled over and asked: "Can somebody help me with some tweezers? I stood on a thorn in the shower." She raised her leg to inspect her foot.

Warren had set up one shower while Ash set up the other.

"Warren and Ash, we've come a long way since Crooks' Corner," I said. "We've learnt a lot and made improvements. We're fast learners and by the end of the first Leg, we were crafting shower floors of stones, leaves or grass. It's what we have come to expect. Raise your game," I teased, "We can't have the ladies getting thorns in their feet."

Clifford, who had been the first to shower, defended Warren. "When I showered, it said 'Welcome' on the ground. You can't do better than that," he said.

It was time for the first celebratory surprise from Marie. She joked about a series of disasters surrounding her preparations before she pulled out a pack of chocolate-coated shortbread biscuits. The sweetness was delightful and exactly what I needed for dessert.

We woke to a clear, starry sky. The ground and tents were as wet as if it had rained. The cold winter's night, with a clear sky and abundant rain the days before, created a heavy dewfall; and it would be like that throughout the Leg. Thankfully, the temperate climate ensured there was no frost. I knew Warren liked us to get moving well before sunrise, so I resigned myself to putting my tent away when it was still wet and plastered with sand and plant material. The tents were unpacked and left to dry at the breakfast or lunch stop.

As we packed up, our early morning chatter revealed lions had loitered around our camp during the night. As usual, I slept through it. I sometimes felt my deep sleep meant I got less value from the Kruger hike than anyone else.

We took to the management road to avoid the wet grass. The road was so muddy, we were forced to make frequent detours through long, damp savanna. The vegetation was mostly thorn-thickets and the relatively small red bushwillow trees with an irregular canopy of long, slender, willow-like branches. A greater honeyguide called out with its rattling chatter; its instinct to guide us to a hive was remarkable and it continued until it went off the road and we did not follow.

Fresh, reddish, still-wet droppings from a porcupine revealed the difference to the older, black and dry porcupine droppings we had observed on the first day. On the road, we weren't as cautious or quiet as when deep in the bush, and our loud chatter scared a steenbok that darted from behind a thorn thicket towards the river. I noticed the outline of zebra grazing higher up the slope through a gap in the bushwillow. These creatures' vivid black, brown and white stripes are effective camouflage that helps zebra better blend into the background. I would have missed them if we were not walking on a road where I could comfortably look up.

We ploughed uphill. The road became sandier and drier as it got steeper. Stopping at the top of the hill for breakfast next to a fallen tree, we weren't done when the cracking of branches, typical of elephants feeding, hastened our departure. The broadleaf trees are a favourite food of elephants and we could hear them at the top of the ridge. Warren asked us to be as quiet as possible while packing up.

Ash climbed on top of a massive termite mound to check how close the elephants were. The vegetation was dense and he was unable to spot the elephants from his elevated position.

Swiftly and quietly, we moved away and soon came across the tracks of a breeding leopard couple heading in the same direction. The leopard tracks were imprinted on the path of francolins, which are early-morning birds, suggesting the leopards must have been there an hour or so after dawn. The road intersected with the H5 dirt road, and we tracked it eastwards before turning into the bush. Almost immediately, we came to a broad, stony, man-made track. I wondered if we would ever be in the real wild that day.

Teacher Warren told us to sit and prepare for an interactive classroom session. His words brought back gloomy memories of my early school days. I found a shady spot in the lee of a thorn-thicket and sat on a cushion of grass.

"What have we just crossed?" Warren asked the class.

"A railway track," Marie replied. Warren would have given her a gold star if he had one. She was the teacher's favourite then, but it would not stay that way for long.

"Where is it going?" Warren asked after confirming it was the ballast, or slab, on which a railway track had been laid.

"What was the railway line used for?" he queried.

We weren't the brightest class in the bush and were not getting any awards for our answers. Or maybe we were the best because we were the only class. Warren told us James Stevenson-Hamilton, the first warden of the Kruger National Park, was instrumental in establishing the Selati railway line to transport gold as well as supplies for his residence and to convey guests. It became the route for a popular nine-stop train trip, which included a halt at what is now Skukuza. Passengers went for walks with guides into the bush, which played a role in establishing Kruger Park as a tourist destination.

The last train to run this line was Locomotive No. 3638, built in 1949 by the North British Locomotive Company; which was withdrawn from service in 1978 when it was given to the National Parks Board of Trustees. The locomotive and a restored carriage are now at the Kruger Station in the Skukuza Rest Camp, with a fine restaurant, café and other amenities.

The railroad tracks and sleepers were removed from the line, and all that remains are rust-covered stones that make up the ballast on which the sleepers and rails rested. The ballast is devoid of vegetation, although half a century has passed since the last locomotive ran. We walked on it for a long, uncomfortable stretch, made worse by the noisy crunch of boots on loose stones. Now and again, a rusted bolt, square washer or bolt assembly lay on the ballast. I picked up a bolt for a closer look before tossing it down. I regretted not holding onto the memento, and it played on my mind as we hiked.

While nothing should be taken out of the Kruger – the adage, 'leave nothing but footprints and take nothing but pictures' comes to mind – a bolt is foreign matter, so I convinced myself an exception could be made. When we stopped for a break on the ballast, I mentioned this to Ash, who conferred with Warren, and he was amenable to my suggestion. Ash, Marie and I made our way back until we found the bolt, which I picked up with gratitude. Marie picked up a handful of nuts and bolts and took them back to the group, some of which were taken by others as mementoes.

A western yellow-bellied sand snake basked on the ballast with its pointed head raised and mouth slightly open; it ignored the loud crunch of boots on gravel as we approached and even after we congregated around it. It looked like a baby snake. However, this serpent is mildly venomous and when it slithered away, its entire body length was almost a metre, which the stones had hidden. One of Africa's fastest snakes, it disappeared quickly into the grass.

We turned off the slab track and found a sun-bleached rhino skull with unmistakable axe marks riven into the bone by poachers as they slaughtered the animal to remove its horn. Stopping beneath a large green thorn tree (*Balanites maughamii*) to admire the panoramic views to the south, I shuffled around a sizeable termite mound to lean against the fluted tree trunk and take the weight off my feet. We debated stopping there for lunch, but decided to press on. Warren climbed a massive termite mound from where he saw a distant cluster of green thorn trees he said would be better for a lunch break and a nap.

Once we got there, I lay out my tent to dry in the sun and hurried through lunch. I used my mobile phone to video interview Arie about the impending end of our extraordinary expedition. He said, "Before doing The Kruger Trail, I had already done the Lonely Bull and Olifants backpack trails. I enjoyed them, although wished they lasted longer than three nights. So, when I heard about TKT, I knew I wanted to do it. A bonus of The Kruger Trail is the bragging rights. Only a small percentage of people can say they hiked the entire length of Kruger Park from top to bottom.

"The best part of the trail is the ability to camp in the wild and have rest stops during the day because that is time to take in your surroundings and consider how fortunate you are. Doing any Kruger hike also allows you to observe things you never ordinarily find in the camps or while driving. Seeing members of the Big Five and hippos on foot is special. Life is about collecting memories for your old age, and The Kruger Trail will supply lots of those."

Putting my phone away, I dispensed with the usual midday nap and chatted to Ashraf about his family and life as a freelance guide. Ash, who works as a quantity surveyor in the mining industry, is passionate about the Kruger and his role as a guide. When guiding, Ashraf carries a CZ550 .458 Winmag calibre rifle that fires Bjinse Visser's Dzombo bullets.

I had just watched the *Top Gun: Maverick* movie and was enthralled when Ash told me about his recent meeting with Tom Cruise, the lead actor. Cruise spent three months at the Safari Moon Lodge in Hoedspruit filming the flying sequences for *Mission Impossible 8*. Ash was part of the team that provided wildlife viewing and security services to the movie entourage.

The heat beat down upon us when we resumed our hike. Having thrown my usual routine out by missing a nap, I shouldered my backpack and stopped myself from asking why we were leaving in the hottest part of the day. African monarch butterflies fluttered about the grass and bushes.

These common medium-sized butterflies are known as the plain tiger. They are found across Africa, Asia and Australia.

Trekking southwards over rolling hills adorned with abundant outcrops of bushwillow and acacia that provided much-needed shade, I spotted a shiny and wet warthog far ahead. The area was filled with small mud holes and when we got close, a family of three warthogs fled, tails erect and in single file.

Following the path up a long uphill, I had no energy to walk around a splattering of flat, round patties of buffalo dung. I stepped on one and almost fell on my back. It looked caked dry from the sun and the wind, but the slippery texture beneath the dried skin had the same effect as if I had stepped on a banana peel. Buffaloes have four-chambered stomachs and I had stepped on the dung that passed through all four. Like cows and other hooved animals, they swallow their food and continue chewing to extract maximum nutrient value. Later, they regurgitate the moist bolus of grass from the reticulum.

My contemplation along the little-used animal path along the top of a ridge ended when Warren stopped and signalled silence. We waited for a long time, not knowing what was going on. Warren said he thought he had heard a rhino. He led us down the slope hoping to flush it out. Instead, we intersected with elephants. They either saw or smelt us and one alarmingly close bull trumpeted loudly. Without saying anything, Warren briskly set off back to the top of the ridge. I was looking the other way and was left isolated and exposed. I hurried to catch up with the back of the line, turning around often to check we weren't being followed.

Once off the ridge, the ground sloped to a broad, bush-filled basin with patches of open grassland where a single file of impala sprinted past. The golden hues of the setting sun glistened on the water of the Mpondo Dam. An older giraffe joined two lightly coloured young giraffes near to where a vulture hunched on the bare branch of a long-dead tree. Close to water, at the time of day when animals like to drink, for safety we made a detour around the small pools of muddy water and the dense and thick bush.

A couple of zebras continued grazing as we passed. They had seen us approach and did not feel threatened. We intersected a dirt road that took us to the dam, where the water level was high from the rains. What was usually a parking and viewing point for tourists was underwater.

"That's where you launch your boat," Warren joked as he pointed to where the road ended in the water.

"Fishing boat or ski boat?" Lourens quipped.

We headed for a motionless glossy, black-feathered, woolly-necked stork on the marshy ground. The setting sun lit up the stork's woolly white neck and drew our eyes to her stare. A giant crocodile in the water was basking in the last rays of the sun.

Time was running out for the promised treat of sundowners at the dam and we should have known better than to take a shortcut to approach the stork. We got mired in mud and had to turn back to avoid getting our boots wet so late in the day.

After precious minutes of wasted daylight, we walked over the man-made dam wall parallel to the S102 dirt road. A pod of three hippos in the centre of the dam grunted before advancing with menace at us. We ignored them and descended cautiously down the steep dam wall before crossing the road and into thicker bush. Camp was quickly set up in an open area dominated by a tall leadwood tree. I was surprised to hear we had hiked only 13.5 kilometres, making it one of the shortest days of the trail.

The sun was sinking and we rushed our showers to return to the dam for the sunset, dressed in shorts and T-shirts and wearing slipslops. Clifford wanted to stage his treat event on the dam wall. A vast pool of muddy water on the dirt road we had easily negotiated earlier with our boots on, slowed us. Most of us got around it by balancing on branches and a narrow ledge at the edge of the puddle. Warren still wore his boots and, despite the rifle, he managed to carry Jennifer on his back to yells of encouragement and applause. When the going is tough, everyone loves a Rambo.

As we reached the wall, the yellow ball of sun in the sunset-streaked sky dropped below the horizon. I knew Clifford had something elaborate planned and I was unsure whether we had enough daylight left for his ceremony before returning to the safety of the camp. There are less than 30 minutes of light after the sun sets at the equator, and about two hours when closer to the poles. We were close to the Tropic of Capricorn at a latitude of about 23 degrees and 26 minutes south of the equator.

We sat in a line along the top of the narrow, sloping dam wall. I was closer to the water's edge than the others. When the three hippos guarding the dam approached again, Warren told me to sit higher up, which I obediently did. I made a snarky comment and Warren told me to keep quiet. I felt like the naughty schoolboy on an outing. The hippos coasted back to the middle, satisfied we were not entering their water.

Expectations around Clifford's treat were high. He unpacked two bottles of wine and set up two gas stoves, including one he borrowed. Clifford took out rolled cinnamon sticks, an orange and a cutting board. He sliced the orange into rounds while he boiled the wine, prepped with cloves and star anise, in the two pans. The glühwein was served hot with pecan-fudge shortbread biscuits and a slice of orange. The timing was perfect, with the spicy hot beverage countering the biting cold that crept across as the sun disappeared.

Our chatter and laughter agitated the hippos and they lumbered back towards our side of the dam. We got the message, scrambled down the wall and rushed back to camp. Jennifer's shoes made it difficult for her to walk through mud, so Warren carried her on his back over the pool of water. Dinner felt mundane after Clifford's treat and I slipped into my sleeping bag and was soon asleep.

A noise woke me. I lay still and listened. The tent nearest me contained Arie and Brigitte. A snore whistled through their tent covering. But that was not the noise that woke me. I lay there, awake and wide-eyed. Clumps of grass were being ripped from the ground around my tent. An elephant was so close I could hear it chomping and its teeth grinding. I sensed other large animals walking past my tent. Curiosity got the better of me and I decided to peek, despite the danger.

Being so close to a well-worn animal path, I had anticipated a busy night and set up my tent to face the track, this time with my head on the side of the zipped door-flap. The trick was to use my arms and not move my body. They say location is everything, but so is timing. I thought my snoring neighbours would provide all the cover I needed. However, snoring wasn't enough to dampen zip noise. Arie or Brigitte turned often and I had to wait for the split second of cover it gave me to slide the zip. I was overly cautious and, by the time I opened the zip enough to look with one eye, the animals were gone.

All that effort and lost sleep for nothing.

I left the zip partially open to react faster next time but fell asleep, and when I woke, the camp was already being dismantled.

I learnt Ashraf had shouted at a hyena that snuffled so actively on his tent fabric the flimsy structure could have collapsed.

"Hey!" was all it needed from Ash, and the hyena scurried away. Perhaps that woke me.

We know when animals are around the tents, we must lie still and not make a sound, but something that could threaten life is an obvious exception.

Biyamiti

I woke with a painful blister on a big toe. I had learnt the hard way these must be dealt with promptly, so I put a plaster on it before exiting the tent. The group was noisy and chatty as we packed. The consensus was the activity during the night rivalled, but did not beat, the carnival during the first night of Leg One. Nevertheless, everyone had stories to tell. Clifford said the shout from Ash woke him up, too.

Marie said, "A hyena bumped one of my tent poles, like a dog bumping something with its snout. My heart was racing and I was ready to raise the alarm, but the hyena moved away. It took a while for the adrenaline to wear off, and I found myself desperate to relieve myself. Although elephants were around, so I had to wait for what seemed like an eternity for the coast to clear."

The guides had chained jerry cans with water to a tree less than 10 metres from the tent Lourens shared with Jennifer. He said, "I woke up during the night and heard the rumbling of an elephant's stomach above me. It was within metres of our tent. It was so close I could hear the elephant's feet brush against the grass as it moved. I feared it would step on our tent.

"A few minutes later, I heard the jerry cans moving and something tugging on the chain holding them together. I wondered why the elephant would do that. I listened to the elephants move off and went back to sleep once all became quiet again. Now I know it wasn't the elephants tugging at the jerry cans, but probably the hyena because the lid from one of the jerry cans was chewed off."

We headed south on the gravel road, where we found the fresh tracks of our night visitors heading to our camp. Hyena tracks were on top of the elephant tracks, so they must have been close behind. We left the road and Ash pointed out a tropical tent-web spider nest with its unusual tent shape and mesh-like appearance. The web was a dramatic work of art, thanks to the dew beads glistening like crystals in the soft early morning sunlight. The thickets around us were colonised by spiders. Tent-webs were everywhere on the bushes, and funnel-shaped spider webs covered the ground. This was not a good day for arachnophobes. I don't like spiders at home, yet I'm unbothered by them when in the bush.

We were discussing the spider webs when a wildebeest walked into the clearing. It saw us, reared and dashed about in circles, bellowing loudly before disappearing behind the trees. Its energetic playfulness helped me understand why 18th-century Dutch settlers to South Africa dubbed these dark and gangly creatures wildebeests, meaning 'wild beasts'.

The bush was dense with poor visibility and we soon found ourselves amid impala. They were as surprised as we were and quickly dispersed. As they ran off, Ash plucked some of the double-lobed capsule-like fruit of a young spike-thorn shrub and offered them to us to taste. I found the fruit sweetly scented although bitter.

Ash later pointed out a pink, dew-filled, wild morning glory crawling along the ground close to two of his favourite grasses, which were side by side. One was the hardy, attractively tufted Natal red-top, which is red in summer and white in winter to attract birds and bees. The other was curly-leaf love grass. In some circles, it is considered a weed because it is long-living and fast-growing, even during drought.

Breakfast was on the banks of the Bume River. Hamerkops, one of my favourite birds, landed amid the scattered water pools with jumbled squawks and courtship croaks. Ash was in reflective mode as we sat and ate: "You meet awesome people on the trail. I've observed closely how nature changes people. It's not about trekking big distances. It is about being in nature. Walking in silence for miles in the wilderness evokes nostalgia, emotion and longing. We recall memories. This time for reflection is rare."

After breakfast and checking there was no danger, we descended to the sandy riverbed to speculate about its recent visitors. There were tracks from a pride of lions and fresh holes dug by elephants for water. The lions came later, as some of their tracks were on those of the elephants. We hiked the river's north bank because it was more open. Later crossing to the opposite side where the vegetation was thinner. A mature giraffe, his colours dark with age, watched us.

The heat and the thick grass we trudged through were energy-sapping. Fortunately, the ground beneath the grass was not stony as it had been in the central parts of the Kruger. It was still early and the grass was wet from the morning dew. I looked forward to lying in cool, damp grass during the breaks.

A young knob-thorn tree caught our attention. Elephants had stripped it of so much of its bark it would probably not survive. Elephants regularly eat the leaves and nutritious pods without damaging the tree. However, during musth, when testosterone levels are higher, they tend to eat the bark.

As we reached the shade of a marula tree for a welcome break, Marie tripped. In keeping with her one fall per Leg, she fell into a pile of elephant dung. We sat comfortably in long, thick grass beneath the tree canopy. Generous Jennifer shared her liquorice. She even let me take her favourite – a ball of liquorice covered in spots of orange candy.

After the break, we crossed the S26 Bume Road, a scenic dirt road popular with tourists. Pausing in the shade of a leafy tree with our backpacks on, someone said it was a 'Louis break'. Ash asked what that was. We told him about Leg Three, where Louis had introduced us to the short, standing stop in the shade. A bull elephant, partly concealed by the trees, stopped grazing to take its measure of us, then turned to walk away. It felt like a snub.

Hiking through trees and thorn thickets in long grass, I felt a sudden sharp stab in my foot. I cried out in pain and hobbled to a stop. Warren ran to my aid, thinking I had twisted my ankle. I had stepped on the fallen branch of an acacia thorn tree hidden in the grass. One of the long white thorns had pierced through the sole of my boot and into my big toe. Warren helped me remove the backpack, and I sat in the grass to pull the thorn out of the boot and my foot. The thorn broke, leaving the sharp point still inside.

"It's in your foot. We must take it out," Warren said.

I was in pain, yet instead of sympathy from my companions, I heard things like "amputate", "Merthiolate" and "use a blunt knife". I had myself to blame. Not long before, I had dismissed someone's pain with, "If you are looking for sympathy, you will find it in the dictionary; somewhere between shit and syphilis." The chickens had come home to roost.

I removed my boot and sock and used the pliers from my Leatherman tool to pull out the thorn. We set off again, Marie soon stopped to attend to her backpack. When we resumed walking, Warren joked: "If you guys want a break, speak up. There is no need for these Swazi tactics to stop. Just communicate."

There was scant flat ground, so we seemed to be constantly ascending or descending. We sat down for another of the frequent short breaks designed to help us recuperate before taking on the next climb. A bateleur eagle skimmed the trees, scanning the ground for a meal. A large family of warthogs ran parallel to us through the trees until they veered away and disappeared. At the top of the hill, we found another sounder of warthog. Whenever I notice warthogs together, I wonder why the collective noun is sounder. At the next opportunity to speak, I asked about the choice of sounder as a collective noun, because it can mean healthier, sturdier or better. Though it can also indicate someone or something that sounds an alarm. Nobody knew the answer. I joked a committee must have devised the collective noun and resolved to stop thinking about it every time I came across a warthog.

The intact skull of a white rhino lay on the path, indicating it appeared to have died of natural causes. Shortly afterwards, we came across another rhino skull. It had also died of natural causes as far as we could tell, though that must have been years ago, as most of the decayed teeth had detached from the jawbone and lay around the skull. Impala scampered through the trees while we chatted. Another rhino skull lay nearby and a shiver went down my spine. We were in a rhino graveyard; this skull was from a white rhino that had been poached. The hack marks on the bone at the base of the horn were visible. The mood changed.

The bush was dense, and animal paths were overgrown from little use. We were in the winter months and I would have expected the grass cover to recede; but was not the case.

We broke into an elevated open area with fewer trees and short, green grass as landscaped as a golf course. The expansive view was magnificent as we looked across the southern reaches of the Kruger and the snaking, greener track of foliage flanking the Biyamiti River. The Biyamiti watercourse is known for various cuckoos, such as the Jacobin, African and red-chested. I did not expect to spot any because all are summer migrants and had long departed for their North African and European breeding grounds.

We began the long, gentle descent to the Biyamiti River and I hoped we would camp for the night on the riverbed and not the riverbank. Warren called me to the front. He told me to hold my walking pole like a rifle and lead the group towards the river. The group fell back to let me get ahead. It felt like it was just me and the African wild. It was a momentous experience, though feeling alone was unnerving despite knowing a line of folk were behind me. Arnold Bam let me do something similar on Leg Two through the mopane, which was more challenging because there were no landmarks, and the mopane all looked the same, making it difficult to judge direction.

As we left the open grasslands and entered an area of denser bush, a giant plated lizard sunned on a rock formation. The lizard remained for a long time despite us stopping and chatting around it. Once it had enough of us, it hurried into a fissure in the rocks. Three giraffes crossed the path in single file ahead of us and stopped to stare. They moved into the trees when we approached.

The Panthera had covered 15.6 kilometres as we stopped on a long, narrow sandbank in the Biyamiti River. Biyamiti originates from the Shangaan *ku biya* (make a barricade) and *miti* (huts). In the 19th century, the Shangaan erected defence systems around their homes to protect themselves from marauding Swazis. But for us tonight, we came in peace, and there was enough space to accommodate the tents in a straight line, with Ash on one end and Warren, bolstered by an imposing solitary rock, on the other.

Nearby were a clean, elephant-dug hole for drinking water and ankle-deep pools good enough to bathe in. The water extracted from the elephant hole was exquisite in its purity. The river systems in the Kruger flow mainly from west to east and drain through Mozambique into the Indian Ocean. The Biyamiti is one of six rivers, including the Tsendze, Mnondozi and N'wanetsi, all with their sources inside the Kruger. These rivers do not experience the same pollution as the five rivers originating outside Kruger.

It was my treat night and I had a lot to do in preparation for a game of beer pong. Before that, I embarrassed myself. I found a small pool of water near where Clifford was bathing next to the elephant hole where everyone was waiting to fill water bottles. I took off my hiking shorts, leaving on my underpants. When I bent over to wash my face, Clifford burst out laughing.

"José, we can all see your butt," he shouted.

While packing for the hike, I discovered a rip in a pair of underpants. Because the tear was tiny, I decided to wear them for the last time during the hike. Early that morning, when I was lying in my tent at the Mpondo Dam, I contorted my body to slip on the torn underpants. I heard the tear rip when I pulled them up, but had no idea how bad it was.

A hyena approached our camp from the riverbed upstream as we returned to the tents after bathing and collecting water. It looked bewildered when it paused to look at the chaos of colourful tents and humans. We hunched down to make ourselves smaller, which seemed to embolden the hyena and it kept walking at us until it stopped about 20 paces away. The odds were not in its favour, so it turned and crossed to the other side of the river. Downstream, a buffalo bull foraged in the reeds and long grass in the middle of the river.

I kept an eye on all the animal activity while setting up for the beer pong.

I substituted the beer with a half-jack of whisky and adapted the rules to entertain those who do not drink alcohol, including the guides who never drink on a hike. Each person had three chances to throw a ping-pong ball, bouncing it off an upside-down pot into a smaller pot. Success was rewarded with a cap of whisky or nominating someone else. Those who missed all three attempts did not get to drink or nominate, but had to share their most difficult or embarrassing moment of the hike. They were allowed a *strafdop* or penalty drink. We shared stories of embarrassing moments in the Kruger long after the game and whisky were finished. As we had come to expect, Warren had lots to share.

The whisky bottle was empty although I still had to carry it. When Jennifer suggested we spin the bottle to decide who would carry it the rest of the way, I was the first to agree. You'd think she would have known better after being the loser on the two occasions we spun empty bottles of wine on Leg Two. Everyone agreed Jennifer should spin the bottle, given her luck. As she spun the bottle, I held my breath. The bottle did two turns in the sand and pointed back at her. Three out of three. There were comments about it being no wonder the heart-attack birds always went for her. We were sympathetic, nevertheless. It was only day three, and mountainous terrain was ahead.

Jennifer would soon have the last laugh.

For the second day in a row, Clifford was packed and ready to go long before anyone else. He was in a good mood after waking to a booming duet of the southern ground hornbill, his favourite bird. I complimented Clifford on his eagerness and he conceded he did not make coffee that morning while everyone else did. "My efficiency changed when I learnt to do two things at once. Such as packing while I'm eating breakfast," he said.

My tent was still up and I felt under pressure. Even though I was rushing to finish packing, I admired the splendour of saddle-billed storks flying in formation downriver.

We were called together by wannabe Sergeant-Major Warren, who jokingly made us stand to attention in a straight line, army-like, for a warning about the day ahead.

"It will be a long, hard day," he said. "You will not have breakfast. You can eat little bits during our short breaks until lunch. Have you got that?"

Then he added with a smile, "At ease. Let's go."

Marie did not understand we would not have the usual breakfast stop and became increasingly frustrated as the morning wore on.

We crossed the river, following the tracks of the hyena from the previous night. The riverbank was higher on the southern side and, at the top, we stopped to listen to the 'unnh-unnh, unnh-unnh' grunts of a giant eagle owl. There was little chance of spotting the owl, but from our elevated position, I noticed a vulture's crouching silhouette on a dead tree.

The rising sun and the river valley behind us created a perfect group photo opportunity, so we stopped and posed on a large, flat rock. The moment was not spoilt by us standing around the fresh poo of a genet on top of an older dropping. Probably not its own.

We exited the bush onto the S114 dirt road, at the intersection with the private road to Biyamiti Bushveld Camp. A sign with aggressive wording warned motorists not to enter. As if in obedience, we went in the opposite direction for the Mhlambanyatsi River, a tributary of the Biyamiti. Hearing that name brought back memories of when I spent weeks in a small forestry town of the same name in Eswatini. Often as the only guest at the Forester's Arms Hotel during the Covid-19 lockdowns, when the South African and Eswatini borders were closed.

On the ridge high above the tributary, we took our first break. It was a quick stop and I only had time to eat a small apple. After we got going, Alice fell in the long grass. A steenbok raced through the bushes while Warren and Ash helped Alice. Resuming the hike, we descended to the river to make a crossing, then stopped halfway to reconsider. Before us was a large group of grazing buffalo, so we retreated to detour around them. After a short stretch at the top of the ridge, we attempted the descent again. They were now agitated. From the way they grunted and moved, we were obviously not the problem. Buffalo are confident animals, and we suspected lions were nearby. The group got into a huddle to plan a way out.

While the guides discussed strategies, I watched a duiker slip through a stand of magic guarri (*Euclea divinorum*) to escape our group. The plant is not a favourite of browsers although birds enjoy its fruit. This remarkable dense evergreen shrub produces a pheromone when stressed by drought. The pheromone floats on the wind and triggers the release of tannin in the leaves of surrounding trees, making them less palatable and increasing their ability to survive drought. A kudu or giraffe will eat a certain amount but, after a while, the leaves become bitter and the animal will move on. Usually upwind, where the trees have not yet been alerted.

As the duiker disappeared, we faced a white rhino. It stood its ground and took more interest in us than I expected. We approached cautiously until a calf, obscured by the trees, ran to its mother. It is always dangerous to get between an animal mother and her offspring. Warren picked up a short stick to throw if needed, before we turned away from them. We stopped a safe distance away to look back. The rhino cow kept us in sight, her calf at her side. We watched in silent admiration until they turned away, the mother following the calf into the dense magic guarri.

Bright green shoots pockmarked a recently burnt landscape on a path that led us closer to the only two tall trees in the area for a break. Below us were views of the hilly Malelane bushveld terrain. The ground dipped towards denser vegetation on the drainage line at the bottom. A small group of elephant sauntered up the slope closer to us while a bateleur eagle soared across the valley. Clifford picked out two white rhinos through his binoculars. The twitch of the rhino's ears caught his attention; otherwise, he might have missed them among the zebra and the elephants.

Taking a wide berth around the elephants and rhinos, we strolled downhill to the drainage line. Another elephant and a white rhino, hidden behind high grasses, forced us to alter course, and yet again, when another white rhino appeared among the trees.

The vegetation thickened and some impala sprinted at us through the magic guarri and past a lone giraffe. More impala fed on leafy bushes and an abundance of grass shoots. To the south, two young giraffes came out from behind tall thickets and jostled to stare at us. Their mother emerged, decided humans were 'meh' and looked elsewhere.

A bull elephant browsed alone in the trees near our crossing of the Mtlowa River. Looking back, our walk had taken us close to two white rhinos and a small group of wildebeest we had not spotted. Another elephant ambled through the trees, heading for the river. It had been a good day for rhino sightings, so much so I would have lost count if I were not keeping notes. It included two white rhino skulls; I was relieved neither had any visible signs of unnatural causes of death.

The plentiful short, steep downhills and inclines when we crossed the streams feeding into the Mtlowa River called for strength and agility with our heavy backpacks. Warren embraced the opportunities to share his useful guidance on terrain management with a captive audience.

"Engage hill descent, four-wheel-drive, and grip-control. Press every button you've got," he blurted out, in different combinations, at every crossing. I heard competing mutters about Land Rover and Ford. Some were complimentary; most were teasingly not.

Because we walked in silence, we sometimes frightened animals that had not seen us. There was a commotion at the front of the line as a kudu bull raced before us while issuing a hoarse alarm bark. Kudu are always alert and have large, radar-like ears, so I was surprised we had got so close without it hearing us.

LEG SIX

A jackalberry alongside the dry riverbed beckoned for a last brief stop before lunch. I was thankful; the sun was well up and I had only eaten an apple and two rusks all day. I was ready to snack on my crackers and cheese, then decided to wait. I heard Marie complaining again about not having had a chance to eat properly.

After we moved away from the river, we hiked through sparse mixed woodland and thorn thickets on marshy ground. The guides stopped to confer and we waited in line behind them. There appeared to be nothing unusual and I wondered why they needed to talk, when Jennifer spoke up.

"What is that? Something shiny. Looks like a rock or something."

I peered through the thickets and there was a small building. I knew we would cross the H-3 tarred road from Malelane Gate to Skukuza, although that did not explain the man-built structure in front of us. I was about to ask, when, without explanation, the guides started walking and we all went into customary silence.

Emerging from the bush, our gleeful team trooped into the picnic area of the Afsaal Trader's Rest. Afsaal, which is Afrikaans for, 'A place to break the journey', is one of the busiest daytime stops for tourists in the Kruger and one of my favourite places for lunch or a coffee break. The transport riders of the 19th century used Afsaal as a camping spot because of its exceptional location next to a strip of gabbro that attracts antelope year-round. The surrounding granite is not appealing to animals and with the gabbro so alluring by comparison, the area has always had lots of wildlife.

Sitting at a long table between the car park and the restaurants, we ensured we were near a bushy area to hang our dew-dampened tents to dry. A few bold tourists asked about the tents and hiking apparel. Warren, worried someone might complain because of our untidy array, asked us to pack up.

We had hiked 10 kilometres and had about eight to go, so I contemplated whether a big lunch would translate into a sluggish afternoon. Carpe diem came to mind, prompting me to order a bacon and egg breakfast with chips and an ice-cold Coke. I would have even had a beer but alcohol was not sold there.

Lourens had a credit card, which was helpful as most of us were not carrying money. Another bonus was throwing out three days of trash to save weight. Jennifer made a show of disposing of the empty whisky bottle she had expected to carry to the end. The other benefit of stopping at Afsaal was its clean ablution facilities we all used with some relief. We filled up with borehole water while we waited for lunch. Borehole water is always better than chlorinated municipal water, yet even Afsaal's water made me appreciate the quality of the water we had enjoyed from the Biyamiti River.

Two men walked past our table from the carpark and headed for the picnic area at the back. I did a double take. Ross Flood and Steve Johnson are friends from Port Elizabeth, my old hometown. They have a timeshare at Ngwenya Lodge, outside the Kruger on the Crocodile River, and are avid fans of the park. While I was delighted to bump into them, I was also uncomfortable. I had told everyone how rough and challenging The Kruger Trails hike was, but here I was, sipping an ice-cold Coke and enjoying the good life among tourists. To make matters worse, I started the day with fresh clothing after three days of wearing the same kit. I felt like I had just walked out of a dressing room. After we said our goodbyes and they went to join their families at the picnic spot, I was taking a mouthful of bacon and egg when I heard someone say, "That's not how it works." I looked up and it was Steve's wife, Jess, looking at me mock-accusingly. Damn timing. With a mouthful of food, I couldn't even defend myself.

After packing and putting on our backpacks, we took pictures at the Afsaal welcome sign. Ross and Steve were leaving with their families and it turned into a photo-op after I crouched to hear a message from Steve and Jess's three-year-old daughter.

Instead of crossing the tarred road into the bush, we headed south on the road to Malelane Gate so we could take pictures around the Jock of the Bushveld plaque at the intersection with the H2-2 road. I cringed every time a car drove past in case my friends caught me walking on the tarred road. As luck would have it, it happened. I surrendered myself to my sorry fate. I knew my friends would remember my hike through the Kruger with an image of me dressed in natty hiking gear, stuffing my face with a bacon and egg breakfast, and ambling along a tarred road. Such is life.

It was too late to save my pride. Anyway, we soon headed east into the gabbro strip of sweetveld between the Biyamiti and Mhlambane river systems. The grass was thick and the ground stony with few trees. It reminded me of the grasslands between Satara and Lower Sabie on Legs Four and Five. Warren was in the lead and almost walked into a hyena sleeping in the shade of a thorn bush. The perplexed looking animal sprang up and ran off.

Warren had warmed to the 'Louis break', and we had a couple of those thrown in during the afternoon, although we could have done with more in the heat. It felt like a treat when at one of those stops Warren gave in to our sighs and said we could take off backpacks. I languished in thick grass beneath a large knob-thorn alongside a smaller marula tree.

After we got going, a breeze took the edge off the hottest part of the day. Every stop was welcome because we had a chance to catch our breath and learn something new. I sighed with relief when Ash stopped to pick up the oval carapace of a long-dead Speke's hinge-back tortoise. The name refers to the hinge at the shell's rear end to protect the retracted legs when taking shelter in tight spaces. Parts of the skeleton fell out when Ash turned it over to show us the concave underside, which indicated it was a male. The carapace was flat, but not nearly as flat as the well-named pancake tortoise native to Kenya and Tanzania.

During a break, Clifford and I discussed our new perspectives. "These days have sparked my sense of adventure," he said. "The night before last, when we were harassed in our campsite by hyenas, hippos and elephants, was fascinating. The experiences on foot in this amazing place with my bush family, the Panthera, are overwhelming. From the butterflies, spiders and grasses to all we learn. There is no other way to take this all in. I enjoy the time away from reality by being in nature and keeping adrenaline alive."

The long grass tugged at my boots as we descended to the Mhlambane River. A rectangular grassy clearing, the size of a football field and surrounded by acacia, marula and bushwillow trees, made it feel like we had walked onto a village green. The only animal visible was a hyena at the edge of the tree line. The wind was in our favour with the setting sun behind us, so the hyena must have struggled to determine what we were. It hesitantly approached until it observed our numbers and ran off in the direction we were headed.

From the elevated bank of the Mhlambane River, the path dropped sharply to the riverbed. A tight bend meant we had to go down one at a time, helping each other to avoid slipping. Warren used his binoculars to identify a motionless silhouette on the riverbank downriver. To the naked eye it looked like a leopard. I was disappointed when he told us it was an oddly shaped rock.

Warren captured our feelings at the base of the slope when he saw the flowing river and threw up his arms in a victory gesture. It had been a long, hot hike of 23.6 kilometres, and we were relieved there was flowing water so we would not have to dig or use an old elephant hole.

I stripped off and washed, concealed from the camp by rocks and the bend in the river. The water was not as cold as the Biyamiti. I sat on a submerged flat rock to wash as the water flowed over me. It was peaceful and invigorating. I was loath to move. But the light was fading fast and I couldn't safely stay out on my own any longer.

A fire pit was dug in an enclave of dense vegetation on one side, and a cluster of boulders on the river side of the sandbank. We prepared and ate the evening meal on soft white sand close to the fire to fight off the encroaching cold. It felt like a beach party. The trill of birds and insects provided the music. While cooking his dinner, Clifford pulled out a cutlery combo with the spoon, knife and fork held together by a carabiner clip.

"Clifford, you know how throughout the hike we keep improving our equipment; how we use it, and what we bring along?" I asked. "There's no point in keeping cutlery clipped together. It's a pain having to unclip the item you need. Rather let the spoon, knife and fork stay separate," I advised.

He didn't seem convinced.

I should have kept my mouth shut.

Marie laughed when she heard loud, crunching sounds from Clifford. She turned to him and asked: "I thought you said you were having pasta for dinner?"

He gave her a look that said, "Don't ask!" then admitted his pasta hadn't cooked properly and he was now munching on uncooked pasta and powdered sauce. Clifford finished his meal, crunching one spoonful at a time, while Marie chuckled.

When we were done eating, Jennifer treated us to a Dutch delicacy. She opened a pack of stroopwafel. Thin, round waffle cookies made from two crisp biscuit layers with a caramel filling. Jennifer encouraged us to eat this in the Dutch way; and most of us made coffee and let the cookie sit on the cup until the filling melted. I was not having coffee, so I ate the delicious cookie as a dessert. It hit the spot. After four days in the bush, a stale rusk would have tasted great.

We spoke at length about poaching and the dehorning of rhinos. Warren was involved in the programme and said he had dehorned hundreds of rhinos. He spoke emotionally about the effects on the animal and himself. The excision of the horn is painless if done correctly. Although, it does not detract from the trauma a rhino experiences through being captured and sedated. I shivered as Warren spoke about the personal strain, the sinister smell that clung to his body, and the blood that ran off him at home in the shower when things did not go according to plan. Later, the conversation lightened and we chatted long into the night around the fire. We laughed and joked noisily.

After 28 nights in the bush, it was the second to last night, and the hole in my heart I knew would come was beginning to take shape. That was probably why we stayed up late into the night before we reluctantly threw sand over the dying embers and headed to our tents. It was the coldest night yet. I woke up shivering countless times. I thought about what more I could do to keep warm. However, there was nothing else I could wear not already on my body.

The early-morning calls of francolins and spurfowl rang across the riverbank and woke us. Nobody was more animated than Clifford; when I climbed out of my tent, he approached with a swagger.

"José, maybe you should clip your fork to a keyring or something," he said with a smirk as he handed over my fork. He had found it lying in the sand beside the fire. I had learnt a lesson and more was to come.

The air was crisp and a fresh breeze brushed my face as I cleaned my teeth in the river. The Mhlambane River, meaning 'small river', is called that because it is little more than a rivulet flowing in a wide riverbed with banks far apart. Making the river appear even smaller. The first rays of sun lit up impala grazing on the riverbank and blanketed the surrounding bushveld in warm golden hues.

After setting off, we stopped to take pictures beneath a large sycamore fig. Warren told us about the symbiotic relationship between the fig tree and wasps. It is a favourite story of the guides and those who had done prior Legs heard it again. I never tire of hearing it. Warren added a fresh twist.

"Vegans won't eat the figs," Warren said, referring to the fact that because a wasp pollinates the fig, some vegans say an animal is involved.

"So, Warren..." I asked, "...vegans who chew their nails, how does that work for them? Are they still vegans?"

After two days of encountering rhino skulls, we spotted a buffalo skull in the sand when we turned to climb up the bank on the other side of the river. Climbing the bank, just two or three metres higher than the riverbed, saw a dramatic temperature change. We would have had a better night if we slept on the riverbank. The warm breeze reminded me of the hot, dry katabatic berg wind that blows from the plateau down to the coast in the Eastern Cape, where I grew up.

We soon descended to the river again to make a crossing. However, the riverbed was marshier than it looked. We walked on the soft, energy-sapping sand until we found a suitable place to cross. A grey lourie called out as we got closer. The go-away bird loves surface water and we were disturbing its peace.

Breakfast called after a long, easy stretch on a management road. We found an outcrop of elevated rocks beneath a jackalberry tree on the outside of a tight bend on the Mhlambane River. The refreshing cool breeze, the soft morning light and the melody of birds and the harmonies found in running water, soothed us. I crunched on an apple, so cold it felt like it had just been removed from a fridge, while watching a bateleur eagle glide above the hills and over the river in search of prey. It was a female with primarily white flight feathers and a narrow black terminal band.

The bush was thicker in the Malelane area than anywhere else in the Kruger, and we were always going up or down the granite koppies and through pockets of thick sweetveld. The area receives the highest rainfall in the Kruger. So there is considerable diversity in plant and animal species in a confined geographical space that ranges from relatively high altitudes to valley woodlands. The red bushwillow and the magic guarri dominate the landscape, although we also came across less common trees, such as the Cape chestnut (*Calodendrum capense*) and the Zulu mulberry (*Manilkara concolor*). A massive mingerhout tree (*Breonadia salicina*) had a thick base and grey longitudinal ridges in the bark reflecting its age and maturity. It was still healthy even though it had signs of being burnt by fire. Stepping over its exposed roots, I reflected it would be a perfect obstacle for a bunny hop on a bike. Throughout the hike when following animal paths, I often imagined racing through the terrain on my mountain bike.

A steep, rocky path took us towards the drainage line, where four kudu cows ran away from us. Lunch was in a small grove surrounded by so dense bushes and trees, I struggled to find enough sun to dry my tent. I heard the cry of an African fish eagle, but thanks to all the trees and thick vegetation, I was unable to spot it.

We reminisced while having lunch. "I had two mind-sets throughout the journey," said Clifford. "Firstly, enjoying a group dynamic that led to a unique experience and lasting friendships. Secondly, holding on to the selfish reason, I embarked on the trail to spend time with my thoughts in an environment I hold dear. The first Leg was the only one in which I carried my phone as a camera. Thereafter, I ditched the phone to feel fully immersed in the experience. I am seldom able to disconnect for days."

Lourens added, "The hike gave me an appreciation of the Kruger and how the vegetation changes as you walk. The part I never expected was getting to meet new people and making great friends, including the 10 rangers on the trail. Each brought something different in terms of personality and knowledge. We shared experiences, jokes and tough times. The camaraderie was special; whenever anybody was in trouble, everybody was there to help."

"The only problem will be when we finish," Lourens continued. "What's next? For all of us, there will be a big hole. How can you match this? I think it's probably impossible."

"I got to experience this with my dad," Jennifer said, putting her hand affectionately on her father's arm.

After lunch, we climbed to the top of the ridge before descending to the Matjulu River. In the distance, an elephant browsed alone in the trees, separate from a group that milled around a small waterhole. Our path took us into thick bush on the drainage line. Warren stopped, before taking us across a creek that filtered into the Matjulu River. He threw a stick into a thicket next to the path. Nothing stirred. It looked like an ideal spot for a leopard to take an afternoon nap, and we didn't want a surprise encounter.

High on the same path, a black rhino midden had been scraped under and around a bush. A black rhino midden contrasts with a white rhino's, because their middens are usually open and unobstructed. The other telltale sign is black rhino dung is reddish-brown due to the tannins in roots and bark. White rhino dung is black owing to the high levels of melanin in the grass the animal eats.

After crossing the brook, we followed wildlife paths on the contour line until we made an abrupt turn to go uphill through sparse grass. To my surprise, we were already where we would camp for our last night in the bush. Warren had concealed water drums nearby. We could have extracted water from the Matjulu River, but Warren did not want us roughing it on the last night. After a relatively short 14.4 kilometres of ups and downs, he had other plans for us that evening.

The campsite on uneven and stony ground was dry, with scattered grass and dull thorn thickets. The views to the south were magnificent from our elevated position. We could see the 630-metre Tlhalabye Hill we would climb the next day. A herd of elephants walked through the trees headed for the twin mounds of the hill.

I pitched my tent between thorn bushes, with Clifford behind me and Warren further back. A ladybird, the same bronze as the poles of my tent, walked up the bare, arched, central support post to the highest point. After a pause, she turned around, walked down again and flew away. Across cultures, ladybugs symbolise good fortune and now, on the thirtieth and final time I was pitching a tent inside the Kruger Park, there was more to it than being lucky. I felt blessed.

I took time to appreciate the glorious surroundings at sunset, including spectacular views of mountains to the west. To the north, the Steilberg Mountain formed a high rocky ridge etched with gold by the rays of the setting sun. Steilberg is an Afrikaans term that translates to 'steep mountain' and I was stunned to see two elephants headed up the sheer incline.

Brigitte put her nursing skills to good use by attending to Alice's feet. During the lunch break, Brigitte also assisted Warren with his aching feet. I had no idea Alice had been suffering with blisters; they did not slow her down, nor did an uncomfortable backpack early in the hike until she modified it.

Clifford was trying to learn Italian and came to my tent to borrow my pen for his lesson, as he did almost every night. Because it was the last night, I told Clifford to keep my spare pen.

I was showered and in slipslops when Warren told us to put our boots back on and bring a cup. He said we were going for a walk. Warren offered to take our cups as he had a small backpack he had concealed with the water drums. We walked to the S110 Matjulu Loop dirt road, with the Steilberg Mountain behind it. The two elephants I had spotted were now close to the summit. It didn't look like they were part of the large troop of elephants halfway up the mountain slope.

We walked to a large flat rock that formed a stage adorned with a fallen marula tree. The tree had a kink, which formed a saddle, and I sat on it to admire the valley. Marie sat higher up on the tree in front of me. I regarded Tlhalabye Hill with apprehension, remembering a tough climb up Lion's Head in Cape Town.

Warren interrupted my thoughts, "What can I do to make this occasion even better?" He pointed to the setting sun between the Khandzalive and Matjulu mountains, then swept his arm over the rolling hills of the Malelane bushveld to the south. Large tracts of land in the southern Kruger were under Swazi control in the 19th century, and Malelane is named after the ilala palms in the area, and the Malelane Regiment of King Mswati II.

Warren took out a bottle of Amarula, the famous cream liqueur made with the fruit of the marula tree. The marula is known in some communities as the 'medicine tree' and is used to treat an array of ailments from constipation to anaemia and malaria. The tree is sacred in traditional marriage and fertility rites in some African cultures.

Warren pulled out a glass from his backpack branded with the Amarula logo, which he presented to Lourens. He complimented Lourens on his vision of putting together a team to hike the Kruger National Park. Lourens' dream was one which we were all fortunate to share. We drank a toast to Lourens. As the sun dipped below the horizon, I enjoyed a second tot of Amarula while toasting Warren. He and Ash made do with sparkling grape juice.

Ash was recording a conversation with me, away from the rocks where the rest of the group noisily carried on with festivities, when Warren motioned to us to keep quiet. He pointed westwards. The flapping ears of an agitated elephant were silhouetted against the setting sun. I crouched behind the rocks while Ash reached for his rifle. At the same time, the elephants I had seen earlier were headed down the slopes of the Steilberg Mountain towards us. We were in their way and they made no effort to slow or turn away.

"Grab your things, let's go," Warren said.

We walked quickly in single file on the road to move out of the way of the elephants. They turned at the flat rock platform we had used and headed in the same direction as us, seemingly content to walk alongside, until the road led us away.

Flakes of ash rained down like black snow as we walked to camp. I had noticed soot lying on the ground earlier in the day. I thought nothing of it because bushfires and controlled burning occur in the Kruger. I looked around, but there was no smoke. The papery ash was from farmers burning sugar cane fields before the harvest. These dark flakes fall at night when insect-eating bats are active, and I wondered if bats might mistake it for food and ingest it to their detriment. Burning makes the sugar cane harvest easier and reduces accidents and costs. Yet it is an air pollutant that has been discontinued in much of the world. There are no such strictures in South Africa.

Back at camp, Warren pointed out a tree he said we should congregate behind if the elephants came through our camp. To me, it was nothing more than a tapered thorn bush, so I took no comfort in that. I suspect at least one lesson in the course for advanced hiking guides is dedicated to always having a plan B. Warren could check that box.

Arie and Brigitte called everyone together for their treat. They brought out two different types of nougat; we could have one of each. One was almond with chocolate, and the other was an Amarula fudge. The fudge was my favourite. I was never a fan of Amarula although that has since changed … maybe because of the bland diet of our hike. More probably because of where we were and what it signified.

Tlhalabye Hill

I woke to the rattling chirps and whistles of francolins and sandgrouse. The tents were wet from a heavy dewfall as the cloud cover from the night before cleared. The camp was eerily quiet as we packed. The silence was made worse because of its contrast to the exuberance of the previous morning on the Mhlambane River. There was sadness in the air. While dismantling my tent, I found the pen I had given Clifford the night before lying between our two tents. I said something to him about having the last laugh, yet I wasn't in the mood for laughing.

Clifford was not the only one losing things. Ash had spent the night panicking his treasured watch was lost. He searched his possessions inside the tent countless times without luck. Ash couldn't look outside until morning. At first light, he retraced his steps of the night before and found the watch on a stone close to where he had showered.

We were ready to go, except for Warren, who had problems with his rifle. When he did the routine morning check of the weapon, the pin kept slipping and would not load the bullet. Warren managed a temporary fix with duct tape, one of two essential items we carry on the hike; the other being cable ties. A round of compliments followed when Warren told us he was ready to go.

We crossed the Matjulu River and stopped when we heard an alarm call of a vervet monkey. The monkey was doing a poor job of hiding in the riverine trees as it climbed higher, possibly to take refuge from a leopard. Everyone was desperate to find a leopard, and this part of the Kruger was our best chance. Ten pairs of eyes searched the trees, but leopards are elusive and do their best to remain hidden. On the other hand, a group of impala didn't seem alarmed by our proximity as we ascended the riverbank. After 30 days of walking in the Kruger, I was now comfortable being close to wild animals; although, I suspect the familiarity was not reciprocal.

A fallen tree at a small waterhole meant we could take an early break and pause for photographs of the group seated on the trunk with the Tlhalabye Hill in the background. The calm before the storm. The terrain changed from a gentle slope to a proper climb. We headed for the saddle between the two mounds of Tlhalabye Hill. As we started up the foot slopes, an impala dashed at us. It stopped, looked at us in bewilderment, made a U-turn and raced back to where it had come from.

Warren told us the cairn where four of us would place the stones we had carried from Crooks' Corner was on the peak to the right. I was thankful we did not have to climb the higher eastern elevation, over which a majestic martial eagle soared, silhouetted by the rising sun. To my surprise, there were fresh mounds of elephant dung on the narrow, steep, zigzagging animal path. It was difficult enough for us smaller creatures to negotiate.

I wondered why an elephant would go up there when there was plenty of food and water at the mountain's base. Although, on the slope and at the top, were several varieties of the broad-leaf trees that elephants love. Still, they were also found on the grassland, so could not have been why an elephant was climbing the hill. Fresh lion tracks on the path brought no comfort.

I was behind the two guides from when we started the climb and I worked hard to stay close to them. I was carrying about 20 kilograms on my back, and without much of a path through the rocks and wet grass, every stop was a welcome respite. Even if it was short-lived. The rest of the group trailed behind. The line lengthening as we climbed higher. I noticed, with disquiet, the unfairness of the short rest stops for those at the back of the line. As soon as the last person caught up, Warren set off again. Not giving those at the back a chance to rest. It frequently happens in cycling, especially with mountain bikers. The front-runners stop to wait for others at the top of a long climb. They get a good rest but race off when the stragglers catch up. The riders at the back often have no chance to recover.

I was at the front with the guides when Marie snapped. Warren had marched on again just as a sweating and panting Marie caught up with the group.

"You've had your break. We need one, too," Marie exclaimed. "Those at the back haven't had a single break."

She chided Warren and Ashraf. "Usually, you walk up mountains at the slowest person's pace to ensure everyone can keep up. Or you take frequent breaks to allow slower walkers to catch up and take a breath."

She complained slower walkers were falling further from the safety of the rifle bearers. Marie expressed concern, too, there is a higher risk of sprained ankles when people try to ascend a mountain fast. The guides admitted they were used to walking on flat terrain, where they need not think about these things. After that, the guides made sure the group stayed closer together and everyone had a chance to rest.

I thought I heard the trumpet of an elephant when I was close to the top of the hill, but I wasn't sure I had heard correctly. I would have dismissed the thought if I had not stepped over elephant dung on the trail.

When we reached the top, a fresh wind blew and the sky was a bright, crisp blue. The elephant I had heard trumpet and whose dung littered the trail browsed the trees in the saddle. The appropriateness of the elephant's presence was not lost on the group. After all, The Kruger Trail is about following in the footsteps of giants, and we had done just that. The words of Sir Edmund Hillary, the first mountaineer to conquer Mount Everest with his Sherpa, Tenzing Norgay, came to mind: "It's not the mountain we conquer, but ourselves."

We had breakfast, took pictures and shot videos with our mobile phones. Warren pointed out the cairn where we should place our stones. It was not what I expected because it included big stones and small rocks that couldn't have been carried from Crooks' Corner. Never mind from the bottom of the hill. The Zulu word for a cairn is *isivivane* and is linked to their cultural tradition of putting up *isivivane* at important sites as an area is traversed. They may have learnt this from Arab traders in ancient times, although it may be something done by all ancient travellers. Stones as markers have been used by everyone from Scottish shepherds and travellers to the Jewish tradition of leaving a stone each time one visits the grave of a loved one. 'Càrn' is a Gaelic term that symbolises peace or gratitude.

I shared my disappointment about the big stones on the cairn with Warren and he speculated there may have been another cairn. Still, we were standing at the official GPS location he had been given.

I walked away from the laughter and banter for a private moment of reflection and stood on a flat rock, looking north to the distant horizon, letting it all sink in. I was relieved the challenge I had embarked on years before had worked out. There were obstacles nobody could have foreseen; the Covid-19 pandemic added a year to the journey and led to my relocation to Eswatini after being stranded there behind closed borders for six months. I survived the physical challenges and the inherent dangers of walking wild. There was much to be thankful for.

Brigitte joined me to gaze at the breathtaking panorama of savanna and woodland we had crossed on foot. From the top of the mountain, we took in the power and splendour of the African wilderness.

"This makes me intensely aware of the greatness of nature that surrounds us everywhere," Brigitte said. "It is challenging mentally and physically, but the reward is fantastic and worth everything. Even being exposed to danger is thrilling. The friendships that develop are amazing. The suffering and laughter bring us together."

Now, we needed to make our way down. The descent from any hill or mountain is always more demanding on the legs than going up, and with the weight on our backs, it was perilous. Warren led us eastwards towards the canyon of dense vegetation that ran from the top of the saddle. I would have gone straight down because it looked less steep. Although with scant shrubbery and few trees, I admit we could not see all the way over the edge. I looked back at Marie, who shook her head in bewilderment, while others in the group muttered protests.

Tension was high, and the group's camaraderie at the top of Tlhalabye Hill dissipated once we started the hazardous descent. The going was challenging, with slippery rocks, thick bush and no clear trail. In response to a snide comment about the route when we stopped for a quick rest, Warren explained he was following the GPS path mapped out by Louis Lemmer. It was Warren's first time there, and he admitted he had not scouted alternatives before we embarked on the descent.

We helped each other where we could. At one stage, we took off our backpacks and passed them down one at a time before we took turns to slide on our backsides down slippery rocks. As we negotiated our way around a mass of tangled vegetation, I heard the rich, throaty chirps and bubbly notes of a dark-capped yellow warbler. The song was soothing. Halfway, we entered a clearing where a pair of klipspringers scurried up the rocky outcrop, before disappearing over the top.

There was a lot of slipping and sliding on the way. Ash fell near the bottom and, without a pause, rolled into a seated position, folded his arms, and mimicked Bugs Bunny.

"What's up, doc?" he asked squeakily, trying to break the tension with levity.

We stood around Ash with some concern. Not that he needed it.

Marie was near breaking point and gestured to a path running south on the other side of the drainage line.

"Warren, do you see that path?" Marie asked. "It's going that way." She swung her arm from the path and pointed to the flat ground and the Malelane Rest Camp beyond, where we would finish.

"Yes. I do," Warren replied frostily.

I knew then we weren't going that way.

Marie told me later: "The route we went down was incredibly unsafe. Had we met a buffalo or an elephant on their way up, there would have been no escape for us or the animal. The guys around me were in full agreement, but no one said a word, so I felt it was my lot to speak up on behalf of the group. My breaking point was one of frustration; not exertion," she said.

Two dainty, striped kingfishers flew over us. They are territorial and their piercing, high-pitched, defensive call made us look up. They landed in a dead tree and I wondered why they were there because there was no water nearby. Warren stopped to explain the striped kingfisher is a subfamily of kingfishers, though it is not a piscivore (a carnivore that primarily eats fish). Striped kingfishers eat mostly grasshoppers, insects and occasionally small lizards and rodents.

Three southern ground hornbills lifted off the path ahead as we started the descent for an outcrop of trees. The elevation gave me a view from above of their white wingtips before they landed among the trees ahead.

I began preparing to surrender myself to civilisation. My thoughts were interrupted by the bloody skull of an impala, with horns still attached. A large piece of the hide lay nearby, next to the bottom part of the jaw. The putrid smell of death wafted over. Ash picked up the skull by the horns, put it over his head, and strutted around as if trying to avoid a predator. The wild is Ash's playground.

Warren reminded us we were not yet done. "Let's go. This trail isn't going to walk itself," he said.

I was surprised when we stopped for another break within sight of the end. On the other side of the Crocodile River, there were buildings and cultivated farmland. The stop was mostly ceremonial, so we could absorb what we had achieved. I complimented Jennifer on having learnt to live with the 'heart-attack' birds. We told hyperbolic Chuck Norris jokes about being tough, instead of reminiscing.

Warren encouraged us to move on by suggesting we go for lunch at the Pestana Kruger Lodge, just outside the Malelane Gate. It has magnificent gardens and a scenic view of the Crocodile River. Nobody was going to say no to that.

I was ready to tuck into a proper meal. "Let's go," I said. "This lunch isn't going to eat itself."

We were lined up behind Warren when he turned around to check everyone was ready to go. We were, but he wasn't. Somebody pointed out the chest strap of his backpack was not clipped in. "It's also a whistle," he said as he clipped it into place.

There is always time to learn. I had hiked more than 600 kilometres over 36 days with an identical buckle. I had no idea a safety whistle was built into it and a surprised Jennifer admitted she didn't know either.

I bade a silent goodbye to the vervet monkeys playing in the trees and two giraffes strolling down a service road. A lone impala grazed next to the fence of the Malelane Rest Camp. We had hiked just 8.2 kilometres when we arrived at the gate that marked the finish of The Kruger Trail. The final Leg was a short, brutal 92.5 kilometres. The Panthera had hiked 605 kilometres from Crooks' Corner to Malelane Rest Camp. We hugged and high-fived each other. I was not the only one drying my eyes. Lourens was emotional as he said, "I was lucky to have my daughter walk the whole Kruger Trail with me, which made the experience so much more special. Jennifer and I grew our existing bond. For me, it was more than a hike in nature, because I did it with my daughter, which made it almost a spiritual experience."

After lunch at the Pestana Lodge restaurant, Ash and Clifford collected the water drums from our first and second night camps, and I drove with Warren to collect the drums from the last. Warren parked the vehicle on the Matjulu Loop Road, and we walked to where we had concealed the empty water drums. I hoisted the unwieldy bundle held together by a chain onto my back to follow Warren to the vehicle. On the way to Lower Sabie Rest Camp, we noticed a white rhino close to the rest camp. Then we drove around people in parked cars viewing a leopard in a tree.

After a hot shower and a change into comfortable clothes and shoes, we met for dinner at the rest camp restaurant. Arie and Brigitte presented us with French champagne, and while sipping it, we watched Lourens lay out his treat.

"We are having a *Shot in the Park*," Lourens announced as he laid out a colourful array of bottles.

"The shot is made up of four liqueurs, each representing something. At the bottom is peppermint liqueur, a cleanser for our gap year because of Covid-19. Above that is Stroh rum for toughness."

My cheer turned to dread. I had bad memories of Stroh rum shots from my younger years.

"Jägermeister is for the animals, and is topped off with Amarula cream for the vegetation and water along the hike."

The concoction was as enjoyable as it was colourful.

After the meal, Lourens brought out genuine Cuban cigars. The table was outside on the balcony and the staff locked the doors and turned off the lights. A haze of smoke on the deck brought the curtain down on the final act. The stars twinkled, hippos grunted and a cool breeze whispered through the reeds and riverside trees. We toasted shared camaraderie; challenges overcome; and memories of the expansive wild we traversed. Amid the dangers, we found comfort and warmth in companionship and serenity in the beauty of nature.

Reflections

Metal washers and a chromic suture loop have held my collarbone in place after a mountain-bike race crash. Though physically fit, I was in my mid-fifties when I mulled hiking 600-plus kilometres with 20 kilograms or more on my back. Could I do it?

One of my favourite sayings, made famous by John Lennon in his ode to his son Sean, *Beautiful Boy*, galvanised me into action. Lennon sang, "Life is what happens to you while you're busy making other plans." Later, I learnt the quote originated with cartoonist and journalist Allen Saunders in 1957. I looked at my feet and remembered the tagline of the sneakers I often wear while jogging: 'Just Do It'.

There is always a way around life's challenges. None could have anticipated a pandemic – Covid-19 – would engulf the world; cause millions of deaths and illnesses, and interrupt the hike for a year. In the dark days of lockdown and isolation, I feared we would never complete our journey. When I began this adventure, I did not know I would move to a neighbouring country.

Today, I look back on our great trek with pride and a sense of triumph. We, the Panthera, overcame the dangers and peripheral challenges, part of walking in the wild of nature. On any day, we encountered and overcame potential life-or-death situations. There was little, if any, room for missteps. I am thankful Clifford had the presence of mind to call me back from the exposed rock on the Letaba River, when I went to collect water from where a crocodile could have dragged me off the rocks. I am embarrassed I put the group and an elephant in danger at the Matiovila hot springs, because I tried to get a picture of me with an elephant in the frame.

The Kruger Trail is a unique experience for those lucky enough to undertake it. The journey I was privileged to participate in is unmatched, even for professional guides. Warren Deyzel told me when he was a child, he was brought to the Kruger several times a year by his mother. By age 10, Warren knew every road, whether tar or dusty sand path, ploughed through the Kruger.

"The Kruger Trail is the cream of the crop, the epitome of guiding in the Kruger National Park," Warren said. He and all the guides do advanced training called Special Knowledge and Skills in Dangerous Game. It took Warren more than 4,500 hours of walking over almost six years and 770 potentially perilous encounters with the Big Five to achieve that qualification. To be certified as competent usually takes 10 to 15 years; Warren did it in half that time. The achievement is a testament to Warren's dedication to nature and love for the Kruger. Fittingly enough, Warren was a finalist in the Field Guides Association of Southern Africa's prestigious 2023 Safari Guide of the Year award. It honours the hard work; sacrifice; training; skills development; knowledge and expertise of field guides across southern Africa.

We and creatures of the wild are social beings, and the protection of the family unit is paramount. Our immersion in the wild also brought awareness of the differences between humans and animals, including the senses and their role in survival. Civilisation has emboldened human beings, and weaponry has numbed us. Survival dictates life for animals in the wild; habitats, prey and defences are constantly adapted to ensure this. Eyesight, hearing, smell and the ability to detect movement are enhanced. Animals also use camouflage. The ability to change skin colour in chameleons can be to avoid detection. It can also be used for mating or in reaction to threats.

Humans have negatively impacted nature. I shudder when I think of the hostility of the elephants at the base of Steilberg Mountain. I was close enough to look into their eyes and understand how much they dislike humankind. Their rage comes from centuries of being hunted for trophies. The rhinos in the Kruger and elsewhere are disfigured with their iconic horns removed. Yet, the slaughter, although diminished, continues with impoverished poachers risking their lives to cater to the desires of wealthy, mostly south-east Asian, markets.

Meat poaching, according to Conservation Action Trust, has surged 200 percent since the pandemic, and is possibly the greatest threat to the Kruger National Park. South Africa has the world's highest Gini coefficient; the statistical measure of economic inequality in a population. Without economic upliftment of the poverty-stricken populations around the Kruger, this wilderness reserve is at risk. Lourens' words ring true: "If we could walk through the Kruger in 36 days, it is not an infinite resource, and if it's not looked after, it won't be there in the future."

Courts have been inconsistent, with the accused in some cases being cautioned and discharged after being apprehended for setting up snares and being in possession of weapons inside the Kruger. Some of the top guides have left the Park for the better-protected and wildlife-rich private reserves around the Kruger.

The Kruger Trail is still in its infancy and after our group concluded Leg Six, the number of hikers who had completed all Legs from start to finish was just 22. Putting together harmonious groups with competent rangers is a mixture of luck and skill. The guides are hand-picked by Louis Lemmer and rotate between the groups. In 2023, Louis had his pick of 14 qualified guides. Exposing the hiking groups to different professional guides adds interest and diversity to the hike. The guides' personal interests range from astronomy to expertise in botany or tracking, and there is much to be learnt from each. We were led by 10 guides, including Mark Montgomery, an extra on Leg Four. Some guides left a lasting impression on the group; Bjinse Visser is one. In addition to having designed a trusted bullet for the personal rifles of numerous guides, he is spoken of with reverence and trepidation. "I have never met him, but I almost feel like I have because the group talked about him so often," says Marie.

I caught up with Arnold Bam, who led us on Leg Two, but left to pursue a career in the banana plantations of Mozambique, to find out how he felt about his guiding experience. "It was an honour and a privilege to have been part of such an organisation, and I miss it with every fibre of my being, every single day. Once you have had the red soil between your toes, tasted the sweet water of the Tsendze and slept under the stars and heard the lions roar, you are forever captivated by the majesty of nature. I have great memories of my time in the Kruger. I have visited amazing places, experienced truly amazing events and, as a guide in the Kruger National Park, I had the privilege of meeting some of the best people from all over the world," he said.

Part of the magic of hiking through the Kruger is an immersion in the biosphere. Learning about the terrain; identifying the smells; sounds and even the waste animals leave behind. I fell asleep to the melodic hoot of an owl, the grunts and roar of lions, and the noisy mating of hippos. I was pricked by thorns; swiped spider webs off my face; smelt the fragrance of the grasses and stepped over mushrooms on slender stalks rooted in elephant dung. We took life-giving water from mossy trickles in rocks and from a sulphuric hot spring where elephants had romped; we also drank the sweet and pure water of the Biyamiti River.

Experts cannot agree on the population size of elephants the Kruger can sustain. African elephants have the most prolonged gestation period of any mammal and they live long. Some argue for a return to culling, which stopped in 1994 primarily as a result of public pressure. Others say it is a myth there are too many elephants in the Kruger, despite their destructive toll on vegetation. Elephants spend more than three-quarters of their time feeding and consume about 150 kilograms of vegetation daily. A balance must be found between biodiversity and the quantity of elephants. The number of trees in the savanna of eastern Kruger has declined significantly, mainly owing to elephant activity. Some alternatives are already being applied. For example, we saw trees in locations where tourists do not go with tree trunks protected by wire mesh.

Elephants had the most important impact on me, and they present the most significant danger to those doing Kruger hikes. There have been a few incidents where elephants have been shot. We are in their environment, placing ourselves and them at risk. Confrontations were a mix of adrenaline and terror. Whether it was from fleeing pachyderms, or guides taking up a defensive position with deadly weapons. Those encounters brought home the resilience of the guides. They must be alert in the face of ever-present, life-threatening danger. Even when they sleep; a loaded rifle is their bedmate.

I was thrilled to receive a parcel from South African National Parks Honorary Rangers after completing the final Leg. The wooden commemorative box contained mementoes, including a carved wooden elephant and a Certificate of Acknowledgement. Whenever I hold the small carving in my hand, I reflect on how my desire to explore the wilds of Africa turned into an adventure, and how the journey touched me in numerous ways. I learnt about fortitude, resilience, humility and appreciation for life. Far more than the physical test of commencing each day with a backpack, heavy with water and provisions, was the exhilaration of anticipation, discovery and connection with nature. Whether walking on parched riverbeds, weaving through endless mopaneveld, hiking on the banks of rivers, crossing paths with imposing elephants, or going around belligerent hippos, each step brought me closer to better appreciating the wild and understanding how nature enriches our souls.

Significant Sightings

Herd animals range from a few, to hundreds. The sighting listed is of a single herd (or animal), but not how many were in a herd.

Sightings		Leg						Sum
		One	Two	Three	Four	Five	Six	
Big Five	Lion				2	2		4
	Leopard		1					1
	Elephant	2	29	8	13	18	14	84
	Rhino				1	6	5	12
	Buffalo	2	9	2	4	3	2	22
Other Mammals	Giraffe	3	9	5	15	9	9	50
	Zebra	3	6	3	16	10	4	42
	Hyaena	1	1		2	1	4	9
	Hippo		3	12	14	5	2	36
	Wild dog					1		1
	Warthog	5	1	1	2	4	6	19
	Black-backed Jackal	1	1		1	2		5
	Honey Badger		1					1
	Baboon	1	2	1	1	1		6
	Vervet Monkey	1				2	2	5
Antelope	Eland	1	2					3
	Kudu		1	3	6	12	3	25
	Waterbuck	1	1	9	16	2		29
	Blue Wildebeest (Gnu)		1		12	5	3	21
	Tsessebe	1						1
	Impala	4	9	9	21	25	18	86
	Nyala		1	1			1	3
	Other Antelope	1	1	1	5	3	5	16
Birds	Eagle	6	3	5	15	7	4	40
	Owl	1	1	2	1		1	6
	Vulture		2		4	6	4	16
	Ground Hornbill				3		1	4
	Secretary bird				1			1
	Kori Bustard		1		1	2	1	5
	Saddlebill Stork	1		2	1	2	1	7
Reptiles	Crocodile		3	8	9	4	1	25
	Snake					1	1	2
	Leguaan			1		3		4
	Water/Rock Monitor				1	1		2
	Giant-plated lizard					1	1	2
	Total	35	89	73	167	138	93	595

Appendix 1:
Booking, Water and Packing

Each Leg of The Kruger Trail is walked over six days, from Monday to Saturday. The walking season is during the cooler seasons in South Africa; from the end of March to mid-September.

The trails are sold annually in October by auction to groups of up to eight persons, to begin the following year. Only the first Leg is sold at auction, and a set fee is charged for the remaining five Legs. To start the auction registration process or receive more information, email auction@thekrugertrail.co.za.

Water was a challenge in the early stages of our journey in the northern reaches of the Kruger. In some areas, there are no natural water sources, and the guides drop off water drums before the hike. Water purification drops, rather than tablets, are critical. A mini-water filter is also recommended. Good quality filters are rated to an absolute filtration level of 0.1 microns to remove particles, bacteria, protozoa and cysts from source water. Most hikers consume three to four litres of water a day, which they tend to carry from the morning start. One litre of water is the equivalent in kilograms.

This was my packing list after much tweaking.

General Items
- Binoculars (optional)
- Insect repellent
- Sleeping bag
- Foam base for sleeping
- Tent and pegs
- Small groundsheet
- Foldable stool (optional)
- Gas stove and gas canister
- Cooking pot – large and small
- Lighter
- Coffee mug
- Cutlery set
- Backpack
- Poncho
- Inflatable pillow
- Pocketknife
- Duct tape – small roll
- Black bag and dirty clothes bag
- Headlamp and spare batteries
- Water bottle and two-litre water bladders x2
- Water sterilisation drops
- Sawyer mini water filter
- Spare laces x1
- Biodegradable multipurpose soap
- Trekking pole x1
- Sunglasses

Clothing
- Slip-on sandals
- Hiking boots
- Gaiters
- Thick outer, and inner socks
- Underwear
- T-shirts (dark)
- Shirts – for hiking
- Long trousers/short combo
- Shorts for night/swim combo
- Thick long-sleeve vest
- Long Johns
- Hat

Personal/Toiletries
- Toothbrush and toothpaste
- Deodorant
- Toilet paper and plastic trowel
- Packet of tissues
- First aid kit incl. antihistamine
- Pink adhesive plaster
- Towel – quick drying

In addition to food, coffee and tea, a daily dose of electrolyte rehydration is recommended. I ate one small apple each day. Debris must be carried to the end of the Leg, so food should be in light packaging.

Lourens's tips for food and nutrition are:
- Breakfast – after trying instant oats and porridge, I preferred one or two rusks and a cup of coffee.
- I carried snacks: peanuts and raisins; a packet of trail mix; biltong; droëwors and sweets. I snacked on these throughout the day.
- Powder milk was a favourite. On a hot day, I made milk with water.
- Lunch – instant soup, salty biscuits, tuna sachet, Crackerbread and instant noodles.
- Dinner – dehydrated meals with instant mash or couscous. I packed salt and a few small butters in a sealed container because they melt.

Things I discarded from the list as the hike progressed:
- Second walking pole – I preferred to have one hand free.
- Half the pegs for my tent – my body weight and backpack kept the tent in place in strong winds.
- Camera – I could not take notes and pictures. Many used mobile phone cameras.
- Clothing was reduced to a spare shirt, trousers, and two pairs of socks.
- Arie stopped taking a plate, fork and knife. He found a spoon and bowl were enough.

Things others found useful:
- GPS – Arie liked, "...to download the track afterwards to see where you walked and slept".
- Matches – "In case the lighter fails," according to Arie.
- Carabiners, a metal loop with a spring-loaded gate to connect components quickly; usually in safety-critical systems.
  Arie believes you can never have too many.
- Cable ties.
- Collapsible 10-litre water carrier to, "...only have to fetch water once," says Arie. Lourens recommends a foldup bucket to place in the camp from which everybody can scoop water, as needed during the evening.
- Small tripod – Arie took one to mount the phone for selfies or group pics.

- Powerbank – Arie carried this to charge phones so you can always take pics.
- Sleeping bag inner – used by Lourens in colder months.
- Inflatable lightweight mattress – with a patching kit in case of punctures.
- Money or a bank card – came in handy on two occasions.
- Painkillers and anti-inflammatory tablets.
- Blister plasters, "Unused, but have a great placebo effect," according to Clifford.
- A beanie in the colder months.
- Portable bush showers – two for a group of eight are helpful. The guides carry at least one.
- Kindle – Clifford read every day. "I'm addicted to reading, so it's with me when I'm on the go."

Appendix 2:
Safe Hiking in the African Wild

- Don't run. Ever. You cannot outrun any animal. Always obey instructions from the guides.
- Do not sleep in a riverbed if rain is expected, or near the snorers. Lourens advises: "Try and find a relatively flat spot to pitch your tent. If using an inflatable mattress, remove anything sharp to prevent punctures."
- Begin the day with enough water. Lourens recommends: "To keep hydrated, we took Rehidrat at night and electrolytes in the morning. Drink quite a lot of water before starting the hike. Carry enough water, plus a litre extra. Some days, you get water during the day; others, you must carry enough for a day, and sometimes even a day and a half. Ensure you have the capacity."
- Use gaiters when wearing shorts. They keep grass and prickly plants out of your socks and help to keep socks dry in the mornings when the grass is wet from overnight dew. Clifford always wore long pants, "They act as gaiters and protect legs from sun, ticks and cuts."
- Care for your feet and sit when you get the opportunity. The day might be extended, the terrain difficult, and the overnight camp far away. Sometimes you are unable to camp where the guides have planned, and you must hike further to find a suitable, safe spot. Clifford's secret for avoiding foot problems is: "Pack three pairs of hiking socks. I doubled up on my socks and rotated the inner and outer with the one unused. I removed my socks to allow my feet to breathe. Any break for 30 minutes or longer and shoes and socks came off," he said. "I never had a blister or other foot problems throughout the hike." Lourens experienced severe foot problems during Leg Three and says, "Shoes must be well worn before you start and must not be too tight. Your feet will swell. Make sure your toenails are short. If you are prone to blisters, take precautions. If you feel a hot spot developing on your feet while walking, stop and put a plaster over the spot. Also, find the correct method to tie your boots."
- Dry out your clothes and towel overnight.

Acknowledgements

Thanks to South African National Parks for allowing *The Kruger Trail* through its reserve. Thanks, too, to Louis Lemmer and the Magalies Region of the South African National Parks Honorary Rangers, who came up with the concept, then implemented it.

Lourens van Aardt attended the auction, took the risk and put together the Panthera. I appreciated the genial company of my fellow Panthera: Henk and Antoinette Jonker; Clifford French; Corrie and Maritha Barnard; the late Ray Brown; Morné Bester; Marie Dahl; Brigitte Ruprecht-Gersteroph; Donna van Schalkwyk; Annemarie de Lange; Grant Goldstone and Alice du Plessis. Three Panthera accompanied me from start to finish: Lourens van Aardt, Jennifer van Aardt-Bester, and Arie Fourie.

Thanks to our guides: Bjinse Visser; Pilot Nxumalo; Arnold Bam; Warren Deyzel; Louis Lemmer; Pete Wilson; Paul Slyer; Howard Spencer-Wilson; Ashraf Sayed and Mark Montgomery. They shared their knowledge; kept us safe; tended our wounds, and answered questions as I took notes.

Thank you to Jen Cowie, who coached me in writing, created the map and contributed interesting animal facts. Leigh Rohroff inspired me to make videos and understand social media. Marie Dahl edited early versions of the text. She checked animal facts, managed social media and administered my Facebook author profile page. Lynette Tredoux, an Honorary Ranger, checked the manuscript and helped with technical matters. Karen McIntosh took on the Facebook author page in the early stages, and did her best to help me find life balance during the writing journey. Dave Mackenzie, a regular visitor to the Kruger Park and to the Mountain Zebra National Park in the Eastern Cape, gave permission for use of his magnificent wildlife pictures on my author page.

Birdwatchers can benefit from consulting Sunbird Publishers' *Pocket Guide to Birds of Southern Africa*; Siyabonga Africa's *Best Birding Guide to Kruger Park*, and the handy smartphone app *Sasol eBirds of Southern Africa*.

I valued the information about animals, trees and plants in *Exploring Kruger* by Brett Hilton-Barber, with Professor Lee R Berger, and *Shaping Kruger* by Mitch Reardon.

Bibliography

About Safari Guide of the Year – FGASA. 2023. https://www.fgasa.co.za/about-safari-guide-of-the-year.

Amensalism – an Overview | ScienceDirect Topics. n.d. https://www.sciencedirect.com/topics/earth-and-planetary-sciences/amensalism.

Birding in Kruger Park, Best Birding Routes & Drives, Activity Guide. n.d. Birding.krugerpark.co.za. https://birding.krugerpark.co.za/.

Bryden, Bruce. 2005. *A Game Ranger Remembers*. Cape Town: Jonathan Ball Publishers.

Bush Meat Poaching Gaining Momentum in Kruger. Lowvelder. 27 October 2023. https://www.citizen.co.za/lowvelder/news-headlines/local-news/2023/10/27/bush-meat-poaching-gaining-momentum-in-kruger/.

Campbell-Staton, Shane C, Brian J Arnold, Dominique Gonçalves, Petter Granli, Joyce Poole, Ryan A Long, and Robert M Pringle. 2021. *Ivory Poaching and the Rapid Evolution of Tusklessness in African Elephants. Science* 374 (6566): 483–87. https://doi.org/10.1126/science.abe7389.

Capparis Tomentosa | PlantZAfrica. n.d. Pza.sanbi.org. https://pza.sanbi.org/capparis-tomentosa#.

Carruthers, Jane. 1996. *The Kruger National Park: A Social and Political History*. Pietermaritzburg, Natal: University Of Natal Press.

Cillié, Burger and Oberprieler, Ulrich. 2012. *Pocket Guide to Birds of Southern Africa*. Cape Town: Sunbird Publishers.

Conservation Action Trust. 2023. *Snaring in Kruger National Park Spikes More than 200% amid Socio-economic Crisis*. https://www.conservationaction.co.za/snaring-in-kruger-national-park-spikes-more-than-200-amid-socioeconomic-crisis/.

Derichs, Peter. 2018. *Kruger National Park*. Johannesburg: Peter Derichs.

De Rosner, Conraad, with Spence, Graham and Bell, Elaine. 2023. *Called by the Wild*. Cape Town: Jonathan Ball Publishers.

Du Toit, Greg. 2022. *Wilderness Dreaming*. Johannesburg: HPH Publishing.

BIBLIOGRAPHY

Flowers, Jane. *Railway History: Selati, the Train Line That Saved Kruger National Park. Blasting News,* 29 October 2017. https://us.blastingnews.com/curiosities/2017/10/railway-history-selati-the-train-line-that-saved-kruger-national-park-002129085.html.

Hilton-Barber, Brett, and Berger, Professor Lee R. 2015. *Exploring Kruger.* Cape Town: Art Publishers.

History of Kruger Park – Harry Wolhuter – South Africa. n.d. https://www.krugerpark.co.za/kruger-park-history-harry-wolhuter.html.

Hughes, Sylvia. 29 September 1990. *Antelope, Activate the Acacia's Alarm System.* New Scientist. https://www.newscientist.com/article/mg12717361-200-antelope-activate-the-acacias-alarm-system.

Ivanova, Kristina. 2021. *Female African Elephants 'RAPIDLY Evolving' to Become TUSKLESS due to Ivory Poaching, Study Warns.* IHeart Intelligence.com. 22 October 2021. https://iheartintelligence.com/female-african-elephants-rapidly-evolving-to-become-tuskless-due-to-ivory-poaching-study-warns/.

KwaZulu-Natal Carried the Brunt of Rhino Poaching in 2023, Says Creecy | Department of Environmental Affairs. n.d. https://www.dffe.gov.za/mediareleases/creecy_relasesrhinopoachingstats2024feb27.

Lekaota, Limpho, Mr Rofhiwa, and S Khashane. 2019. *Local Communities' Perceptions on the Role of Tourism in Protected Areas. African Journal of Hospitality, Tourism and Leisure 8 (5).* https://www.ajhtl.com/uploads/.

Liebenberg, Louis. 2016. *First Field Guide to Animal Tracks of Southern Africa.* Cape Town: Struik Nature.

LLC, Sauber Legal Services. n.d. https://sauberlaw.com/the-cairn.

Marías, Javier. 2023. *Tomás Nevinson.* New York: Knopf.

Mhlongo, Gugu. n.d. *Traditional Zulu Clothing.* Eshowe. https://eshowe.com/traditional-zulu-clothing/.

Monadjem, Ara. 2023. *African Ark.* Johannesburg: Wits University Press.

Murray, Christopher JL. 2022. *COVID-19 Will Continue, but the End of the Pandemic Is Near. The Lancet* 399 (10323). https://doi.org/10.1016/s0140-6736(22)00100-3.

Poaching Numbers | Conservation | Save the Rhino International. 2023. Save the Rhino. https://www.savetherhino.org/rhino-info/poaching-stats.

Pooley, Elsa. 1999. *First Field Guide to Trees of Southern Africa*. Cape Town: Struik Nature.

Rangers, SANParks Honorary. *K9 National Project. SANParks Honorary Rangers*. 15 February 2022. https://www.sanparksvolunteers.org/k9-national-project.

Reardon, Mitch. 2012. *Shaping Kruger*. Cape Town: Penguin Random House.

Rhino Poaching in South Africa in 2021 | Department of Environmental Affairs. n.d. https://www.dffe.gov.za/RhinoPoachinginSouthAfricain2021.

Saayman, Melville, Riaan Rossouw, and Andrea Saayman. 2012. *Does Conservation Make Sense to Local Communities? Development Southern Africa* 29 (4): 588–609. https://doi.org/10.1080/0376835x.2012.

Hinde, Gerald, and Taylor, Will. 2022. *Safari Secrets*. Johannesburg. HPH Publishing.

Sasol eBirds of Southern Africa. 2022. https://apps.apple.com/us/app/sasol-ebirds-southern-africa/id1505731669.

Shingwedzi Routes – Game Drives around Shingwedzi. n.d. Www.krugerpark.co.za. https://www.krugerpark.co.za/Self_Drive_in_the_The_North-travel/explore-kruger-park-around-shingwedzi.html.

Siyabonga Africa | Poverty and Hunger Alleviation, Skills Development, Community Upliftment. n.d. Www.siyabongaafrica.org.za. https://www.siyabongaafrica.org.za/.

Snaring – Africa Wild. n.d. Africawild-Forum.com. https://africawild-forum.com/viewtopic.

Starr, Michelle. 2018. *Hippos Poop so Much, Sometimes Their Waste Kills All the Fish*. ScienceAlert. https://www.sciencealert.com/hippopotamus-faeces-causes-water-hypoxia-kills-fish.

The Difference between the White and Black Rhino | Londolozi Blog. 2016. 21 January 2016. https://blog.londolozi.com/2016/01/21/the-difference-between-black-and-white-rhino/.

The Kruger Red Rocks. 2016. Notes from Africa. https://notesfromafrica.wordpress.com/2016/10/12/the-kruger-red-rocks/.

BIBLIOGRAPHY

The Man-Eaters of Kruger. 2021. Leisure Wheels. 20 July 2021. https://www.leisurewheels.co.za/travel/man-eaters-kruger/.

Trees in Kruger Park – Kruger National Park, South Africa. n.d. https://www.krugerpark.co.za/Kruger_National_Park_Wildlife-travel/kruger-park-trees.html.

Tropic of Capricorn | Definition & Facts | Britannica. 2020. In Encyclopædia Britannica. https://www.britannica.com/place/Tropic-of-Capricorn.

Two Lions, 110 Vultures Poisoned at S. Africa's Kruger Park. n.d. Phys.org. https://phys.org/news/2016-03-lions-vultures-poisoned-safrica-kruger.html.

Van Hoven, W. 1991. *Mortalities in Kudu (Tragelaphus Strepsiceros) Populations Related to Chemical Defence in Trees*. Semantic Scholar. 27 March 1991. https://www.semanticscholar.org/paper/Mortalities-in-kudu-(*Tragelaphus-strepsiceros*)-to-Hoven.

Volunteer. n.d. SANParks Honorary Rangers. https://www.sanparksvolunteers.org/volunteer.

Walters, Tiara. 2023. *Court Gives Two Accused Snare Poachers a Slap on the Wrist despite 'Admission' of Guilt. Daily Maverick*. 19 November 2023. https://www.dailymaverick.co.za/article/2023-11-19-skukuza-court-gives-two-accused-snare-poachers-a-slap-on-the-wrist-despite-admission-of-guilt.

Why Does Your Soil Smell like Ammonia? How to Fix Smelly Soil. n.d. WikiHow. https://www.wikihow.com/Why-Does-Your-Soil-Smell-Like-Ammonia.

WHO. 2022. *14.9 Million Excess Deaths Associated with the COVID-19 Pandemic in 2020 and 2021*. 5 May 2022. https://www.who.int/news/item/05-05-2022-14.9-million-excess-deaths-were-associated-with-the-covid-19-pandemic-in-2020-and-2021.

World Population Review. 2023. *Gini Coefficient by Country 2022*. World Population Review. 2023. https://worldpopulationreview.com/country-rankings/gini-coefficient-by-country.

WWF – Building a Future in Which Humans Live in Harmony with Nature. n.d. https://wwf.panda.org/.

Zoo, Toledo, and Buckeye Broadband. 2017. *Have You Visited Our Hippos Lately?* BCAN. 16 October 2017. https://www.bcanarts.com/have-you-visited-our-hippos-lately/.

About the Author

An accomplished corporate executive, José Neves is also a sportsman and father.

A Nomads golfer and endurance athlete – which includes completing 10 Ironman events – José heard about the opportunity to hike the length of the world-famous Kruger National Park, and he felt compelled to accept the challenge. Walking Wild is the personalised account of his 605 kilometre backpacking journey through the world-renowned wildlife destination.

José worked for 22 years in leadership positions within the Coca-Cola system in three southern African countries. He now consults on supply chain and logistics in the public health sector.

ABOUT THE AUTHOR

www.ingramcontent.com/pod-product-compliance
Lightning Source LLC
Chambersburg PA
CBHW051938290426
44110CB00015B/2025